Jenny Han

MASTER TREE FINDER

About the Nature Study Guild . .

The founder of the Nature Study Guild of Berkeley, California, in 1938, **May Theilgaard Watts** received her training in botany at the University of Chicago and served as staff naturalist and education director at the Morton Arboretum in Lisle, Illinois. Her contributions to the field have been recognized by the Garden Club, the Audubon Society, and the American Horticultural Society. In addition to having written and edited books for the Nature Study Guild, she is the author of *Reading The Landscape* and *Reading The Landscape of Europe*.

Tom Watts holds a Bachelor's degree in biology from North Central College, Naperville, Illinois, and has a Master's in social science from the University of Chicago. A retired instructional technologist, who has written many of the Guild's books himself, he now heads the organization his mother started and carries on her legacy—increasing the public's awareness and appreciation of plants through books.

This volume incorporates *Master Tree Finder, Desert Tree Finder, Rocky Mountain Tree Finder, Pacific Coast Tree Finder,* and *Winter Tree Finder,* originally published separately by the Nature Study Guild.

Also from
The Nature Study Guild

Master Flower Finder

Published by
WARNER BOOKS

MASTER TREE FINDER

NATURE STUDY GUILD

WARNER BOOKS

A Warner Communications Company

WARNER BOOKS EDITION

This Warner Books Edition was originally published in five volumes entitled: *Master Tree Finder* by May Theilgaard Watts; *Pacific Coast Tree Finder* by Tom Watts; *Winter Tree Finder* by May Theilgaard Watts and Tom Watts; *Rocky Mountain Tree Finder* by Tom Watts; and *Desert Tree Finder* by May Theilgaard Watts and Tom Watts. Published by arrangement with Nature Study Guild, Box 972, Berkeley, California 94701

Cover design by Barbara Buck
Cover art by David Heffernan

Warner Books, Inc.
666 Fifth Avenue
New York, N.Y. 10103

Printed in the United States of America

First Warner Books Printing: April, 1986

10 9 8 7 6 5 4 3 2 1

CONTENTS

BOOK I: MASTER TREE FINDER

BOOK II: DESERT TREE FINDER

BOOK III: ROCKY MOUNTAIN TREE FINDER

BOOK IV: PACIFIC COAST TREE FINDER

BOOK V: WINTER TREE FINDER

MASTER TREE FINDER

By May Theilgaard Watts

A MANUAL FOR THE IDENTIFICATION OF TREES BY THEIR LEAVES

T O U S E T H I S K E Y

1. Select a typical leaf from the tree you wish to identify. Avoid freaks.

2. Start at the top of Page 5 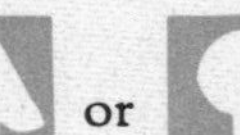 or 

3. Proceed step by step, considering both choices under each symbol 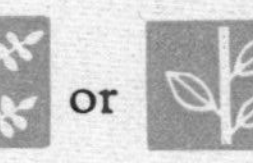 or 

4. When you have made the final choice, arriving at the name of the leaf, compare your leaf with the illustration, and check the other features shown.

advice: examine pages 1, 2, 3, and 4, before starting on page 5

(1)

THE DISTRIBUTION OF NATIVE TREES

The areas shown on the small green maps beside the trees are those in which the tree grows wild. Some of these trees are planted by people over a much wider area.

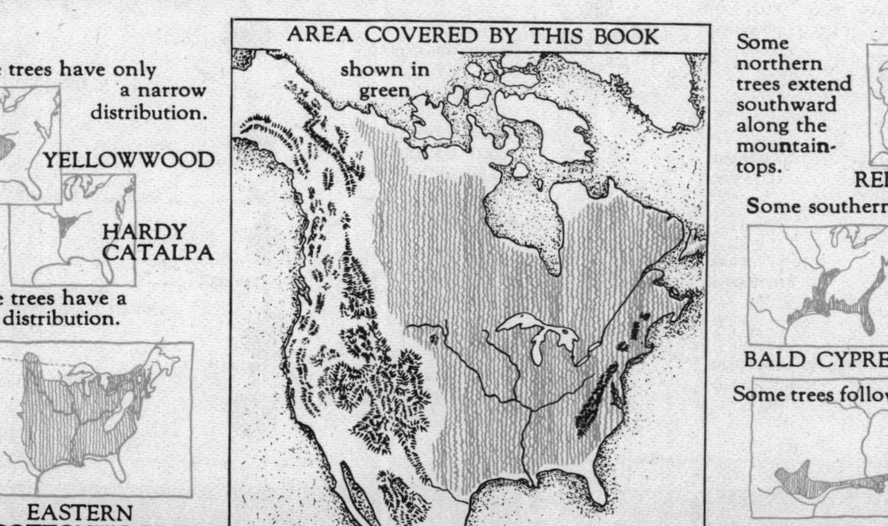

the HABITAT of a tree, the place where it is likely to grow naturally, is indicated beside the leaf of each NATIVE TREE

lowland . . . .

banks of streams and lakes . . .

bogs . . . . .

upland . . . .

sand and gravel . . . .

the edge of the forest . . . .

small tree in the shade of tall trees . . . .

mixed forest of evergreen and deciduous trees . . . .

evergreen forest . . . .

deciduous forest . . .

tolerating moderate shade . . . .

tolerating heavy shade . . . .

eastern mountains . .

Most of the habitats indicated in this book are a combination of two or more of the situations shown on this page and the next.

the PLACE of a tree in Association with PEOPLE is shown beside the leaves of introduced trees and some native trees

3

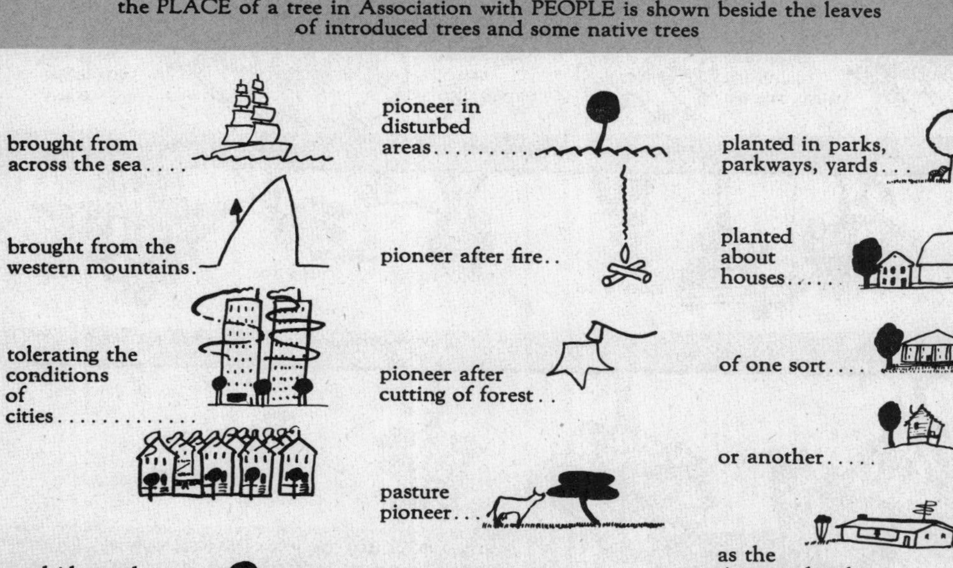

the same kinds of trees are found in fence-rows, pastures, and the edge of the forest.

4

SHAPES

The tree shapes shown in this book are the shapes of mature trees. Tree shape can change with age. Below are shown six stages in the life of an American Elm.

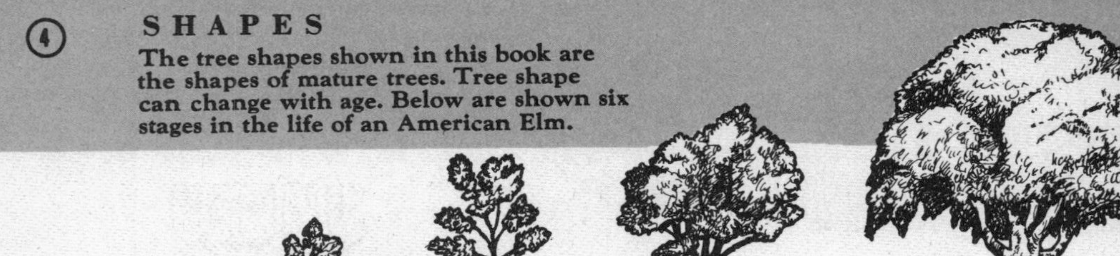

The tree shapes shown below have been modified by:

The leaf shape may depend, in part, on its position on the tree:

on a vigorous seedling....

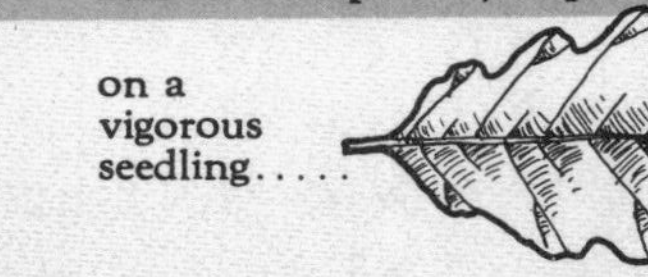

BUR OAK

on shaded lower branches....

BUR OAK

on the sunny topmost branches....

BUR OAK

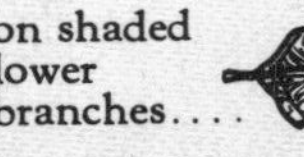

START HERE →

If the tree has needles, start with this symbol, this page

If the tree has leaves, start with this symbol, page 14

If the needles are long, ½ inch to 18 inches,
go below, to

If the needles are short, scale-like, overlapping,
go on page 13, to

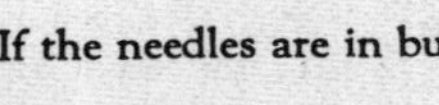

If the needles are in bundles or tufts,
go below, to

If the needles are borne singly,
go on page 10, to

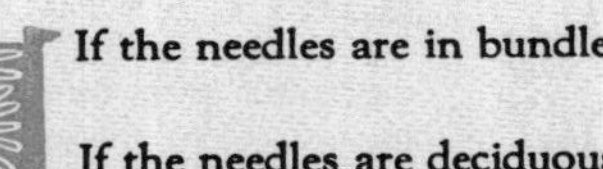

If the needles are in bundles of 2 to 5,
go on page 6, to

If the needles are deciduous, many in a tuft,
go on page 6, to

LARCHES

If the branchlets are drooping, and the cones are about 1 inch long,

it is **EUROPEAN LARCH**
Larix decidua

If the branchlets are not drooping, and the cones are about ½ inch long,

it is **AMERICAN LARCH or TAMARACK**
Larix laricina

PINES

If there are 5 needles in a bundle,

it is **WHITE PINE**
Pinus Strobus

If there are 2 or 3 needles in a bundle,

go on next page, to

If there are 2 needles in a bundle,
go on page 8 to

If there are 3 needles in a bundle,
go below to

If the needles are less than 5 inches long, yellow-green, twisted, the trunk and branches may be bearded with needles,
it is **PITCH PINE**
Pinus rigida

If the needles are 5 or more inches long,
go below to

If the needles are stout, long, 5″ to 8″, not twisted, (some bundles have only 2 needles),
it is **PONDEROSA PINE**
or WESTERN YELLOW PINE
Pinus ponderosa

If the needles are slender,
go below to

if the needles are 6″ to 9″, rather stiff, it is **LOBLOLLY PINE**
Pinus Taeda

If the needles are very long, 8″ to 18″, with a ragged sheath, it is **LONG-LEAF PINE**
Pinus palustris

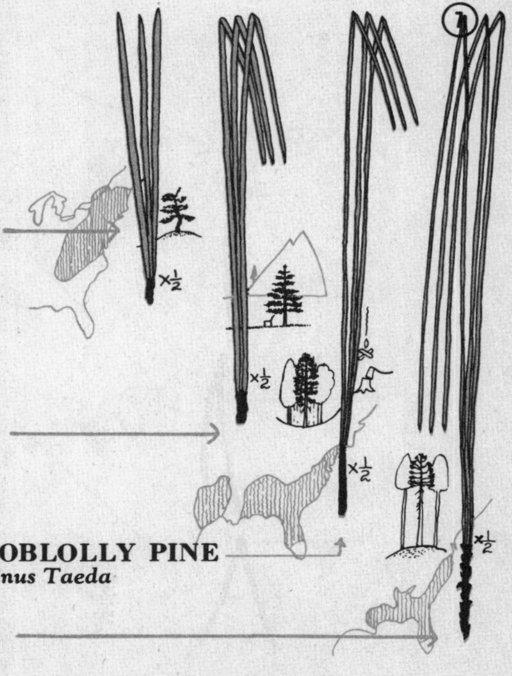

×½ ×½ ×½ ×½

If the needles are short, less than 3″,

go below to

If the needles are long, 3″ to 8″,

go on page 9 to

If the needles are 1½″ long, thick, spreading away from each other (divergent),

it is **JACK PINE**
Pinus Banksiana

If the needles are 2″ to 3″ long, slender, slightly twisted, slightly divergent,

it is **SCRUB PINE**
Pinus virginiana

If the needles are 2″ to 3″ long, slightly twisted, and the tree has branches of orange color,

it is **SCOTCH PINE**
Pinus sylvestris

If the needles are slender, 3″ to 5″ long on a whitish twig, (some bundles with 3 needles),

it is **SHORTLEAF PINE**
Pinus echinata

If the needles are slender, brittle; the twigs not white; the sheath long,

it is **RED PINE**
or NORWAY PINE
Pinus resinosa

If the needles are stout, curved, not brittle, the sheath ragged, short,

it is **AUSTRIAN PINE**
Pinus nigra

If the needles are stiff, sharp, 4-sided, (can be twirled between the thumb and finger), and leave the twig rough when they fall off,

go below to

If the needles are flat and pliable,

go on page 12 to

If the needles are *extremely sharp*, and the branches form a flat, horizontal spray,

it is **COLORADO SPRUCE**
Picea pungens

If the needles are not very sharp, nor the branches noticeably horizontal,

go below to 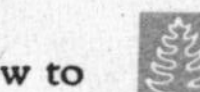

If the branchlets droop, and the cones are 4" to 6" long,

it is **NORWAY SPRUCE**
Picea Abies

If the branchlets do not droop, and the cones are shorter,

go on next page, to 

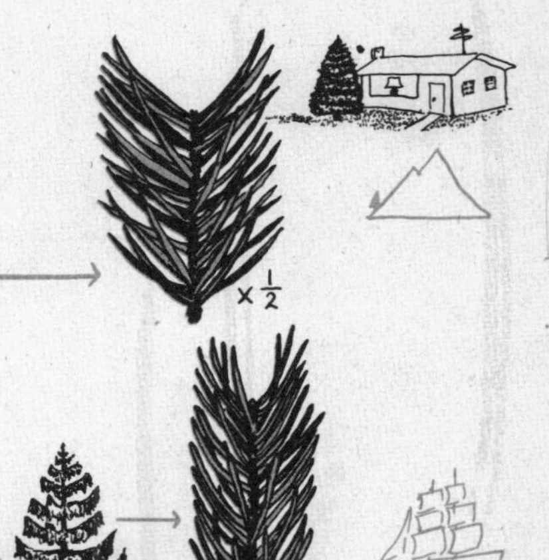

If the needles are short, less than ½", and the buds and twigs are hairy,

it is **BLACK SPRUCE**
Picea mariana

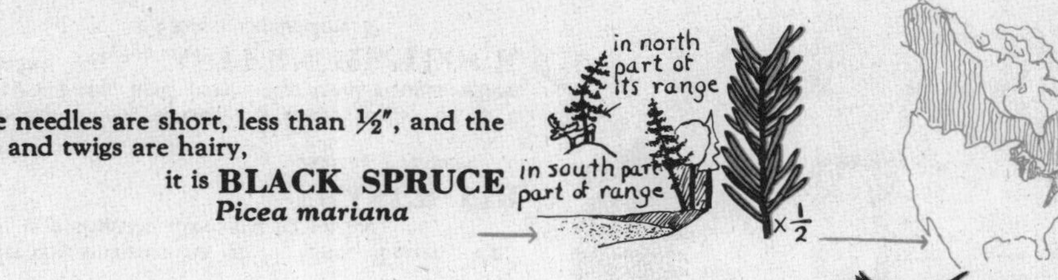

If the needles are ½" or more, and the twigs and buds are hairy,

it is **RED SPRUCE**
Picea rubens

If the needles are blue-green, and the twigs are hairless,

it is **WHITE SPRUCE**
Picea glauca

(12)

If the needles are 2-ranked, (like hair divided by a comb), go below to

If the needles are not 2-ranked, branchlets drooping, buds red-brown, pointed,

it is **DOUGLAS FIR**
Pseudotsuga menziesii

If the needles are whitened beneath, go below to

If the needles are not whitened beneath, but of graduated lengths along the twig that is shed with them, it is **BALD CYPRESS**
Taxodium distichum

If needles have broad bases, and leave twig smooth when they fall,

it is **BALSAM FIR**
(upper right) *Abies balsamea*

In the mountains of N. Car., Tenn., Va., it is a slightly different fir called,

FRASER FIR
Abies Fraseri

If needles are about ½ inch long, have a narrow base, and leave the twig rough when they fall, it is **EASTERN HEMLOCK**
Tsuga canadensis

×½ ×½ ×½ ×½

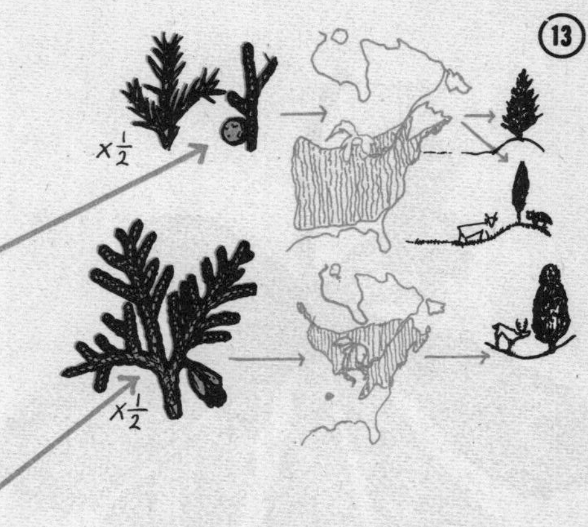

If all the needles are scale-like

go below to

If part of the needles are small and scale-like and part are sharp and prickly,

it is **RED CEDAR**
Juniperus virginiana

If the needles are flat, forming a flattened spray; and if there are numerous ½″ cones; and the tree is in a swampy or limestone area,

it is **ARBOR VITAE**
Thuja occidentalis

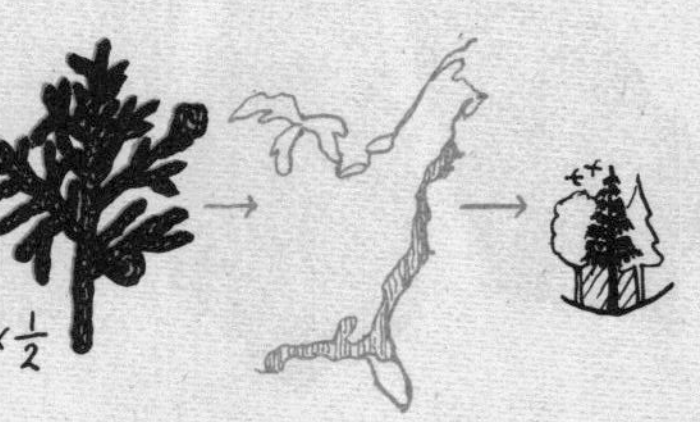

If the needles are narrow scales, not in flat sprays, and if the numerous ¼″ to ½″ cones are globular, and if the tree is in a coastal swamp,

it is **ATLANTIC WHITE CEDAR**
Chamaecyparis thyoides

If the leaves or buds grow opposite like this,

go below to

If the leaves or buds grow alternately like this,

go on page 21 to

If the leaves are compound, composed of several leaflets, (you can tell leaves from leaflets because there is no bud at the base of a leaflet),

go below to

If the leaves are simple, (not composed of leaflets),

go on page 18 to

If the 5 or more leaflets radiate from one point,

go on page 15 to 

If the leaflets do not radiate from one point, or if there are only 3 leaflets,

go on page 16 to

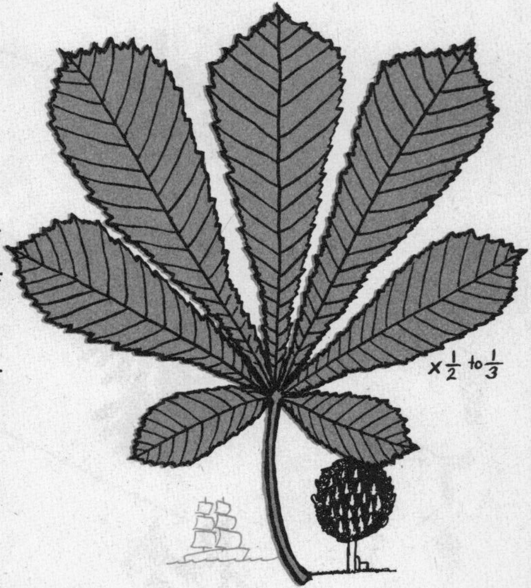

$\times \frac{1}{2}$ to $\frac{1}{3}$

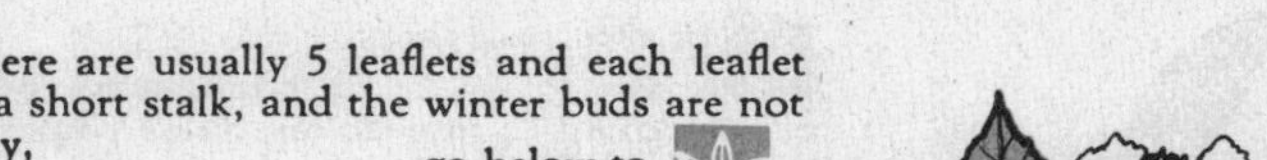

If there are usually 5 leaflets and each leaflet has a short stalk, and the winter buds are not sticky, go below to BUCKEYES

If there are usually 7 leaflets, doubly-toothed, and the leaflets have no stalks, and the winter buds are sticky,

it is **HORSE CHESTNUT**
Aesculus Hippocastanum
See illustration on page 14

If the leaflets are irregularly and bluntly toothed, and the end buds are keeled, and the twigs have a disagreeable smell when bruised,

it is **OHIO BUCKEYE**
Aesculus glabra

If the leaflets are regularly and finely toothed and the end buds are not keeled, it is

SWEET BUCKEYE
YELLOW BUCKEYE
Aesculus octandra

×½

×½

If the leaflets are of different sizes and shapes,
it is **BOX ELDER**
Acer Negundo

If the leaflets are similar in size and shape,
go below to

If each leaflet has a short stem,
go below to

If the leaflets have no stem,
it is **BLACK ASH**
Fraxinus nigra

If the leaflets are regularly toothed, and the twig is square, or with 2 long lines from leaf scars,
it is **BLUE ASH**
Fraxinus quadrangulata

If the leaflets are not regularly toothed, or only toothed along the tip half of the margin, and the twig is round,
go on next page to

If the twigs and leaf stalks are hairy,
it is **RED ASH**
Fraxinus pennsylvanica

If the twigs and leaf stalks are not hairy,
go below to

If the leaflets are whitish beneath,
it is **WHITE ASH**
Fraxinus americana

If the leaflets are green on both sides,
it is **GREEN ASH**
Fraxinus pennsylvanica subintegerrima

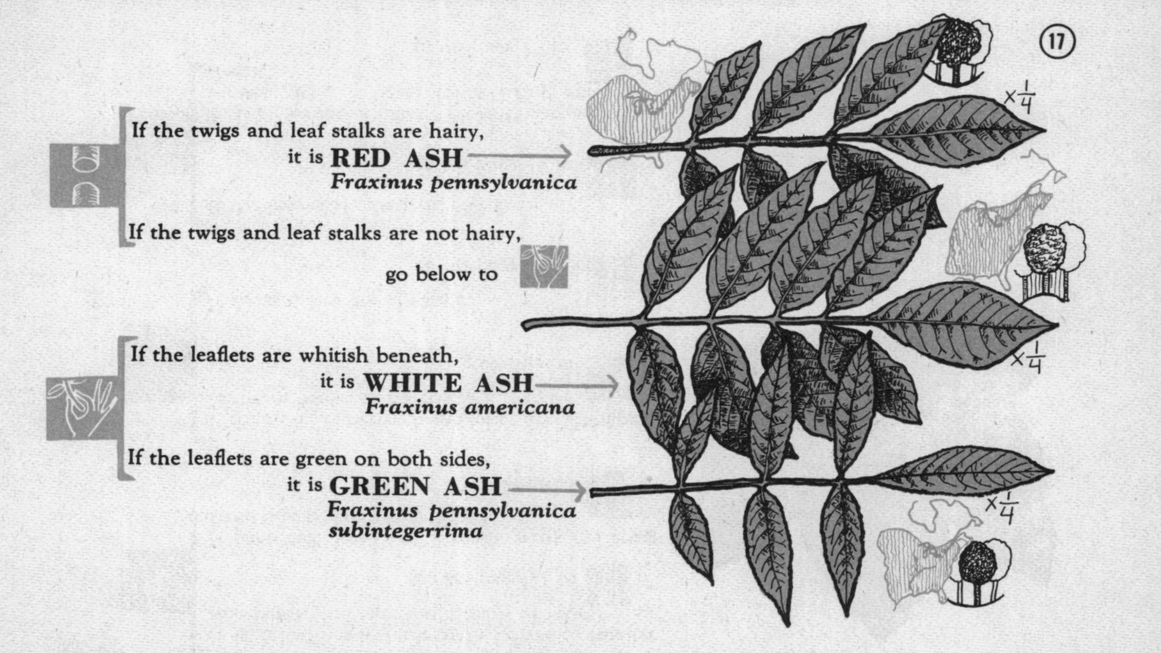

If each leaf has a single main vein with smaller side veins, and is without teeth or lobes,

go on page 21 to

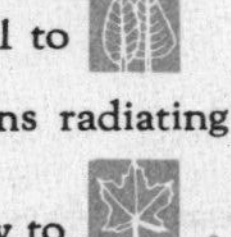

If each leaf has 3 to 7 main veins radiating from one point, and is lobed,

go below to

If the notches between the lobes are V shaped, (either a broad or narrow V),

go below to

If the notches are U shaped,

go on page 20 to

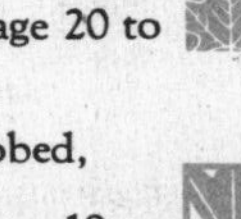

If the leaves are distinctly 5-lobed,

go on page 19 to

If the leaves appear 3-lobed rather than 5-lobed, (the 2 basal lobes being small or absent),

go on page 19 to

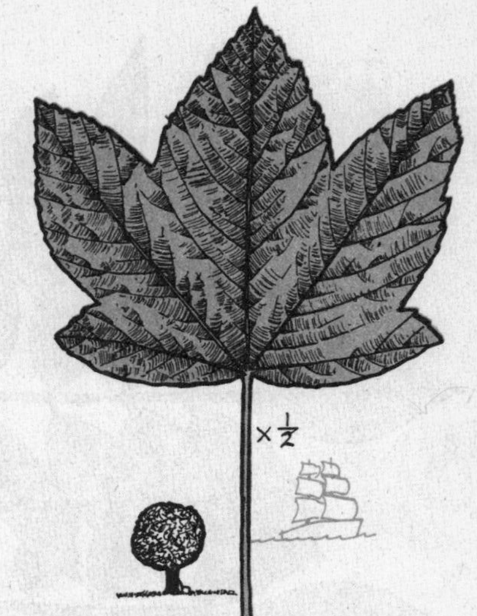

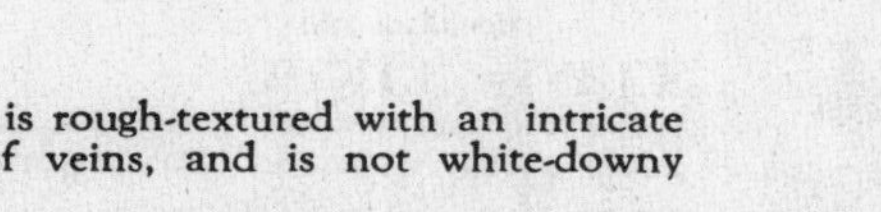

If the leaf is rough-textured with an intricate network of veins, and is not white-downy beneath,

it is **SYCAMORE MAPLE**
Acer Pseudo-Platanus

picture on page 18

If the end lobe narrows toward its base, and the notches between the lobes are deep, and the under-surface is white-downy,

it is **SILVER MAPLE**
Acer saccharinum

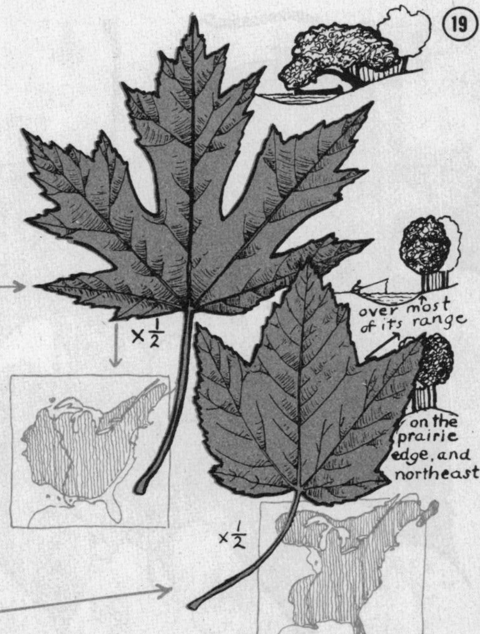

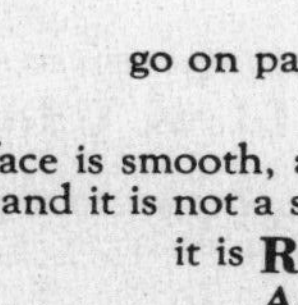

If the leaf surface is rough with a network of depressed veins, and the lobes are drawn out to long tapering tips, and the teeth are all of somewhat the same size, and the tree is small, shrubby,

go on page 20 to 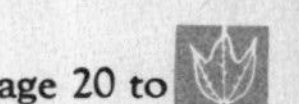 

If the leaf surface is smooth, and the teeth of irregular sizes, and it is not a shrub,

it is **RED MAPLE**
Acer rubrum

If leaves are finely-toothed, hairless; bark green with white stripes, it is

STRIPED MAPLE
Acer pensylvanicum
(upper right)

If leaves are coarsely toothed, and white-hairy beneath with hairy twigs, it is

MOUNTAIN MAPLE
Acer spicatum (upper left)

If leaf stem shows a milky juice when broken; leaf usually wider than long; base of leaf not curving,
it is **NORWAY MAPLE**
Acer platanoides (lower left)

If there is no milky juice; leaf about as long as wide; base of leaf curving, it is

SUGAR MAPLE
Acer saccharum (lower right)

(A similar tree, but with leaves hairy beneath, 3 lobed, with sides drooping, is
BLACK MAPLE
Acer nigrum)

$\times \frac{1}{2}$ $\times \frac{1}{2}$ $\times \frac{1}{2}$ $\times \frac{1}{2}$

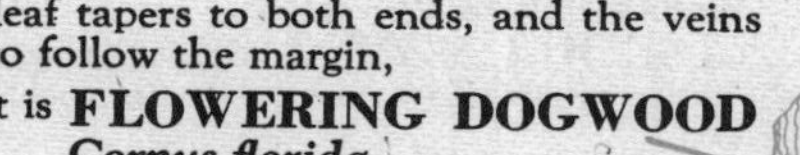

If the leaf tapers to both ends, and the veins curve to follow the margin,

it is **FLOWERING DOGWOOD**
Cornus florida

If the leaf is 6″ to 12″ long, heart-shaped,

it is **HARDY CATALPA**
Catalpa speciosa

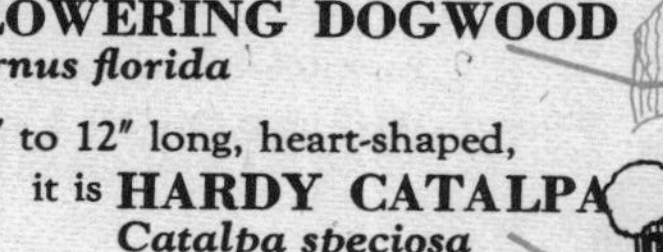
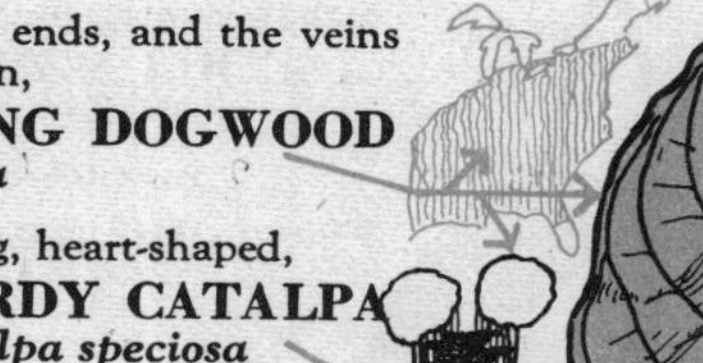

If the leaves are compound, composed of several leaflets, (you can tell leaves from leaflets because there is no bud at the base of a leaflet),

go below to  

If the leaves are simple, not composed of leaflets,

go on page 28 to 

If the margins of the leaves are not toothed at all,

go on next page to 

If the margins of the leaves are toothed, or partly-toothed,

go on page 24 to

If tree is small, growing in a bog or ditch; leaflets more than an inch long, tapering to a V shape at both ends, (it may have drooping clusters of white berries.) Don't touch it!

it is **POISON SUMAC**
Toxicodendron vernix

If the tree is not in a swamp or bog, and the leaflets, or most of them, are rounded at one end or both, (the tree may have pea-like pods)

go below to LEGUMES

If the leaves, or some of them, are doubly compound, dividing and subdividing,

go on next page to

If the leaves are singly-compound,

go below to

If leaf tips are pointed,

it is **YELLOWWOOD** (center)
Cladrastus kentukea

If leaf tips are rounded; twigs have short, paired thorns, it is **BLACK LOCUST**
Robinia Pseudo-Acacia

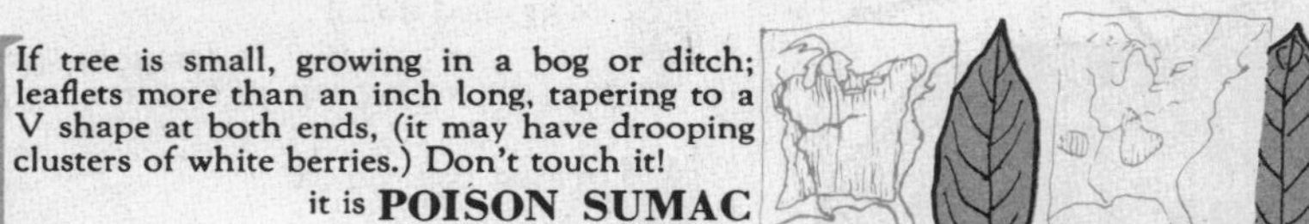

If the leaflets are less than 1½″ long,

go below to 

If the leaflets are 2″ to 2½″ long, it is **KENTUCKY COFFEE-TREE**
Gymnocladus dioicus →

If each leaf is a fern-like spray of hundreds of small asymmetrical leaflets, shaped like flattened pea pods, and the tree has no thorns,

it is **MIMOSA SILK TREE**
Albizia julibrissin
(center leaf)

If each leaflet is symmetrical, and the tree has some compound and some doubly-compound leaves, and the tree has large thorns, usually branched, (lacking in some horticultural varieties),

it is **HONEY LOCUST**
Gleditsia triacanthos
(lower right)

If there is one tooth, (occasionally 2), at each side of the base of each leaflet,

it is **TREE OF HEAVEN**
Ailanthus altissima

If there are teeth continuously along the margins of the leaflet, (in some cases the basal sections of the leaflets are without teeth),

go below to 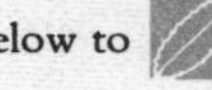

If the leaf has milky juice, and the base of the leaf is enlarged to a cone that encircles next year's bud, and the leaf stem and twig are hairy, and the tree is crooked, shrubby, not tree-shaped,

it is **STAGHORN SUMAC**
Rhus typhina

If there is no milky juice and the tree is tree-shaped,

go on next page to 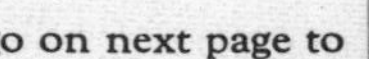

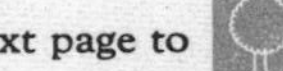

If all the leaflets are small, (not more than 1½"), on a small leaf, (usually not more than 6" to 7"), on a small tree with clusters of white flowers or showy fruit,

go below to 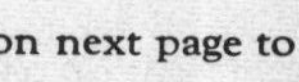

If the leaflets are large, (usually 1½" to 8" long), on large leaves, (usually 8" or more), and there is some evidence of nuts on or under the tree,

go on next page to NUT TREES

If the leaflets have somewhat blunted tips and are hairy beneath,

it is **EUROPEAN MOUNTAIN-ASH**
Sorbus aucuparia

If the leaflets have pointed tips and are hairless,

it is **AMERICAN MOUNTAIN-ASH**
Sorbus americana

×½

×½

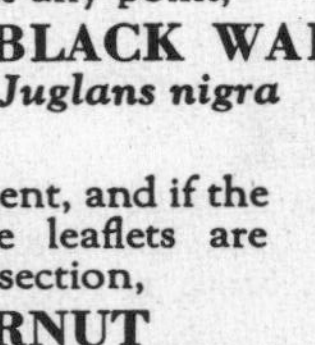

If the crushed leaf is aromatic, and the end leaflet, if present, does not narrow gradually to an elongated, straight-sided V-base, and a long section of the twig reveals layered pith, and the husks of the nuts do not separate into sections,

go below to

If the end leaflet narrows gradually to a long, straight-sided V-shape, and the 3 end leaflets are usually distinctly larger than the basal leaflets, and the husks of the nuts separate,

go on next page to

If the end leaflet is small or lacking, and the side leaflets all taper continuously so that the sides are not parallel at any point,

it is **BLACK WALNUT**
Juglans nigra

If the end leaflet is present, and if the sides of some of the leaflets are parallel along the mid-section,

it is **BUTTERNUT**
WHITE WALNUT
Juglans cinerea

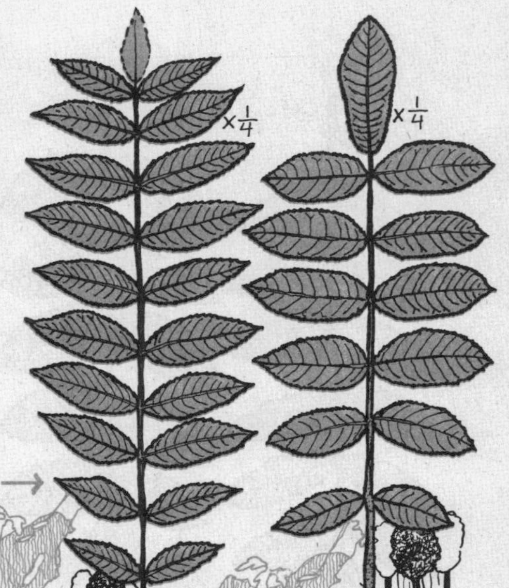

HICKORIES

If the leaflets at the tip of the leaf are much larger than the others, and if the leaf has only 5 to 7 leaflets, go below to

If the 3 tip leaflets are not much larger than the others, and the leaf has 7 to 11 leaflets, go below to

If the underside of the leaves, and the stems and twigs, are covered with a dense, matted wool,

it is **MOCKERNUT HICKORY**
Carya tomentosa

If leaves and stem are smooth, and buds are yellow or have yellow hairs,

go on next page to

If the leaf is 6″ to 12″ long, and the twig is slender without an especially big end bud, it is **PIGNUT HICKORY**
Carya glabra

If the leaf is 12″ to 20″ long, and the twigs are thick, with very big end buds,

it is **SHAGBARK HICKORY**
Carya ovata

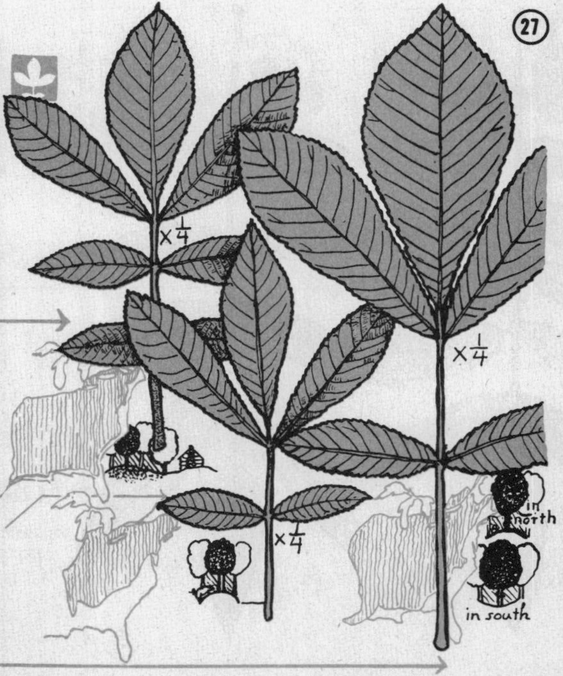

If the leaf is small, (usually less than 12"), and the leaflets, (usually 7), are slightly hairy beneath, and the buds are mustard yellow,

it is **BITTERNUT HICKORY**
Carya cordiformis

If the leaf is 12" to 20" long, with 9 to 17 leaflets, and the buds have yellow hairs,

it is **PECAN**
Carya illinoensis

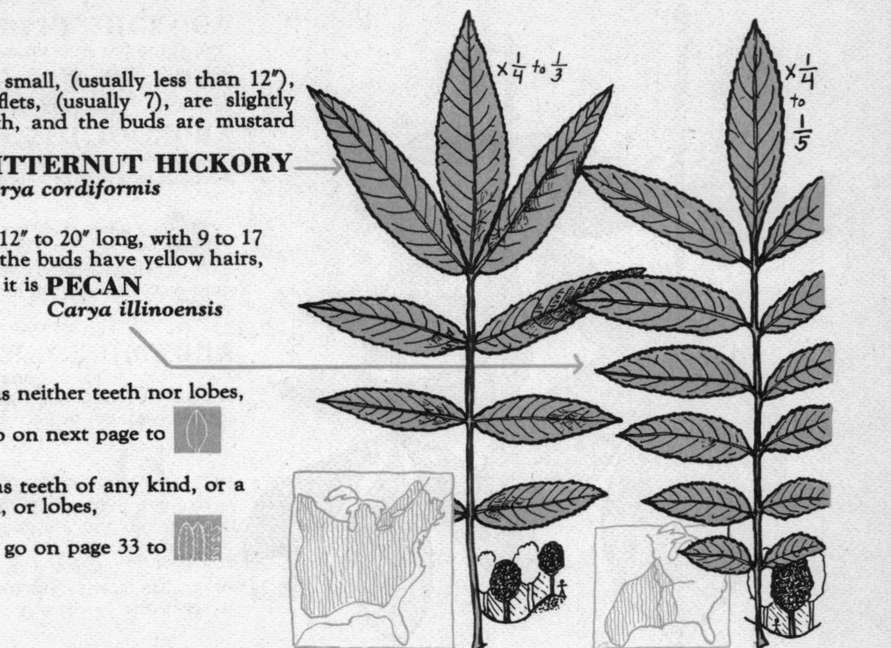

If the leaf has neither teeth nor lobes,

go on next page to

If the leaf has teeth of any kind, or a wavy margin, or lobes,

go on page 33 to

If the leaf is tipped with a single bristle (like the tip of a needle),

go below to

If the leaf has no bristle at its tip, (the leaf may be pointed or not),

go on next page to

If the leaf is dark green above and hairy beneath,

it is **SHINGLE OAK**
Quercus imbricaria

If the leaf is light green above and veiny beneath, with a yellow midrib, and is ¼″ to 1″ wide,

it is **WILLOW OAK**
Quercus Phellos

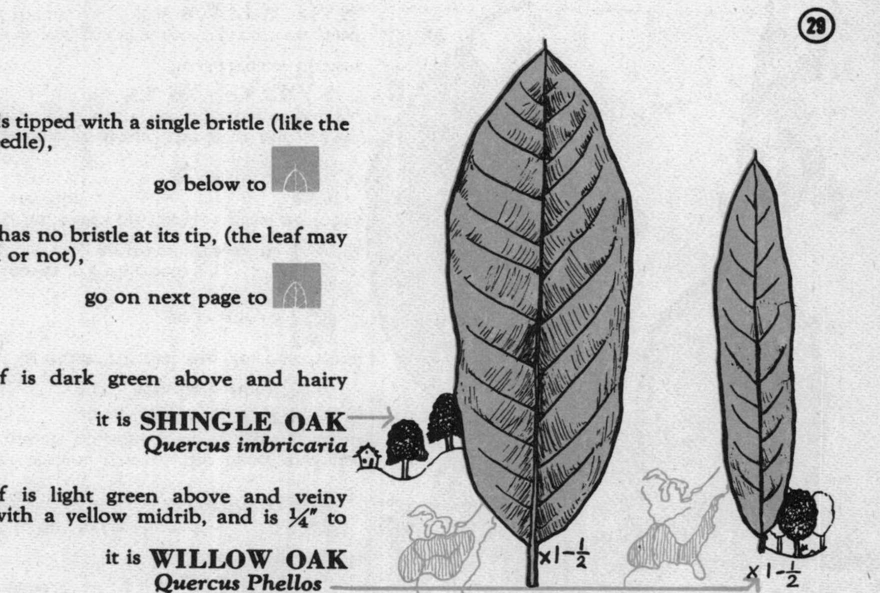

If the leaf is heart-shaped, with veins branching from the base, it is **REDBUD**
Cercis canadensis

If the leaf is not heart-shaped, go below to

If the leaf widens toward the base, and the veins are much branched, on a thorny, small tree, it is **OSAGE ORANGE**
Maclura pomifera

If the leaf is widest toward the tip, or toward the middle, go below to

If all the leaves are unlobed, go on next page to

If some of the leaves on the tree have no lobes but some are lobed, go below to

If the leaves are thin and the bark and leaves are aromatic, and there are 3 forms of leaves, it is **SASSAFRAS**
Sassafras albidum

If the leaves are thick, almost evergreen, and of several forms, it is **WATER OAK**
Quercus nigra

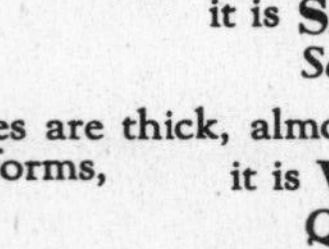

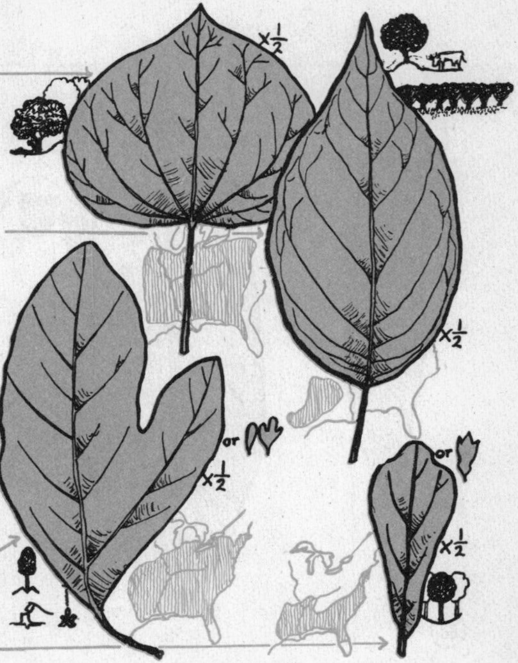

If the leaves are only 2″ to 5″ long, thick, and shiny, go below to

If the leaves are 5″ to 20″, go below to

If the leaf is evergreen, with thickened in-rolled edges, dark green and lustrous above, and silvery-white and hairy below, it is **LIVE OAK** *Quercus virginiana*

If the leaf is deciduous, net-veined, with slender stem, go below to

If the leaf is widest near the tip end and has a broad, flat midrib, it is **SOUR GUM or TUPELO** *Nyssa sylvatica*

If the leaf is widest at the middle, with conspicuous, netted veins, curving with the undulating margin, it is **PERSIMMON** *Diospyros virginiana*

If there is a line, or scar, completely encircling the twig at each leaf, and the end buds are large, go on next page to

If there is no line, and the buds are woolly, without scales, and the leaf stems are very short, it is **PAWPAW** *Asimina triloba*

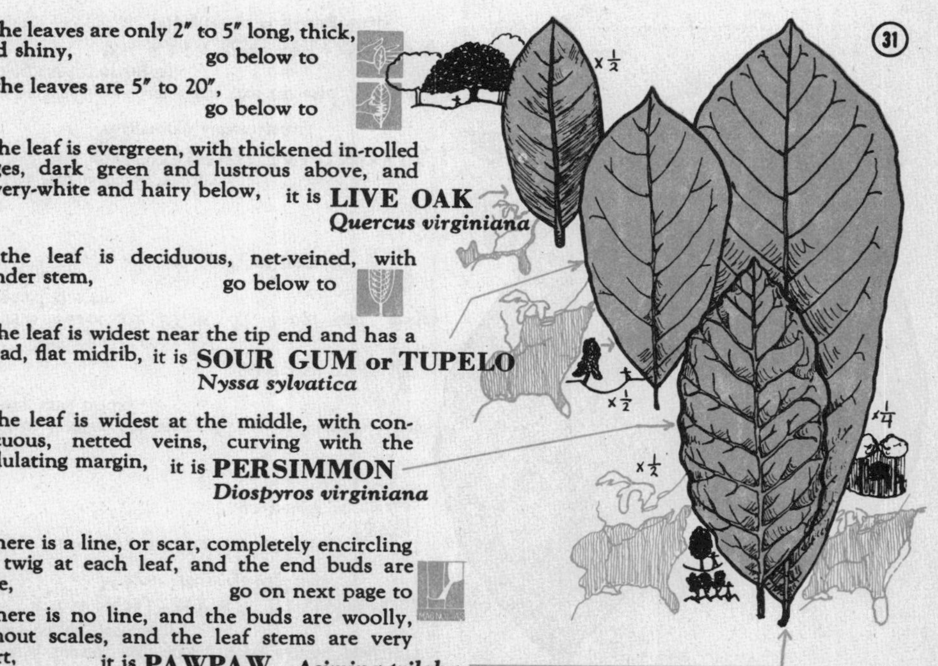

(32)

MAGNOLIAS

If the leaves are evergreen, thick, leathery, rusty-hairy beneath,

it is **SOUTHERN MAGNOLIA**
Magnolia grandiflora

If the leaves are deciduous and thin,

go below to

If the leaves are only 6″ to 10″, with silky-hairy end buds,

go below to

If the leaves are 10″ to 35″ long, and wider toward the tip,

go on next page to

If the leaf is oval, thin,

it is **CUCUMBER MAGNOLIA**
Magnolia acuminata

If the leaf is widest near the tip end, with an abruptly-tapering tip,

it is **SAUCER MAGNOLIA**
Magnolia soulangeana

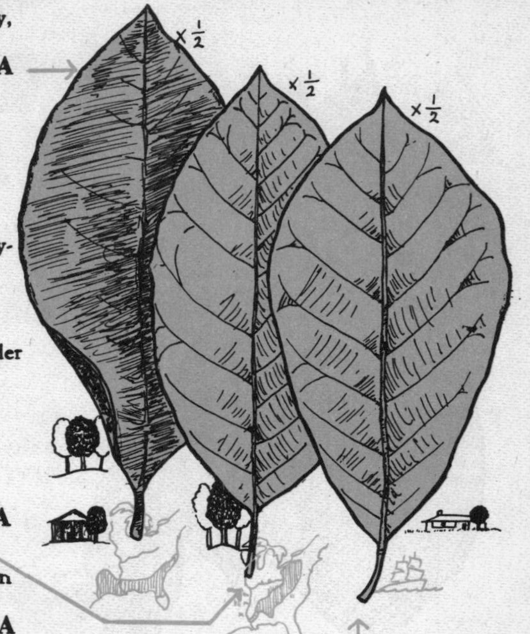

If the base of the leaf is heart-shaped, or ear-lobed,

go below to

If the base of the leaf is tapered,

it is **UMBRELLA MAGNOLIA**
Magnolia tripetala

If the base of the leaf is deeply ear-lobed, and the leaf is 8″ to 18″ long,

it is **MOUNTAIN MAGNOLIA**
Magnolia Fraseri
Center leaf

If the base is heart-shaped, and the leaf is whitish-hairy beneath, 12″ to 36″,

it is **LARGE-LEAVED MAGNOLIA**
Magnolia macrophylla
Right hand leaf

If the leaf is evergreen, tipped with stiff, sharp spines,

go on next page to

If the leaf is not evergreen,

go on next page to

33

34

If the surface of the leaf is dull, and the edge is not wavy, it is **AMERICAN HOLLY**
Ilex opaca

If the surface of the leaf is glossy, and the edge is wavy, it is **ENGLISH HOLLY**
Ilex aquifolium

If the tree has thorns or thorn-like twigs, and is small,
go on page 46 to

If the tree has no thorns or thorn-like twigs,
go below to

If the margin is toothed, or doubly-toothed continuously along all or almost all of its margin,
go below to

If the leaf is either deeply or shallowly lobed or waved, (but not continuously saw-toothed),
go on page 51 to

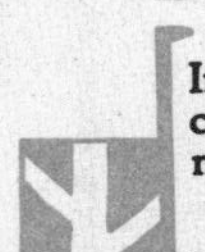

If the leaf is lobed as well as saw toothed, and is about as long as wide, with 3 to 5 main veins,
go on page 54 to

If the leaf is not lobed,
go on next page to

If the teeth are all of about the same size, go below to

If the margin is doubly-toothed, with small teeth between the larger ones, or with slightly deeper notches regularly spaced between teeth, go on page 45 to

If the teeth are of the same number as the side veins and terminate them, go below to

If teeth are more numerous than side veins and do not terminate them, go on page 37 to

If the leaf is 5″ to 8″ long, with teeth curving toward the tip of the leaf, go on next page to

If the leaf is thin, (2½″ to 5″ long), with shallow teeth, go below to

If the leaf is 2″ to 4″ long, not twice as long as wide, with inconspicuous teeth; and there are only 5 to 9 pairs of veins,

it is **EUROPEAN BEECH**
Fagus sylvatica

A variety with bronze-purple leaves, is **COPPER BEECH**
Fagus sylvatica purpurea

If the leaf is 3″ to 5″ long, more than twice as long as it is wide, and the teeth are more conspicuous; and there are 9 to 14 pairs of veins, it is

AMERICAN BEECH
Fagus grandifolia

If the leaf is canoe shaped, with a short stem,
it is **CHESTNUT**
Castanea dentata

(This tree was mostly destroyed by chestnut blight)

If the leaf is thick and pale beneath, with a slender stem,
it is **CHINQUAPIN OAK**
Quercus Muehlenbergii

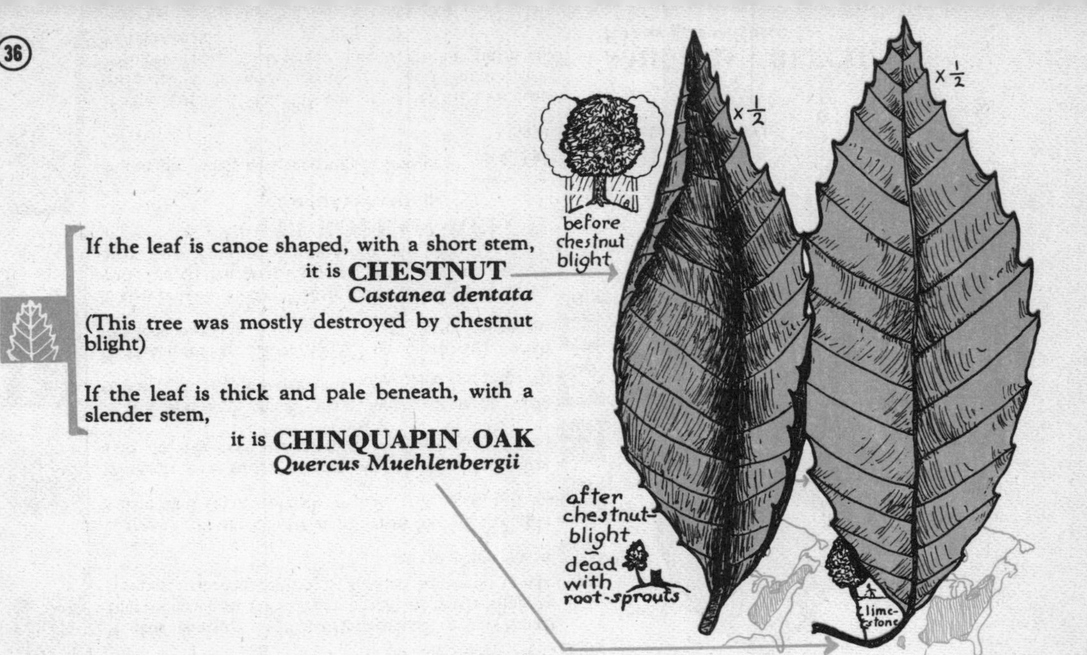

If the leaf stem is long, (at least half as long as the blade), and the teeth are somewhat blunted, and the blade is wide, with firm texture and meshed veinlets, go below to

If the leaf does not have this combination of characteristics, go on page 40 to

If the stem of the leaf is flattened, go below to

If the stem of the leaf is not flattened, go on page 39 to

If the leaf blade is triangular, flat at the base, go below to

If the leaf base is rounded, go on page 38 to

If there are no glands on the leaf-stalk; the leaf has a translucent border and is finely-toothed; (12 or more teeth to an inch), and the tree is shaped like an exclamation point,

it is **LOMBARDY POPLAR**
Populus nigra* variety *italica

If the leaf stalk has 2 or 3 glands at the base of the blade, and the teeth are coarser, (about 5 to 8 to an inch), go on next page to

If the buds are sticky, and the leaf has a wide mid-vein,

it is **EASTERN COTTONWOOD**
Populus deltoides
figure on page 37, bottom

If the buds are slightly hairy, the mid-vein is narrow and the leaf narrows suddenly to a long, tapering tip,

it is **PLAINS COTTONWOOD**
Populus deltoides occidentalis
figure on page 37, right

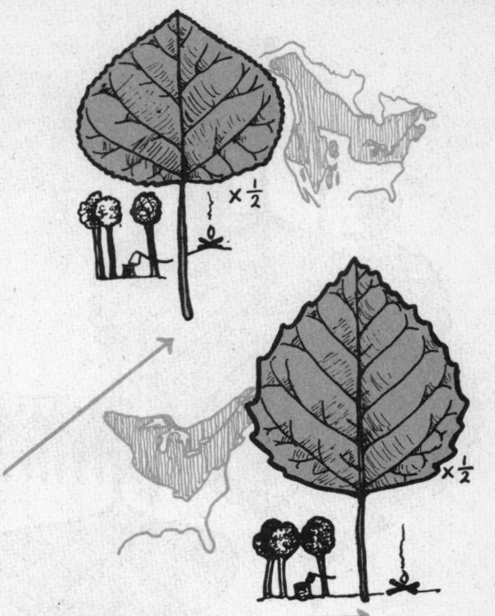

If the leaf is not longer than it is broad, and the teeth are many and fine,

it is **TREMBLING ASPEN**
Populus tremuloides

If the leaf is longer than broad, with teeth coarse and few,

it is **BIG-TOOTHED ASPEN**
Populus grandidentata

If the leaf has a rounded, or only slightly pointed tip; and a heart-shaped base; and is hairy, (sometimes only when newly unfolded),

it is **SWAMP COTTONWOOD**
Populus heterophylla

If the leaf has a pointed tip, and fragrant buds,

go below to 

If the leaf is oval, with a rounded base, and a smooth, slender stem and twigs,

it is **BALSAM POPLAR**
Populus balsamifera

If the leaf is heart-shaped, and hairy on the under-surface, stem and twigs,

it is **BALM OF GILEAD**
Populus gileadensis
(of unknown origin)

If the two side veins starting from the base of the blade are longer and more conspicuous than the other side veins,

go below to

If the side veins are all of about equal importance,

go on page 41 to

If the base of the leaf is definitely not symmetrical,

go below to 

If the base is symmetrical, or only slightly asymmetrical, and the juice is milky, and some leaves are lobed, others unlobed,

go on next page to 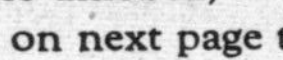

If the leaf is broad,

go on next page to 

If the leaf is narrow, long-pointed with a short stem, and no teeth at the base,

it is **HACKBERRY**
Celtis occidentalis

If the leaf is hairless, it is **LINDEN**
AMERICAN BASSWOOD
Tilia americana

If the underside of the leaf is velvety-white,
it is **WHITE BASSWOOD**
(upper right) *Tilia heterophylla*

If the leaf is rough above and hairy beneath, sometimes 2 or 3 lobed,
it is **RED MULBERRY**
Morus rubra

If the leaves are smooth above and not hairy beneath, usually lobed,
it is **WHITE MULBERRY**
(lower right) *Morus alba*

If the leaves are long and narrow, many-veined, tapering gradually and steadily to a long point, and the twigs are slender and limber, with only one scale covering each bud,

go on next page to

If the leaves and twigs are not thus, and the buds have more than one scale,

go on page 43 to

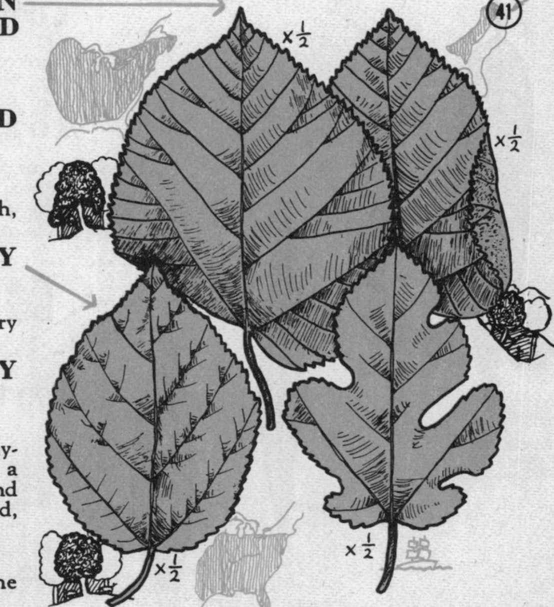

42

If the leaf has white, silky hairs, and tapers to both ends,

it is **WHITE WILLOW**
Salix alba

If the leaf has no silky hairs,

go below to

If the leaf and twigs are drooping,

it is **WEEPING WILLOW**
Salix babylonica

If the twigs are not drooping,

go below to

If the leaf is narrow, deep green on both sides, often sickle-shaped, with a downy stem, and a rounded base, (vigorous sprouts have leaf-like appendages called stipules, at the base of the leaf stem),

it is **BLACK WILLOW**
Salix nigra

If the leaf is wide at the middle, pale green above, paler beneath, and drooping,

it is **PEACH-LEAVED WILLOW**
Salix amygdaloides

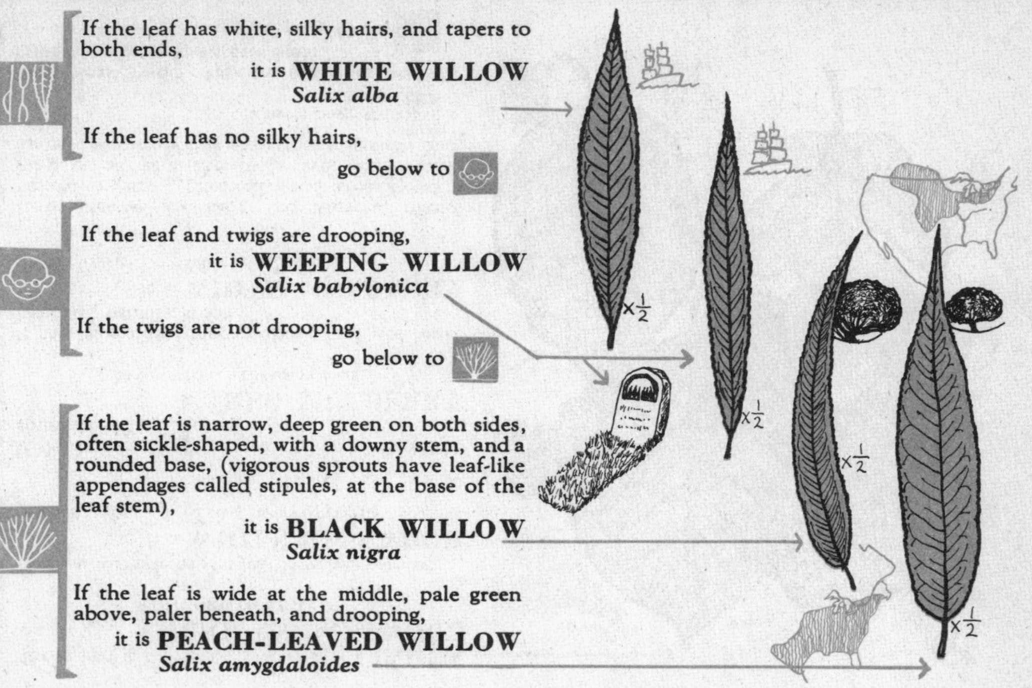

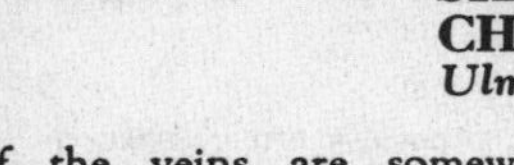

If the veins are straight, parallel, seldom branched, it is **SIBERIAN ELM**
CHINESE ELM
Ulmus pumila

If the veins are somewhat curving and branching,
go below to

If the leaf is 5″ to 7″ long and acid, and if there are large, one-sided clusters of flowers or dried fruit, it is **SOURWOOD**
Oxydendrum arboreum

If the leaf is 4″ or less, go below to

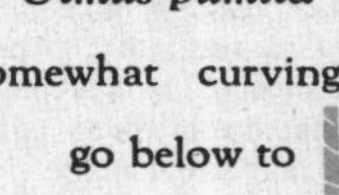

If the leaf stem is about ⅓ to ½ as long as the blade, and the base of the leaf is broadly rounded or slightly heart-shaped, and the stem and undersurface are somewhat downy,
it is **SERVICEBERRY**
JUNEBERRY
Amelanchier arborea

If the leaf stem is short, and the base of the leaf is not rounded or heart-shaped, and the leaf and twig are bitter-tasting,
go on next page to

(44)

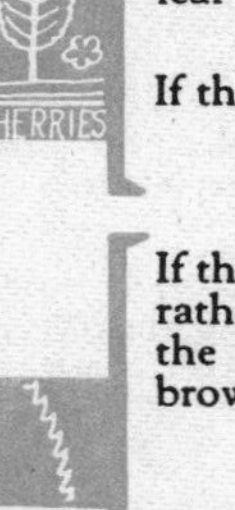

If the leaf is soft, and the veinlets form a dense net-work (especially conspicuous on the under-surface), and the leaf narrows abruptly to a long, tapering tip, and the tree has thorn-like, short twigs, and shaggy bark,

it is **AMERICAN PLUM** →
Prunus americana

If there are no thorn-like twigs, nor dense net-work of veins, nor abruptly tapering point,

go below to CHERRIES

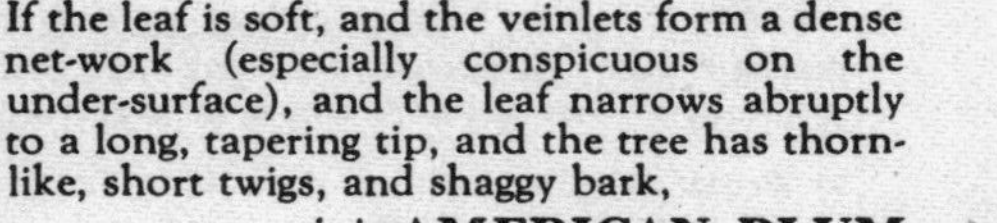

If the teeth are somewhat incurved, and the leaf is narrow,

go below to

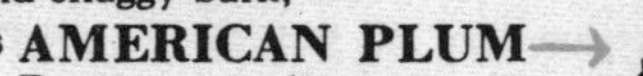

If the teeth are out-curved and the leaf is oval,

it is **CHOKE CHERRY** →
Prunus virginiana

If the leaf is firm and somewhat leathery with a rather broad mid-rib that is conspicuous on the undersurface, where it sometimes bears brownish hairs toward the base of the leaf,

it is **BLACK CHERRY** →
Prunus serotina

If the leaf is thin, hairless,

it is **PIN CHERRY** →
Prunus pensylvanica

If the base of the leaf is lop-sided,

go below to

If the base of the leaf is symmetrical,

go on page 49 to

If the leaf is rough beneath, as well as on the upper surface, and if a flake of bark shows layers of red,

it is **SLIPPERY ELM**
Ulmus rubra

If the leaf is not rough beneath,

go below to

If the leaf base is only slightly lop-sided, and there are usually some twigs with corky wings,

it is **CORK ELM**
Ulmus Thomasi

If the leaf is distinctly lop-sided, and either sand-paper-like or smooth above,

it is **AMERICAN ELM**
Ulmus americana

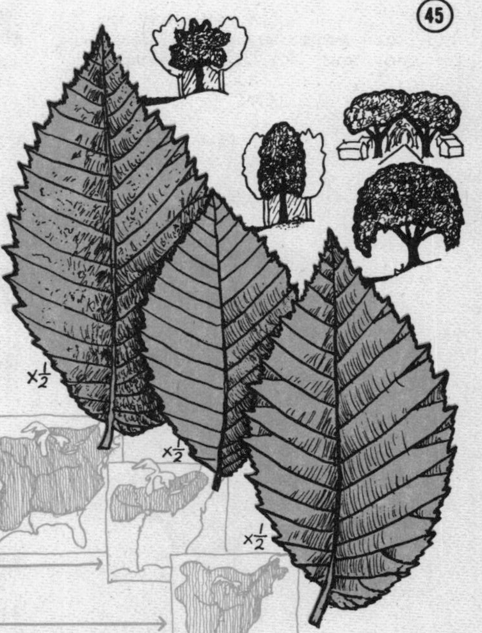

If the thorns are smooth, tapering, often more than an inch long,

go below to

If the thorns are like stunted, pointed twigs, or stubby, blunt spurs,

go on page 48 to

If the leaves are widest at the base,

go below to

If the leaves taper to the base,

go on next page to

If the triangular leaf is hairy, soft, with a thick, hairy stem,

it is **DOWNY HAWTHORN**
Crataegus mollis

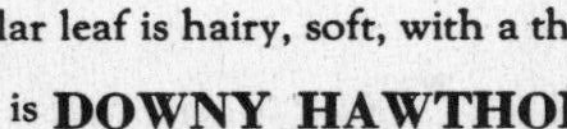

If the triangular leaf is smooth with a slender, smooth stem,

go on next page to

NOTE:

Hawthorns are too numerous to cover completely, these are the common ones.

If some of the leaves are deeply 3-lobed, and some unlobed, and the leaves are long-stemmed, with orange midribs,

it is **WASHINGTON HAWTHORN**
Crataegus Phaenopyrum

If the triangular leaf is smooth, not deeply 3-lobed,

it is **THICKET HAWTHORN**
Crataegus pruinosa

If the margin has two sizes of teeth, and the leaf has deeply set veins,

it is **DOTTED HAWTHORN**
Crataegus punctata

If the margin has only one size of teeth, and the leaf is smooth and leathery,

it is **COCKSPUR HAWTHORN**
Crataegus crus-galli

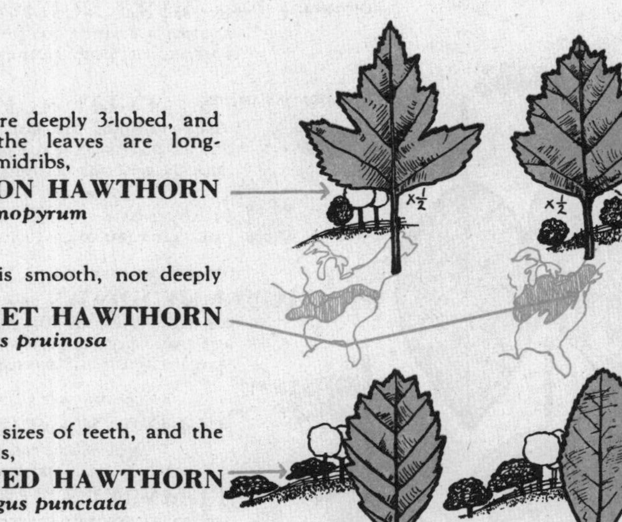

If the leaf is not lobed, go below to

If the leaf is usually somewhat lobed, go below to

If twigs, leaf stems, and undersurfaces are woolly, it is **PRAIRIE CRABAPPLE** *Malus ioensis*

If the leaves and twigs are not woolly, it is **WILD CRABAPPLE** *Malus coronaria*

If the leaf surface, especially the undersurface, shows an intricate network of veins, and the leaf has a long, tapering tip, and the spurs are slender, it is **AMERICAN PLUM** see illustration page 44 *Prunus americana*

If the surface shows no intricate network, and the spurs are stout, go below to

If there is soft, woolly hair on the new shoots, and on the underside of the leaves, and on the leaf stems, and the spurs are seldom sharp-tipped, it is **COMMON APPLE** *Malus sylvestris*

If the leaf surfaces are smooth, and the margins have rounded teeth, and the spurs are usually sharp-tipped, it is **COMMON PEAR** *Pyrus communis*

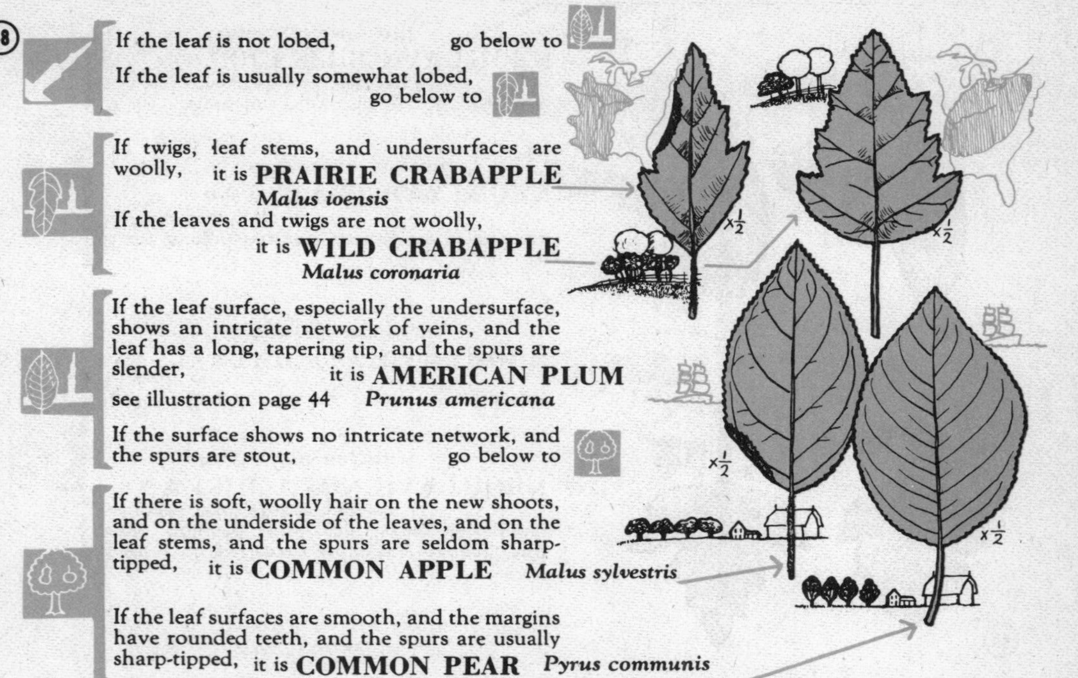

If the leaf has a blunt tip,
it is **EUROPEAN ALDER**
Alnus glutinosa

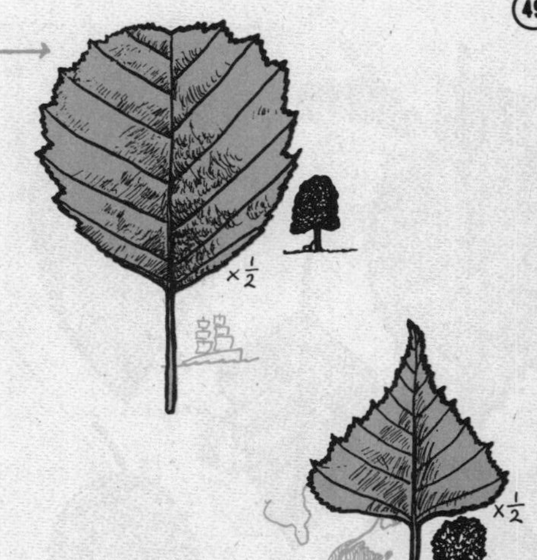

If the leaf has a pointed tip,
go below to

If the bark (except on old trunks) is paper-smooth, or shiny, or peeling, or ragged,
go below to

If the bark is grey-scaly, or dark blue-grey,
go on page 51 to

If the trunks are white,
go below to

If the trunks are yellowish to red-brown,
go on next page to

If the leaf is triangular with a long tapering tip,
it is **GRAY BIRCH**
Betula populifolia

If the leaf is oval,
go on next page to

If the buds are shiny with resin,
it is **EUROPEAN WHITE BIRCH**
Betula alba

If the leaf buds are not sticky and shiny,
it is **AMERICAN WHITE BIRCH**
PAPER-WHITE BIRCH
Betula papyrifera

If the base of the leaf is slightly heart-shaped,
go below to

If the base of the leaf is wedge-shaped, the bark ragged and shaggy, it is **RED BIRCH**
RIVER BIRCH
Betula nigra

If the bark is dark brown, not peeling,
it is **CHERRY BIRCH**
Betula lenta

If the bark is bronze, or silvery, peeling in thin, curly flakes, it is **YELLOW BIRCH**
Betula alleghaniensis

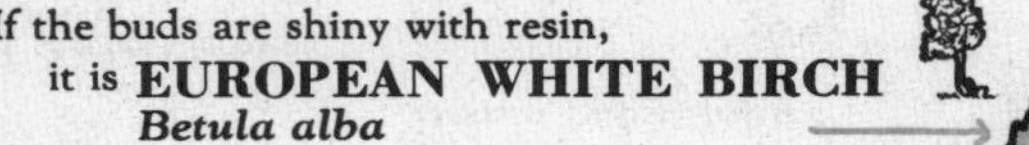

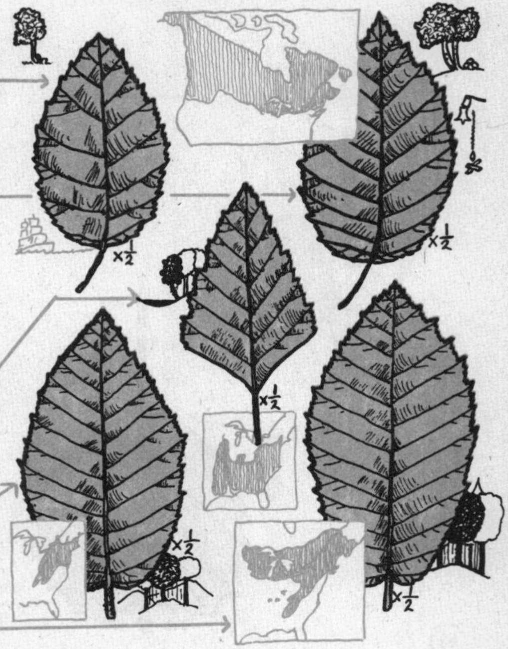

If the veins are unbranched, the base of the leaf is rounded,

it is **BLUE BEECH**
AMERICAN HORNBEAM
Carpinus caroliniana

If the veins are somewhat branched, and the base of the leaf slightly heart-shaped,

it is **IRONWOOD**
Ostrya virginiana

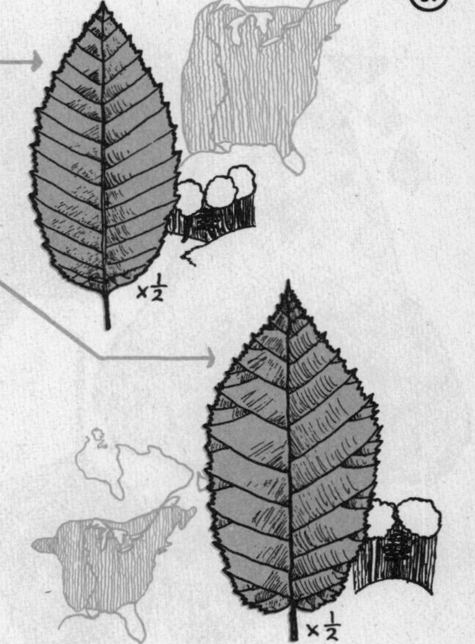

If the margin has waves, hardly indented deeply enough to be called lobes,

go below to

If the leaf is lobed,

go on page 53 to

If the leaf stem is long, (about as long as the blade, or longer),

go on next page to

If the leaf stem is not as long as the blade,

go on next page to

52

If the leaf has a felt-like, white undersurface, (some of the leaves may be lobed),

it is **WHITE POPLAR**
Populus alba

If the veins are arranged like the ribs of a fan,

it is **GINKGO**
Ginkgo biloba

Figure page 54

If the leaf is usually bristle-tipped, and widest at the tip, and some leaves on the tree are lobed,

go below to

If there are no bristle tips,

go on next page to

If the leaves are small, 2″ to 4″, shining on both sides, almost evergreen, and there may be both lobed and unlobed leaves, and wavy-edged leaves, and leaves with and without bristles, all on the same tree, it is **WATER OAK**
Quercus nigra

If the leaves are 4″ to 6″ long, usually with bristles on the 3 to 5 waves or lobes, (sometimes without bristles), and the underside is rusty-hairy, it is **BLACKJACK OAK**
Quercus marilandica

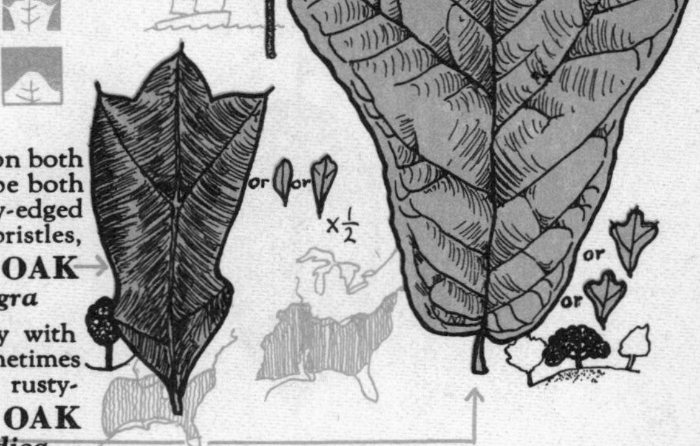

If the waves are regular, and rounded, and the leaves are broadly oval,

it is **CHESTNUT OAK**
Quercus Prinus
(left leaf)

If the waves are irregular, sometimes almost deep enough to be called lobes, and the leaves are soft and hairy beneath,

it is **SWAMP-WHITE OAK**
Quercus bicolor
(right leaf)

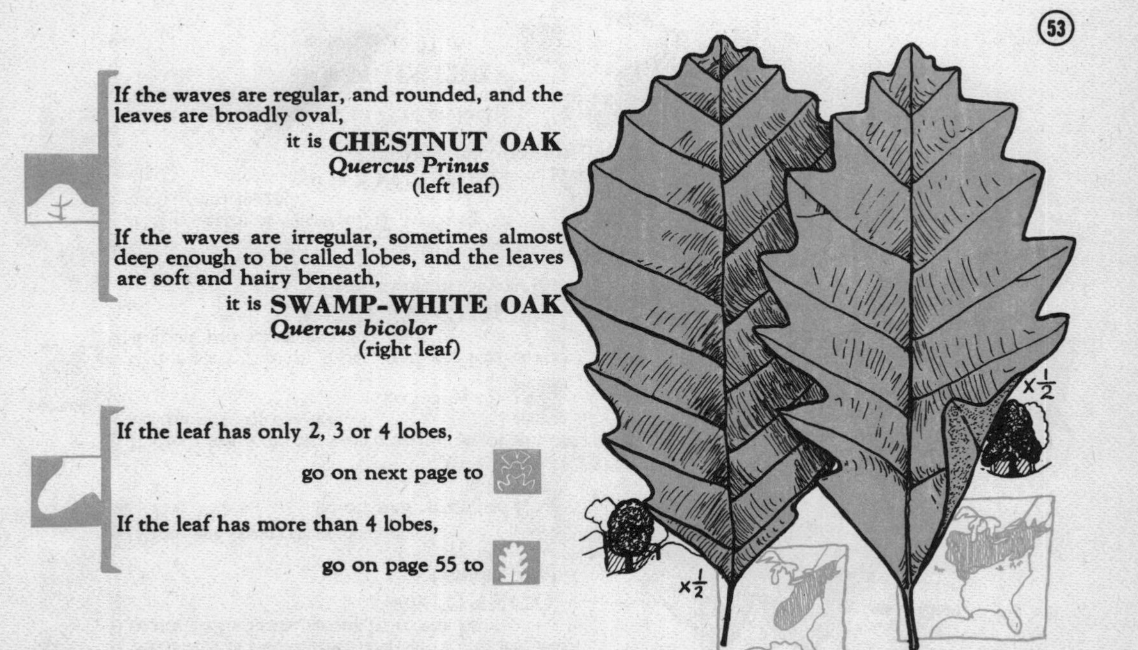

If the leaf has only 2, 3 or 4 lobes,

go on next page to

If the leaf has more than 4 lobes,

go on page 55 to

If the leaf is fan-shaped with only 2 lobes, with many veins fanning out from the base,

it is **GINKGO**
Ginkgo biloba

If the leaf is not thus,

go on next page to

If there are 3 main veins starting at, or almost at, the base of the leaf,

go below to

If there are 5 main lobes, and the leaf is star shaped and aromatic,

it is **SWEET GUM**
Liquidambar Styraciflua

If the teeth are coarse, (2 to 3 to an inch), and jagged,

it is **SYCAMORE**
Platanus occidentalis

If the teeth are fine, (10 to 15 to an inch), and rounded,

it is **MULBERRY**

go on page 41 to

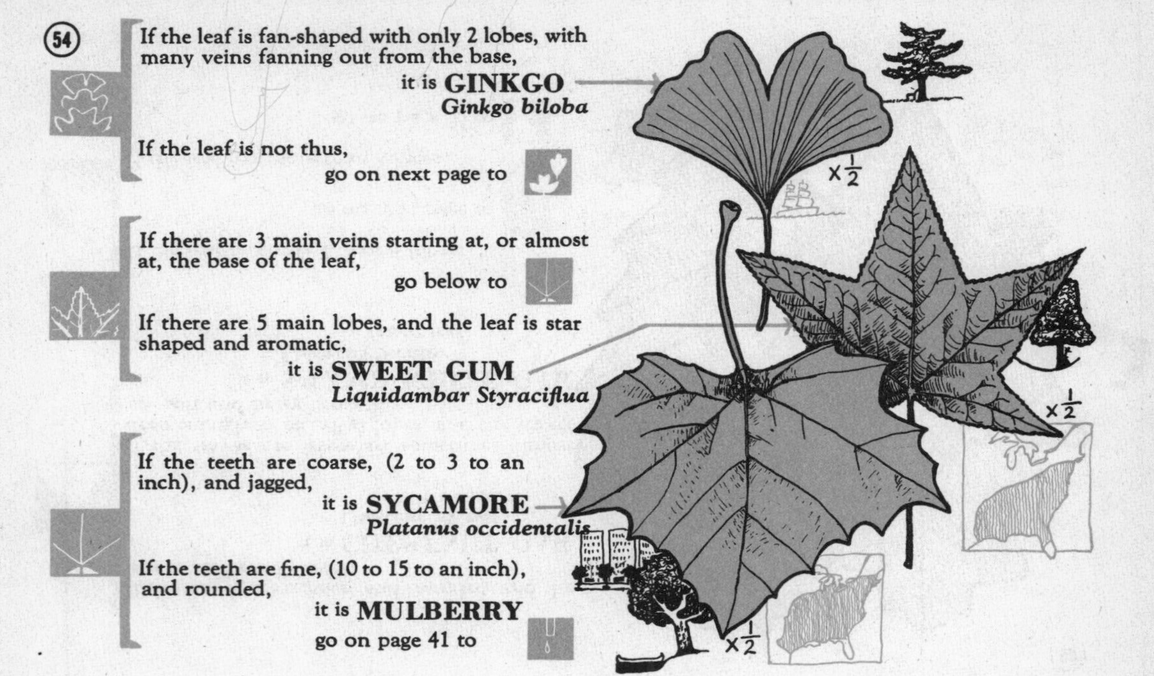

If the tree has some lobed leaves and some unlobed leaves,

go below to

If the main vein ends in a notch, and the tip looks cut off, it is **TULIP TREE**
Liriodendron Tulipifera
right-hand leaf

If the leaf is thin and some leaves are mitten-shaped, it is **SASSAFRAS**
Sassafras albidum
left-hand leaf

If the leaf is thick and leathery,

go on page 52 to

If the lobes are bristle-pointed,

go below to

If the lobes are rounded,

go on page 58 to

If the leaf is not deeply lobed, (not more than half-way to the mid-rib),

go on next page to

If the leaf is deeply lobed, (more than half-way to the mid-rib),

go on next page to

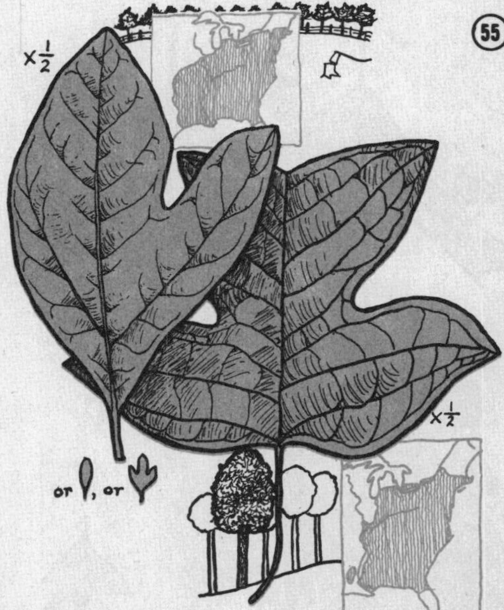

If the leaf is small, white-downy beneath on a small tree,
it is **SCRUB OAK**
BEAR OAK
Quercus ilicifolia

If the leaf is not thus,
go below to

If the tip end of the leaf is narrow, long, (about ⅓ to ½ the length of the blade),
it is **SPANISH OAK**
Quercus falcata
(lower right leaf)

If the leaf is not thus,
go on page 57 to

If the leaf is thin, firm, smooth beneath, 5" to 9" long, with lobes that taper toward their tips, usually more than 7-lobed,
it is **RED OAK**
Quercus rubra

If the leaf is thick, leathery, usually widening toward the tip, usually 7-lobed, somewhat hairy beneath, (the tree usually has several different forms of leaves), and the buds are angled,
it is **BLACK OAK**
Quercus velutina
(upper right leaves)

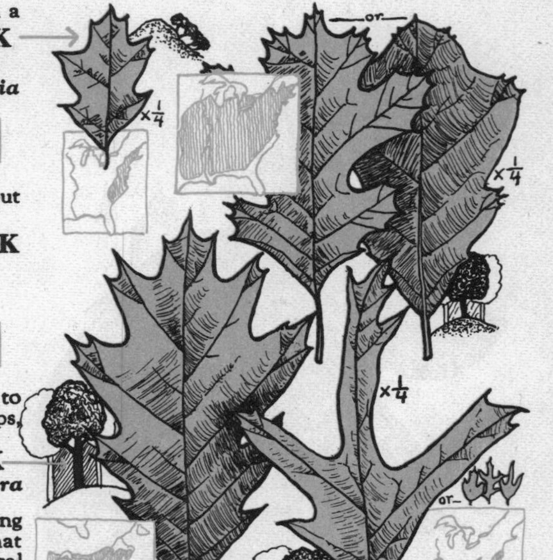

If the lobes taper toward their tips and the leaf is small, (3″ to 4″), often only 5-lobed, with a wedge-shaped base,

it is **PIN OAK**
Quercus palustris

If the lobes broaden toward their tips,

go below to 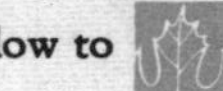

If the leaf is dark green, shining, oval, on an untidy-looking tree, usually with the lowest branches dead,

it is **HILL'S OAK**
JACK OAK
Quercus ellipsoidalis

If the leaf is thin, delicate, with lobes sometimes almost enclosing oval spaces, and with a yellow mid-rib,

it is **SCARLET OAK**
Quercus coccinea

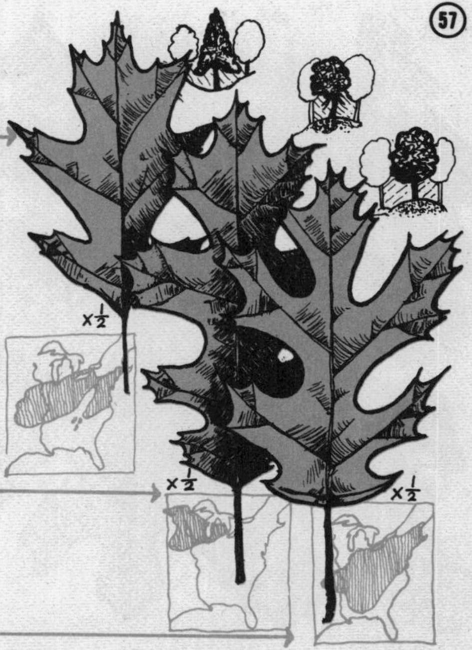

x ½

x ½

x ½

If the leaf is small, (2″ to 4″), and has ear-like lobes at the base, and a *very* short stem,

it is **ENGLISH OAK**
Quercus Robur
(lower right leaf)

If the leaf is not thus,
go below to

If the lobes are square cut, with the 3 end lobes much larger than the others, it is **POST OAK**
Quercus stellata
(lower left leaf)

If the lobes are not thus,
go below to

If the lobes are somewhat similar in size and shape,

it is **WHITE OAK**
Quercus alba
(upper left leaf)

If the middle of the leaf is cut nearly to the midrib, on most of the leaves, and the upper half of the leaf is not deeply lobed,

it is **BUR OAK**
Quercus macrocarpa
(upper right leaf)

Desert Tree Finder

a pocket manual for identifying desert trees

by May Theilgaard Watts
Tom Watts

To identify a tree, begin on the next page with the first choice:

either  or

...and go on from there. After a few more choices, you'll come to a drawing and the name of your tree.

advice: See pages 2-7 before you begin.

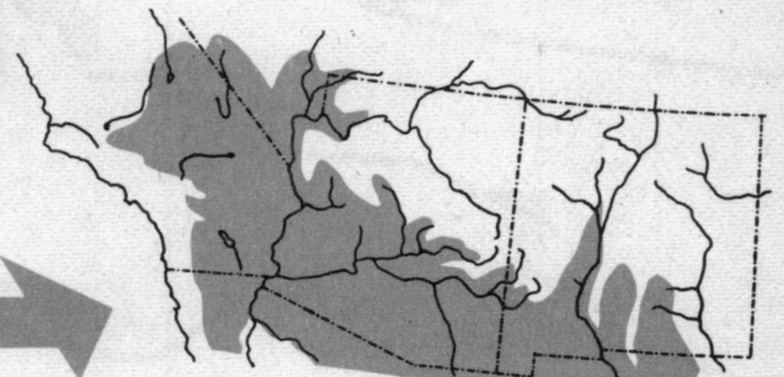

area covered by this book

This book is for identifying trees of the desert and dry desert hills, and some trees commonly grown in Man-made oases. For higher altitudes which have enough rainfall for pine trees, use:

the ROCKY MOUNTAIN TREE FINDER (Arizona, New Mexico)
the PACIFIC COAST TREE FINDER (California)

You can tell pine trees by their long needles bundled together at the base:

Begin here

(1)

If the tree you are identifying grows among:

fire plugs, grassy graves, water tanks,

putting greens, orange blossoms,

fountains, pools,

or sounds of lawnmowers and air conditioners,

you are in a Man-made oasis. Go to this symbol on page 54.

If there is no water supply in pipes or ditches, go to this symbol page 8.

(2) **Maps in this book show the natural ranges of trees**

These symbols show how or where desert trees are likely to grow:

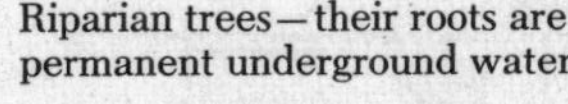

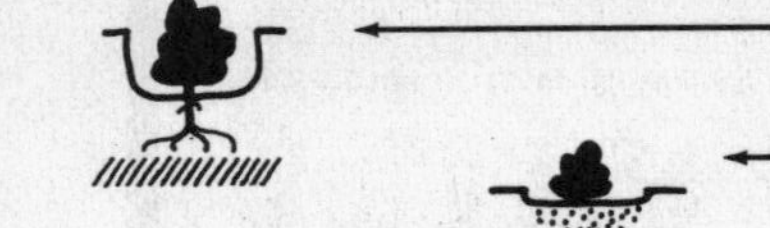

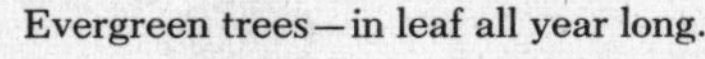

Riparian trees—their roots are in permanent underground water.

Trees of desert washes—they grow where flood waters gather after a thunderstorm.

Evergreen trees—in leaf all year long.

Trees leafless in dry seasons—they leaf out only after a good rain.

Trees leafless in winter only.

Trees of the oak-juniper woodland. These trees of higher altitudes also grow in canyons and cool slopes at the edge of the desert.

Trees introduced by Man which have escaped from cultivation and are now growing wild.

Domesticated trees of the desert, planted in parks, yards and cemeteries.

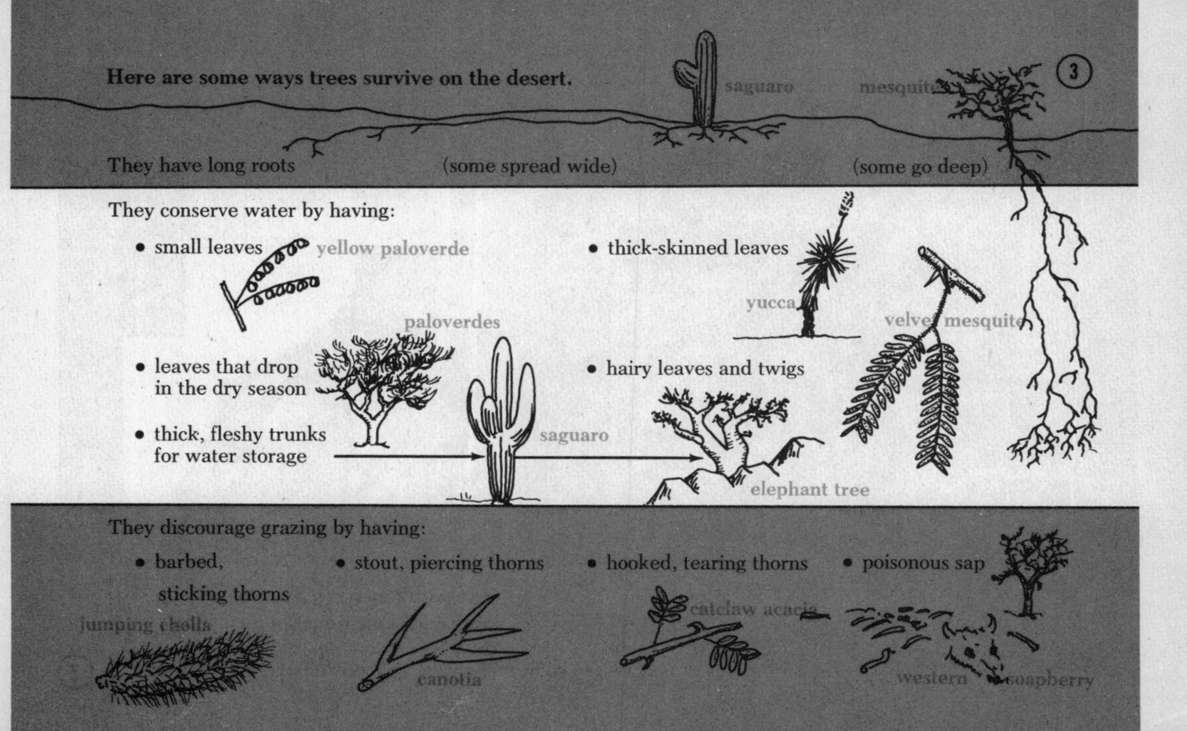
3
Here are some ways trees survive on the desert.
saguaro
mesquite
They have long roots
(some spread wide)
(some go deep)
They conserve water by having:
• small leaves
yellow paloverde
• thick-skinned leaves
yucca
velvet mesquite
paloverdes
• leaves that drop in the dry season
• hairy leaves and twigs
• thick, fleshy trunks for water storage
saguaro
elephant tree
They discourage grazing by having:
• barbed, sticking thorns
• stout, piercing thorns
• hooked, tearing thorns
• poisonous sap
jumping cholla
canotia
catclaw acacia
western soapberry

Rainfall Most of the rain in the desert region falls in the cool higher altitudes of the surrounding mountains. Lower altitudes are warmer, but the rainfall there may dry up in mid air. The high-rainfall areas on this map show also where the high mountains are:

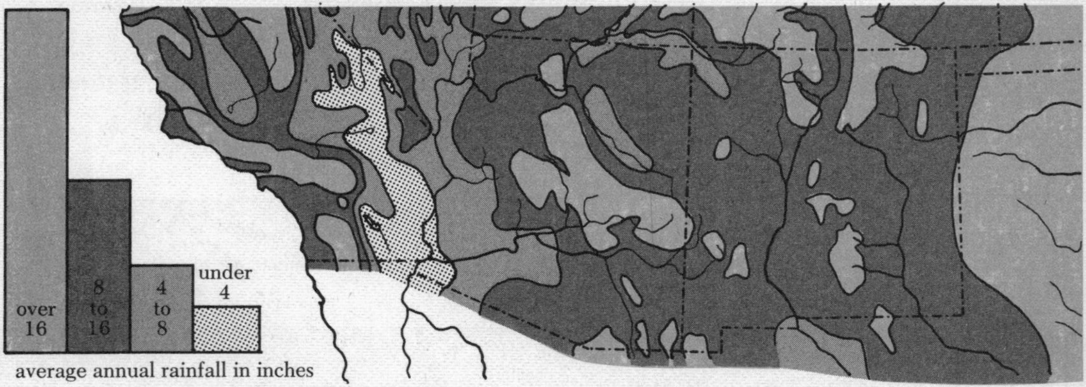

over 16
8 to 16
4 to 8
under 4

average annual rainfall in inches

Where the average yearly rainfall is under 16 inches, it makes a great difference to trees how much the amount of rain varies from year to year, and what season the rain falls—matters which depend on seasonal winds from the Atlantic and Pacific Oceans.

Winter Rain

Weakened remnants of the winter storms which drench the California coast can bring sparse, gentle rain east as far as the Continental Divide. But many desert trees can't benefit from rain in winter when it's too cold for their roots to grow or seeds to germinate. Winter rains seldom reach the Chihuahuan Desert. It has dry, frosty winters.

Summer Rain (5)

Monsoon winds can bring unstable, tropical air from the Gulf of Mexico. The resulting thundershowers soak unevenly into the soil, but they come at the best season for trees. Summer rains are most reliable in the eastern end of the Sonoran Desert (the desert with the most abundant trees). To the west, the rains thin out, may skip a year. The trees are smaller and farther apart too.

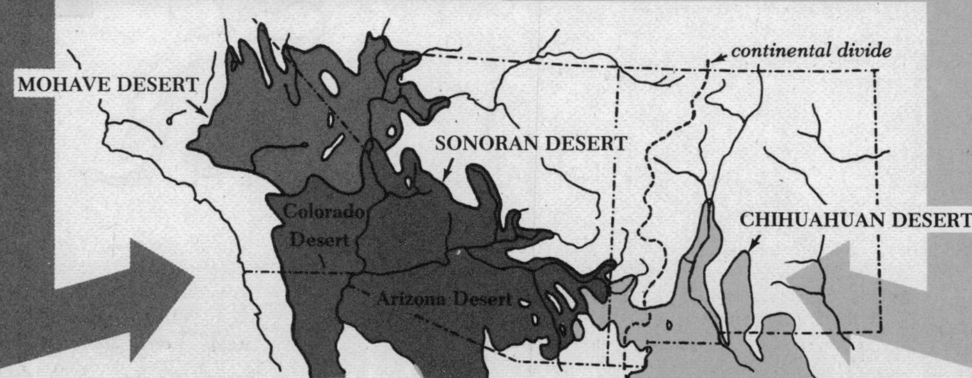

6

Desert Soils

Desert mountains stand knee-deep in their own debris—eroded rock, gravel, sand and clay—which forms long bajadas (slopes) leading down to an intermountain basin or valley. In the desert dryness, soil changes along these slopes can mean life or death for trees. Violent, splashing rain causes sheet erosion which makes a network of temporary watercourses emptying into

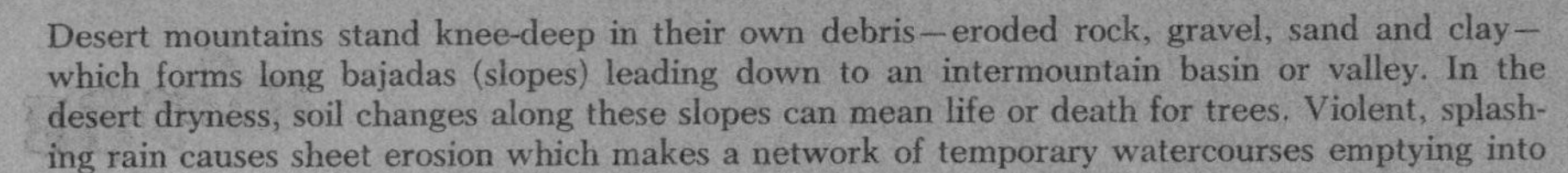

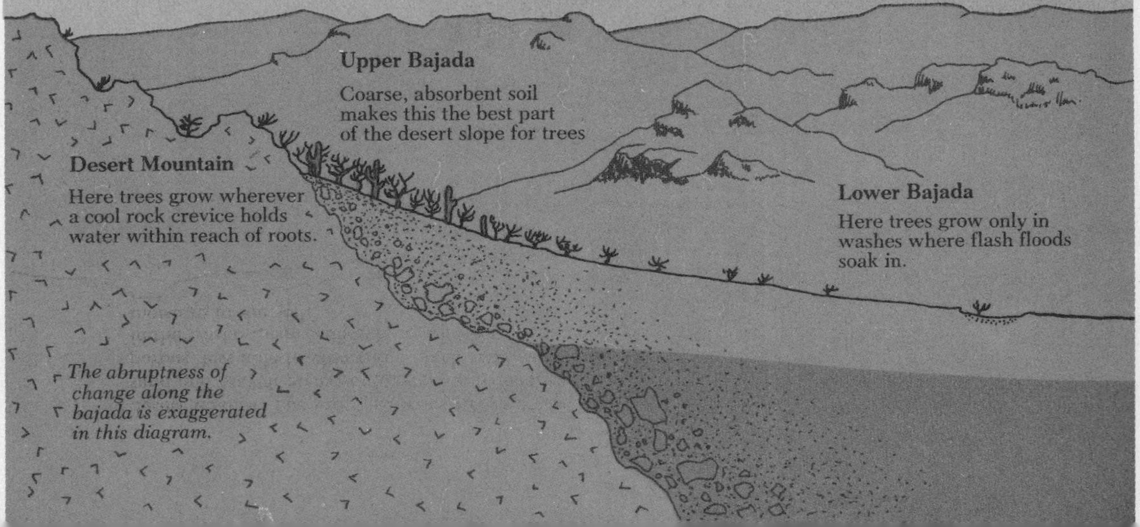

7

desert washes. The erosion carries the finer soil particles farther down slope than the coarser sand and gravel. So as you descend a bajada, the trees thin out because soils become finer, less porous, less able to absorb the quick rains which run off and collect in the washes. Trees grow in the washes, especially where a layer of windblown sand collects in the depressions and holds moisture in the soil.

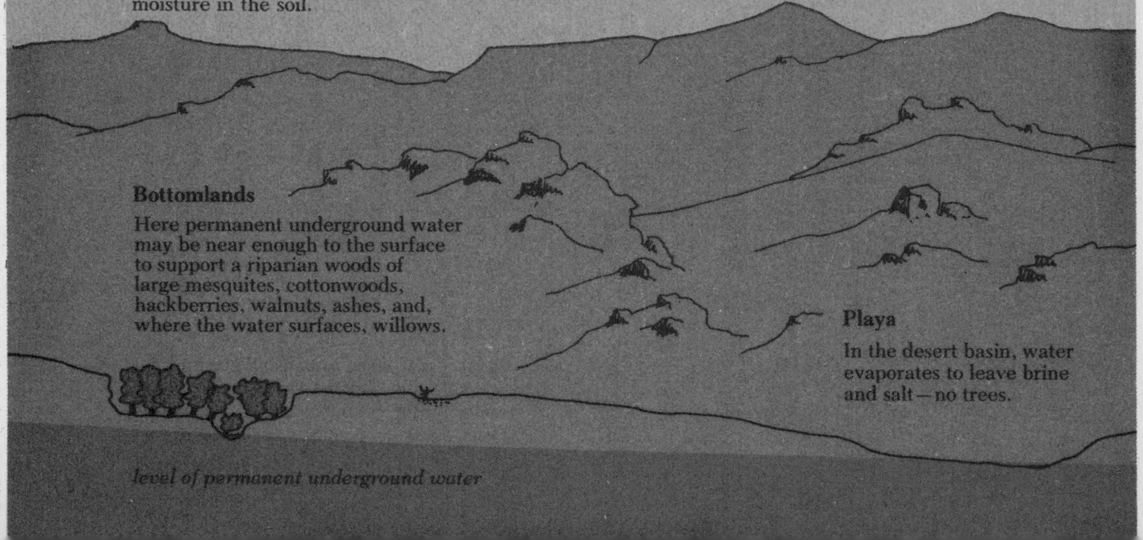

Bottomlands

Here permanent underground water may be near enough to the surface to support a riparian woods of large mesquites, cottonwoods, hackberries, walnuts, ashes, and, where the water surfaces, willows.

Playa

In the desert basin, water evaporates to leave brine and salt—no trees.

level of permanent underground water

If the tree is a cactus, fleshy outside, woody within; and bears clustered spines, go to →  below

If it's not a cactus, go to →  page 12

If there are many jointed-looking branches which divide into smaller branches pointing in all directions, it's a CHOLLA. Go to →  page 11

If the branches are few; or if they all come up from the ground, go to →  next page

If a single trunk rises from the ground, it is **SAGUARO** *Cereus giganteus*

Sajuaro branches are crowned with waxen, night-blooming flowers in April, and edible red fruit in June (harvested by Papago Indians). After rain, trunk corrugations flatten out as flesh absorbs water and swells.

If there are many erect branches coming up from the ground, go to next page

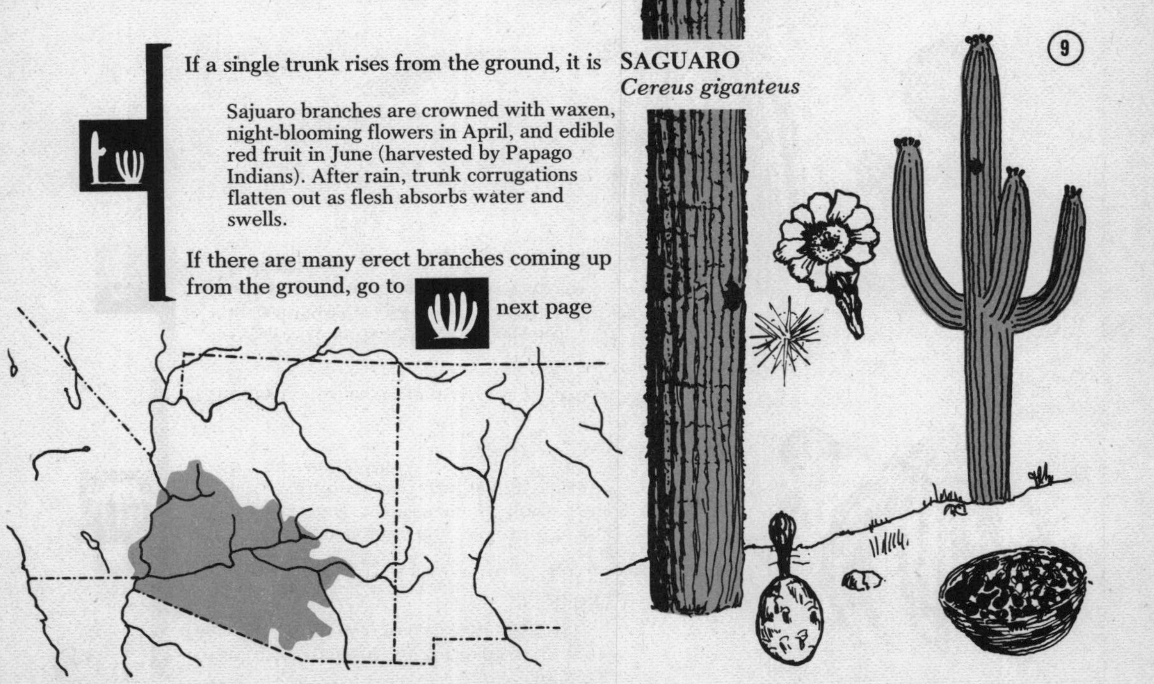

10

If the upper parts of the branches are bearded with grey, twisted spines, it is

SENITA
Lophocereus schottii

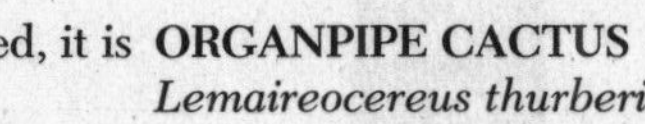

Senita branches are crowned April to August with pink, night-blooming flowers, and later with small, red fruits eaten by cattle. It's rare in the U.S.

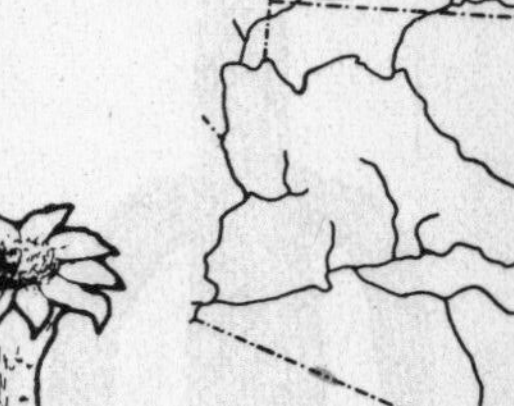

If the branches aren't bearded, it is **ORGANPIPE CACTUS**
Lemaireocereus thurberi

From May to June there are greenish-brown flowers; and later, many juicy, sweet, red fruits harvested by Papago Indians.

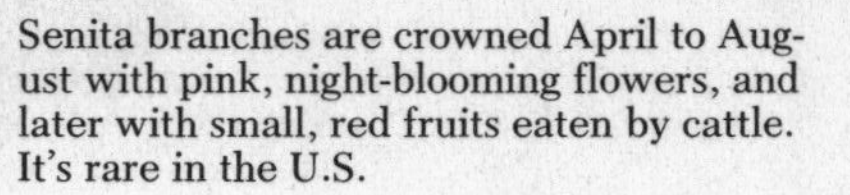

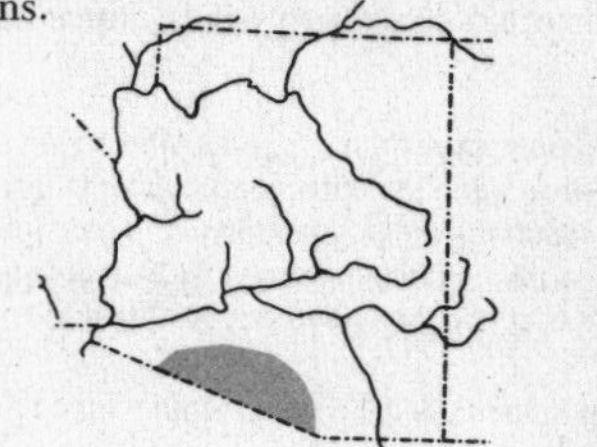

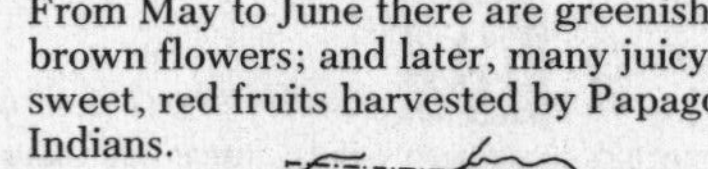

(11)

If the jointed branches are densely covered with straw-colored spines; the trunk bark black; and the fruits dangle in long clusters, it is

JUMPING CHOLLA
Opuntia fulgida

The joints, which can sprout a new plant, detach or "jump" at a touch. Barbed spines discourage a second touch.

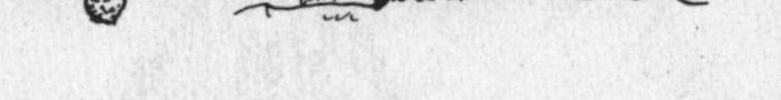

If the spines are dark, of uneven length and the trunk bark is lighter, it is

STAGHORN CHOLLA
Opuntia versicolor

Flowers are orange to brown. Fruit persists on the plant through the winter.

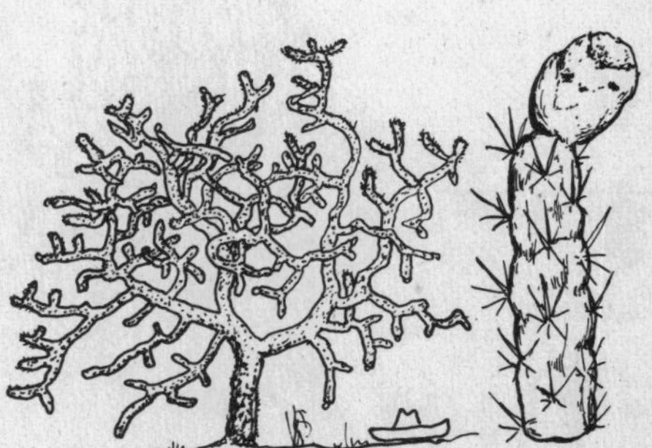

If all leaves are clustered at the tip of a single trunk, or at the tips of the branches, go to below

If they are not so clustered, or if the tree is leafless, go to page 16

If the leaves are long-stemmed, fan-shaped it is **CALIFORNIA FAN PALM**
Washingtonia filifera

If the leaves are stemless, spear-shaped, it's a YUCCA. Go to next page

If the tree has many branches; and if there are small, sharp teeth along the leaf edges, it is **JOSHUA TREE** *Yucca brevifolia*

If there are only a few branches, or just a main trunk; and if the leaves are edged with peeling fibers, go to next page

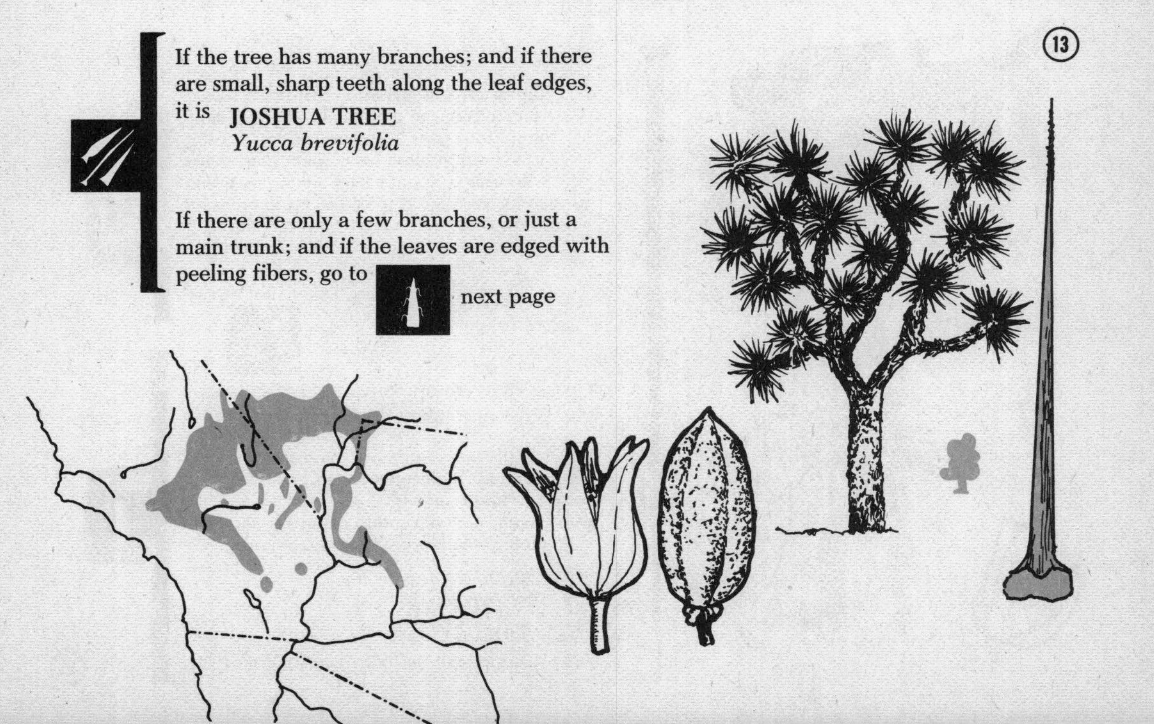

14

If the leaves are flexible, grasslike, it is

SOAPTREE YUCCA
PALMILLA
Yucca elata

The flower stalk is long, bearing many flowers on its upper part, but naked on its lower part. Seed capsules open in three parts to release seeds, and remain on the stalk through the winter.

If the leaves are stiff, daggerlike; and dead leaves cover the trunk almost to its base, go to

next page

On dry yucca seedpods you'll find a small hole made by the escape of a larva that fed on some of the seeds. It grew from an egg laid by a female yucca moth, whose instinct then made her pollinate the yucca flower, thereby ensuring seed formation. This probably happened at night, when desert creatures do business after hiding from the hot daytime sun.

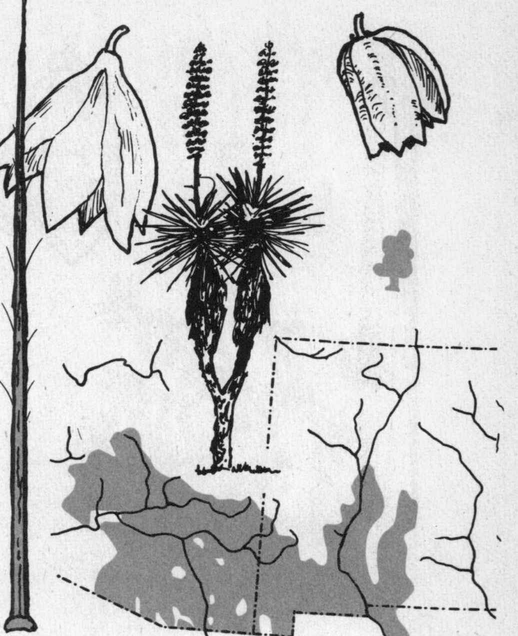

If the leaf is edged with coarse, splinter-like fibers; and the flower cluster is shorter, it is

MOJAVE YUCCA
Yucca schidigera

If the leaf has many whitish threads along its edge; and flower clusters are three to four feet long, it is **TORREY YUCCA**
Yucca torreyi

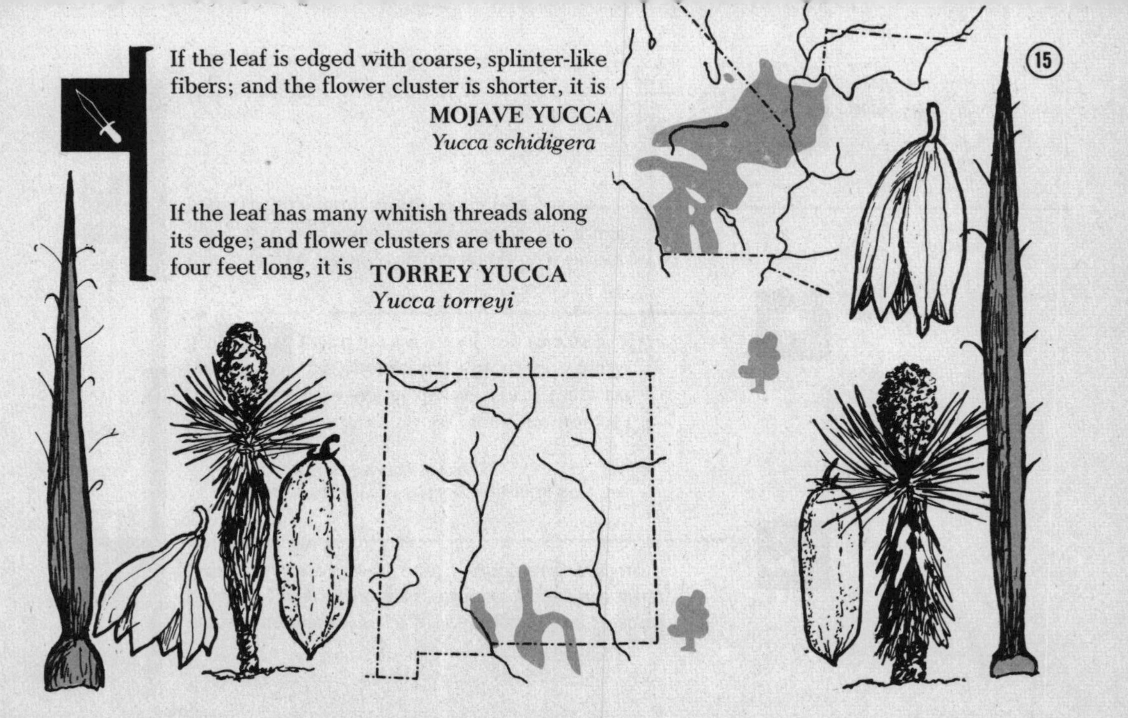

If the tree has green or grey twigs ending in sharp, tapered thorns or spines; and the leaves are either totally absent, or else small, ephemeral, and unimportant, go to ——→ below

In winter, or the dry season, you may have to look under the tree for its leaves.

If there are thorns or spines along the side of the twig rather than just at the end; or if there are some leaves big enough for a fly to hide under; or if there are just leaves without any thorns at all, go to ——→ page 21

If almost the whole tree has smooth, yellow-green bark; or if there are yellow flowers, bean-like pods, or tiny compound leaves, it is ——→

If the tree isn't like that, go to ——→ page 18

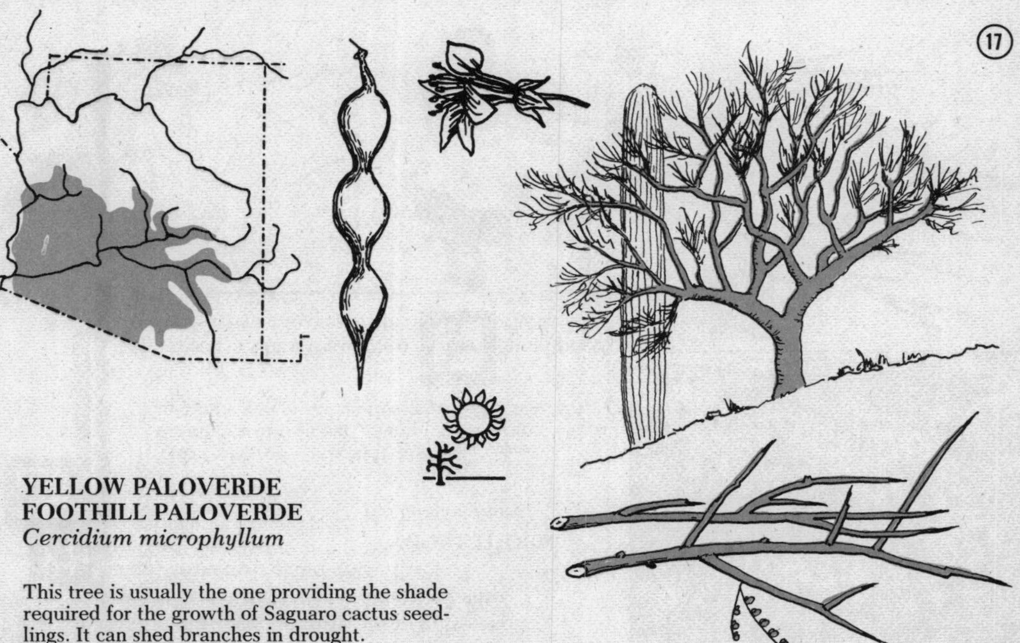

17

YELLOW PALOVERDE
FOOTHILL PALOVERDE
Cercidium microphyllum

This tree is usually the one providing the shade required for the growth of Saguaro cactus seedlings. It can shed branches in drought.

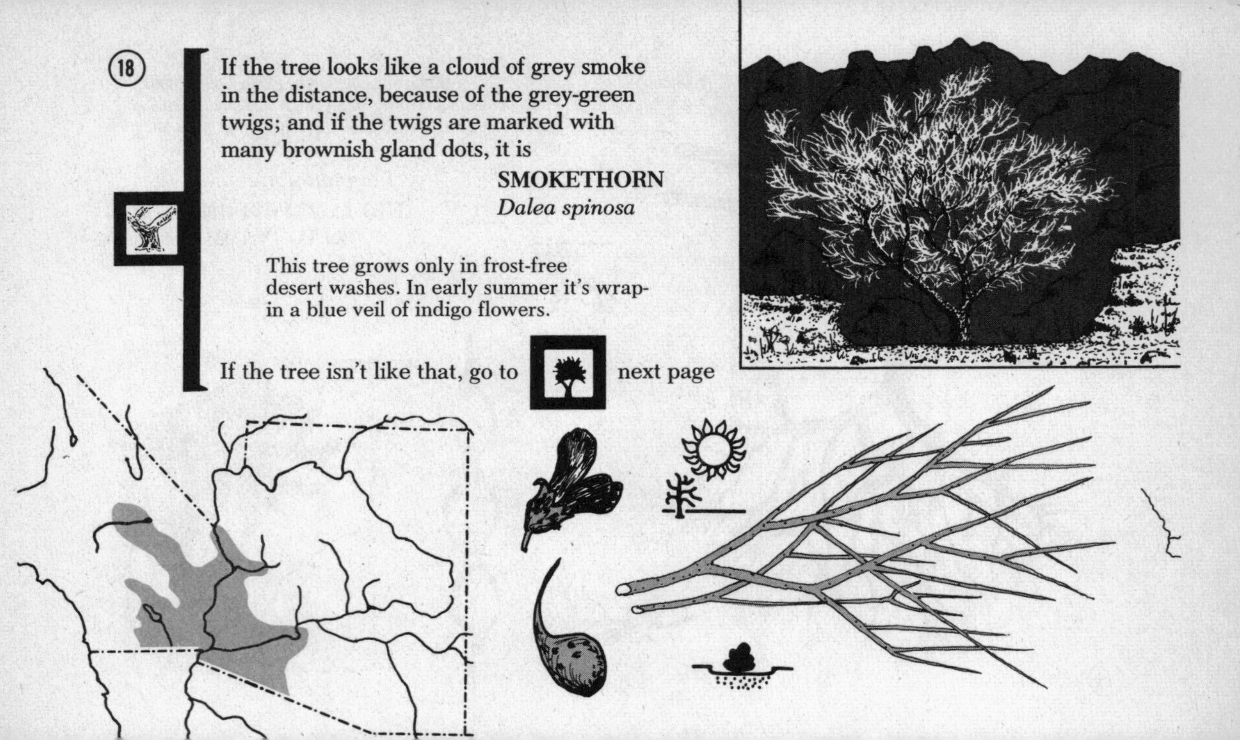

(18)

If the tree looks like a cloud of grey smoke in the distance, because of the grey-green twigs; and if the twigs are marked with many brownish gland dots, it is

SMOKETHORN
Dalea spinosa

This tree grows only in frost-free desert washes. In early summer it's wrap-in a blue veil of indigo flowers.

If the tree isn't like that, go to [symbol] next page

If the branches grow at a wide angle (almost a right angle); or if there are dark berries, it is **ALLTHORN CRUCIFIXION-THORN**
Koeberlinia spinosa var. *tenuispina*

You'll find bad-smelling flowers March to June.

If the branches grow at a more narrow angle, forming broomlike masses, go to next page

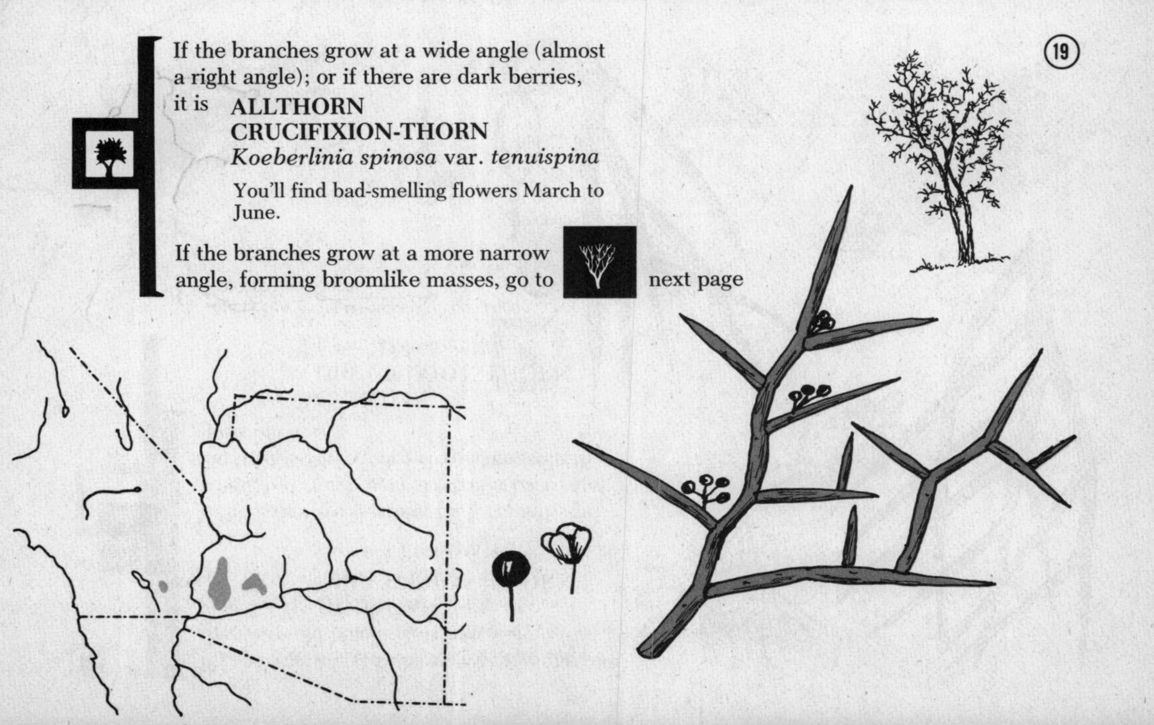

20

If the twigs are stiff, hairy when young; and there are old black fruits hanging on for years, it is **HOLACANTHA CRUCIFIXION-THORN**
Castela emoryi

If the twigs are flexible; bark smooth and green, but rough near the trunk base; and the fruit is a hard, egg-shaped capsule that splits open, it is

CANOTIA CRUCIFIXION-THORN
Canotia holacantha

This is the most common of the three "crucifixion-thorns".

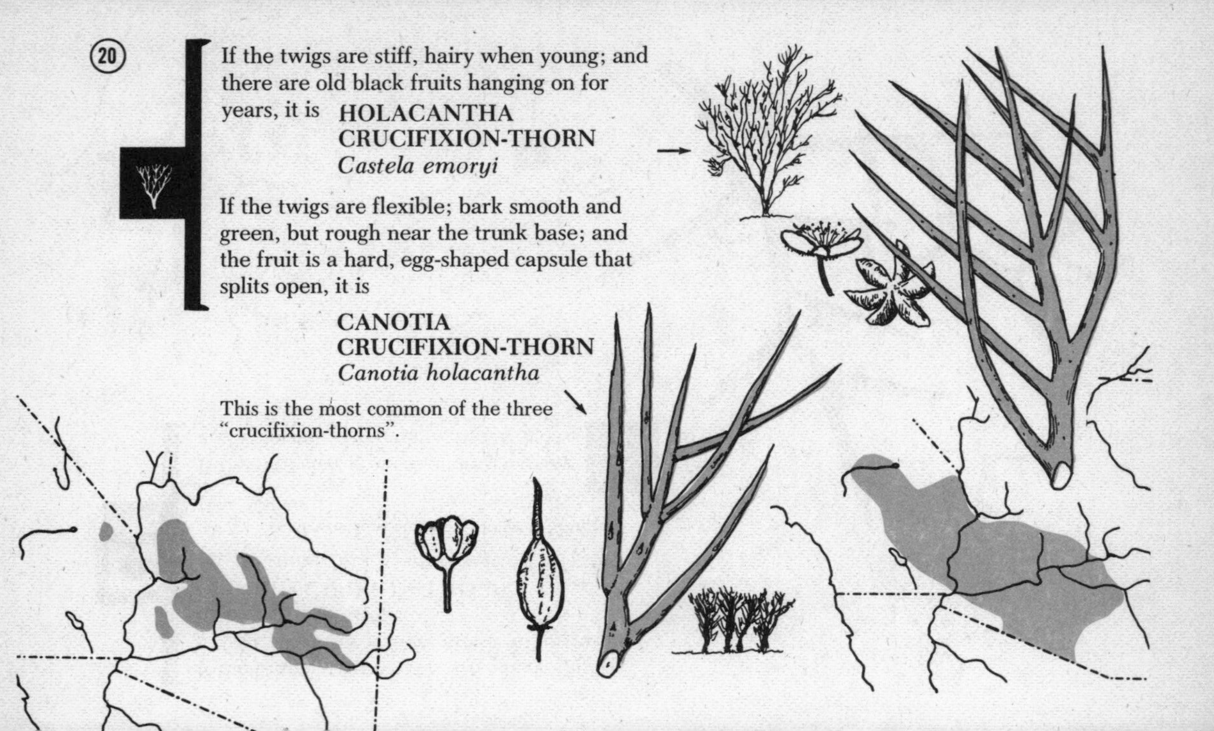

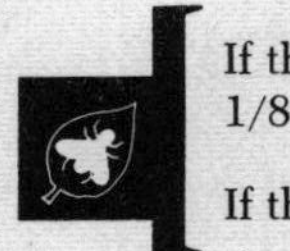

If the sides or tips of the twigs have spines 1/8 inch or more long, go to ⟶ below

If the tree is not spiny, go to ⟶ page 32

If the tree has pods, a wide-spreading top, clustered flowers, and compound leaves (composed of many small leaflets), go to ⟶ page 24

If it's not like that, go to ⟶ next page

22

If the tree is composed of long, thorny, twigless branches, it is **OCOTILLO**
Fouquieria splendens

You'll see only thorns on ocotillo unless there has been rain to bring out leaves along the branches and red flowers at the top.

If some or all of the twigs are tipped with spines; or if the branches divide into smaller branches, go to next page

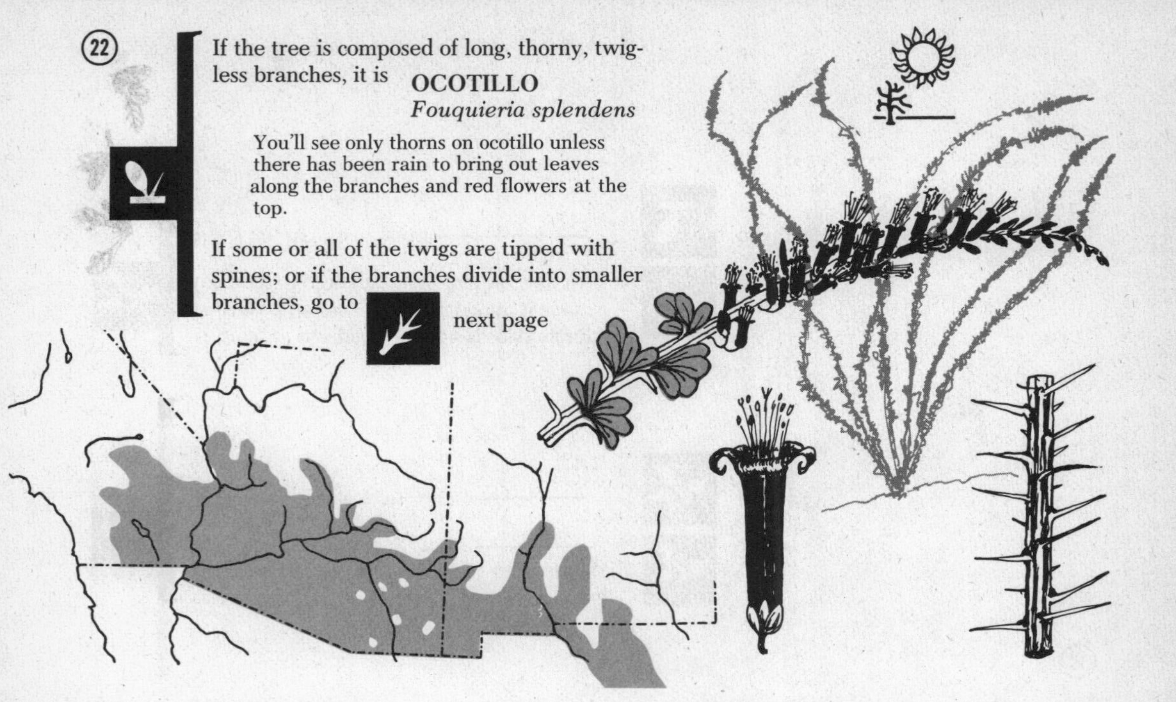

(23)

If there is a spine, not only at the tip of a twig, but also at the base of an occasional leaf; and the leaves have matted hair on their undersides, it is **GUM BUMELIA**
Bumelia lanuginosa

This is a relative of the tropical tree, Sapodilla, which exudes chicle, the source of chewing gum.

If the spines occur at the twig tips only, and the fruit is extremely bitter it is

BITTER CONDALIA
Condalia globosa

(24)

If the bark, except at the base of the trunk, is smooth and green, it's a PALOVERDE. Go to below

If the bark is not smooth and green, go to page 26

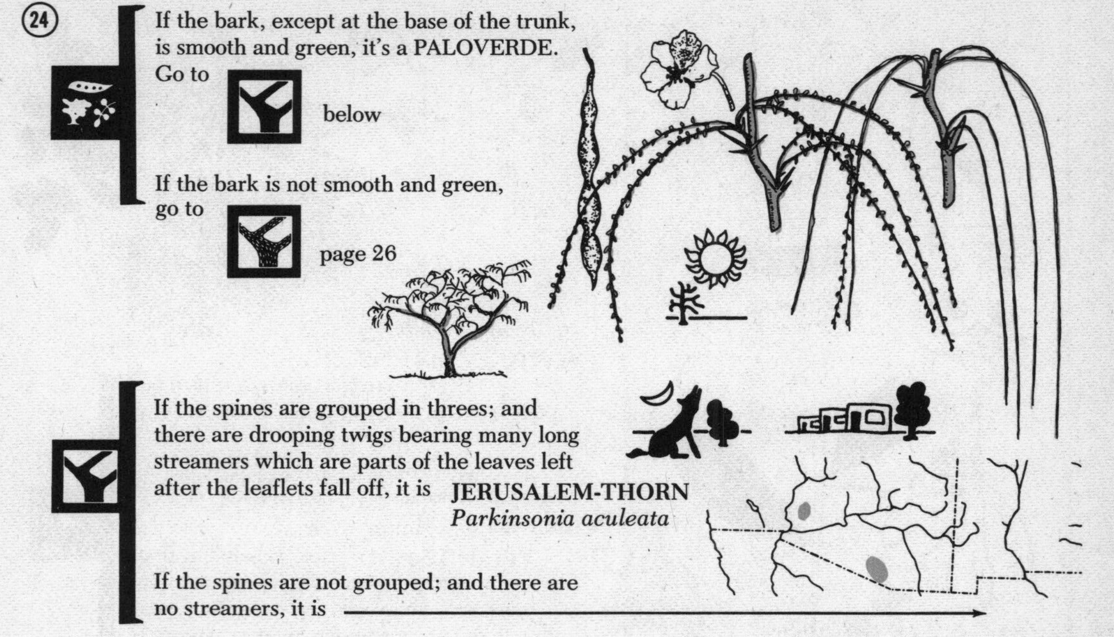

If the spines are grouped in threes; and there are drooping twigs bearing many long streamers which are parts of the leaves left after the leaflets fall off, it is **JERUSALEM-THORN**
Parkinsonia aculeata

If the spines are not grouped; and there are no streamers, it is →

25

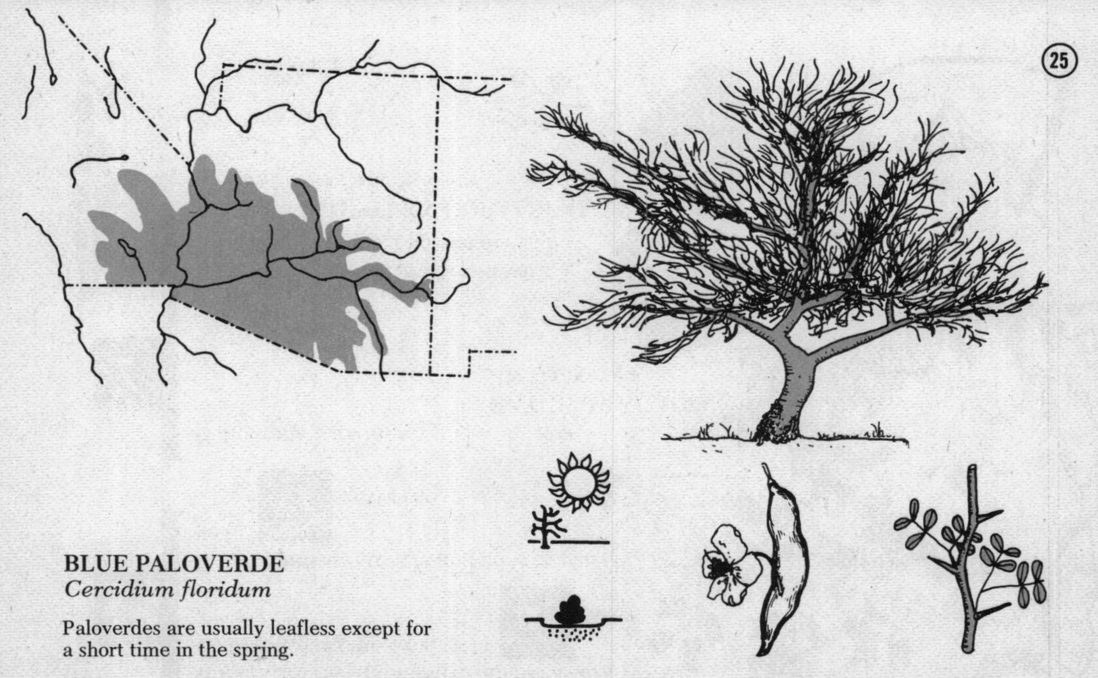

BLUE PALOVERDE

Cercidium floridum

Paloverdes are usually leafless except for a short time in the spring.

26

If there are single spines curved like hooks scattered along the twig, go to [hook-spine symbol] below

If the spines are straight and grow in pairs, go to [paired-spine symbol] next page

If the trunk bark is grey and scaly, it is

CATCLAW ACACIA
Acacia greggii

If the trunk bark is light brown with whitish lines running up and down, it is

SOUTHWESTERN CORALBEAN
Erythrina flabelliformis

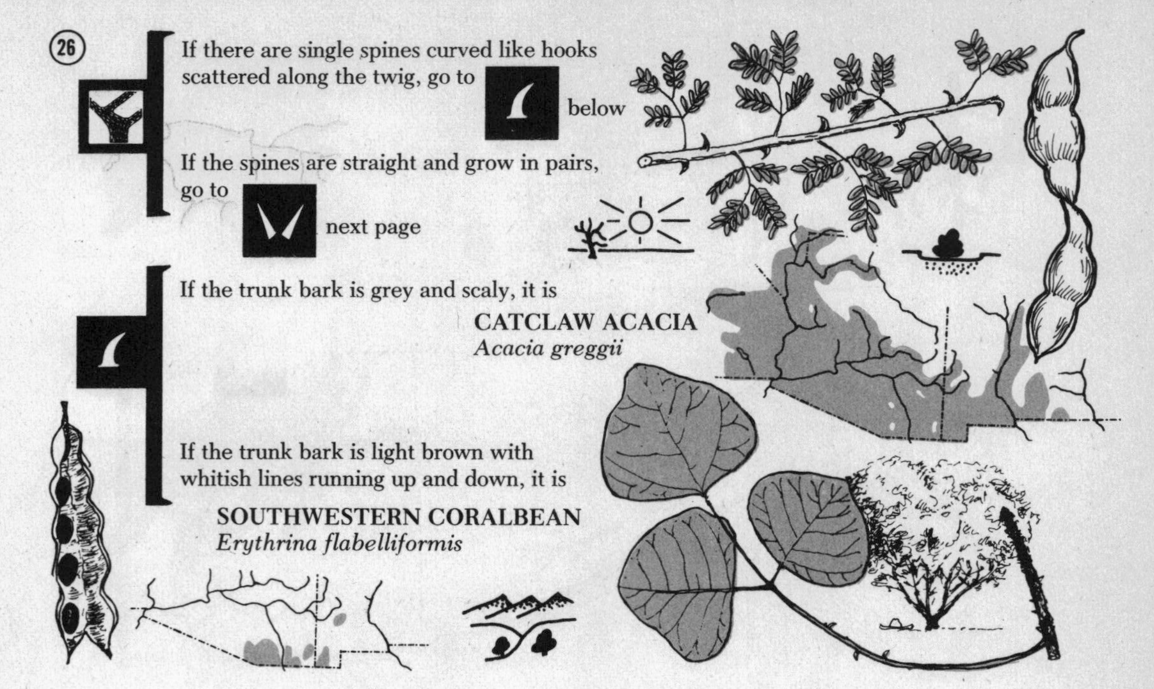

(27)

If the whole tree looks grey-green, with hairy leaves and twigs, and a grey trunk, it is

IRONWOOD
Olneya tesota

The presence of this evergreen tree indicates a climate warm enough for citrus. The wood is hard enough to dull tools, and will not float.

If it's not grey-green (or not evergreen) go to next page

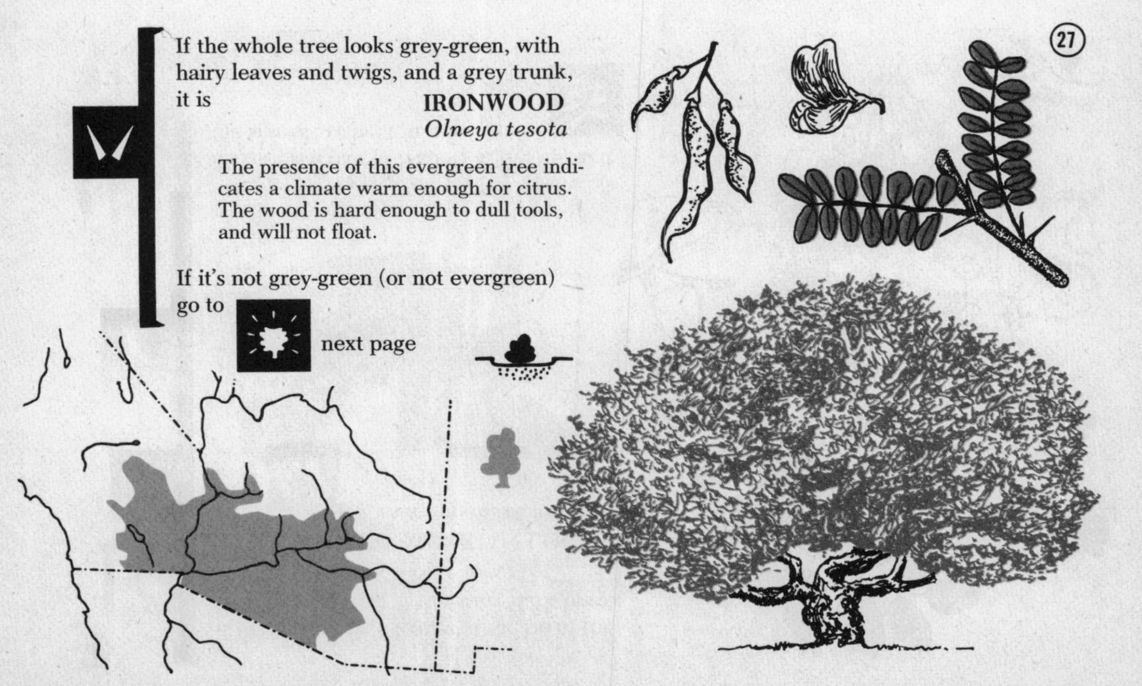

If there is a single leaflet at the tip of the compound leaf, or if there are dark brown or reddish spines, it is

NEW MEXICAN LOCUST
Robinia neo-mexicana

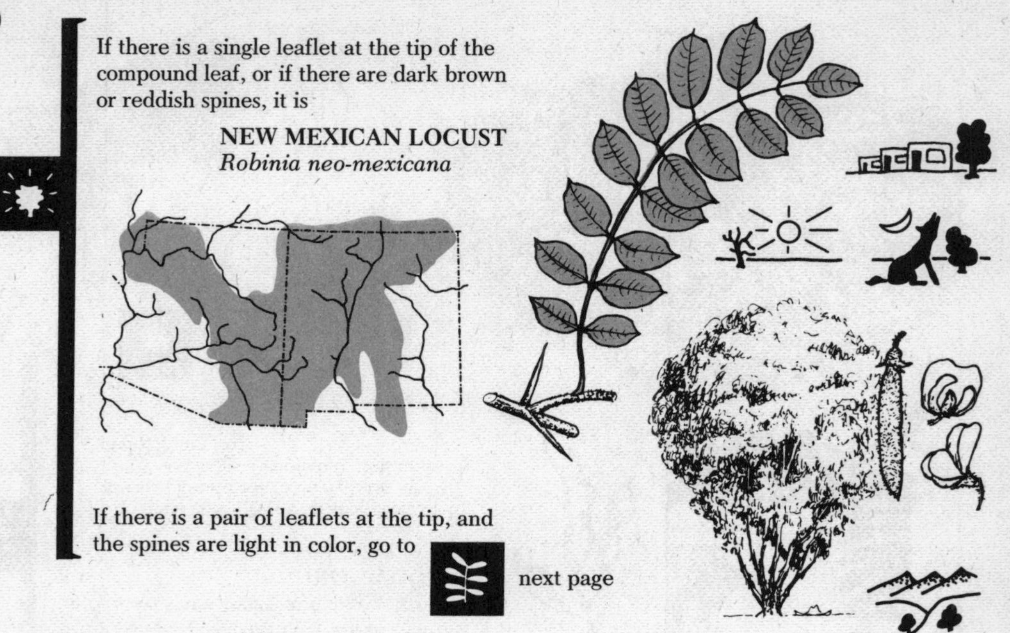

If there is a pair of leaflets at the tip, and the spines are light in color, go to next page

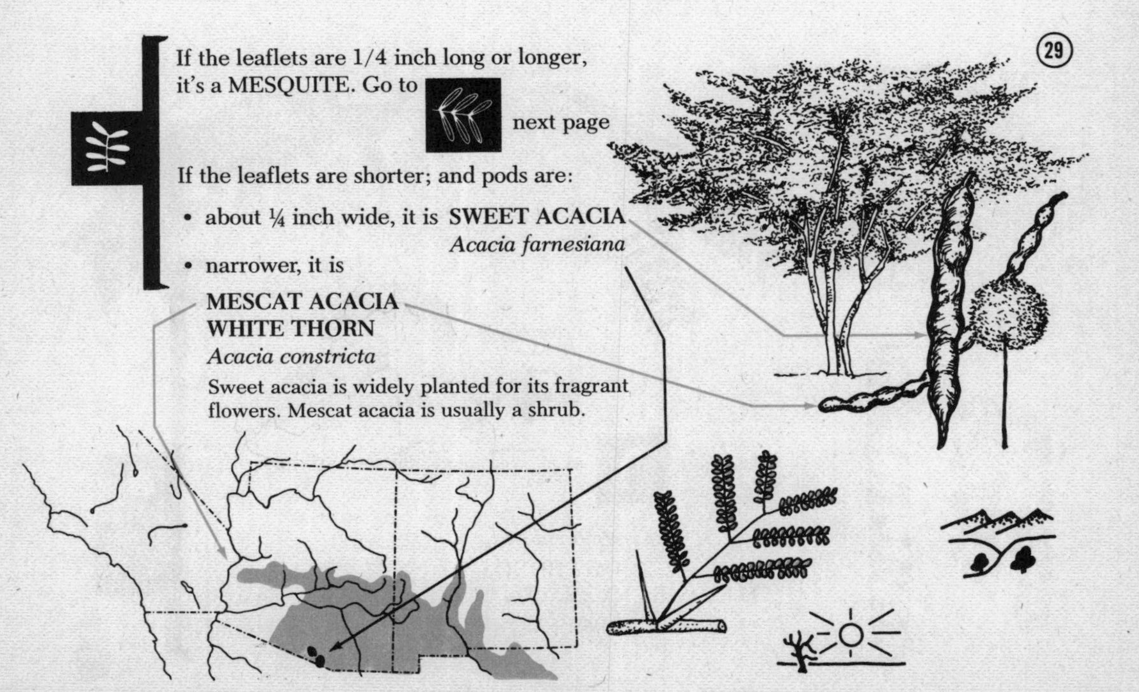

If the leaflets are 1/4 inch long or longer, it's a MESQUITE. Go to next page

If the leaflets are shorter; and pods are:

- about ¼ inch wide, it is **SWEET ACACIA** *Acacia farnesiana*
- narrower, it is

MESCAT ACACIA
WHITE THORN
Acacia constricta

Sweet acacia is widely planted for its fragrant flowers. Mescat acacia is usually a shrub.

30

If the pods are twisted and screwlike; and the spines are whitish, it is **SCREWBEAN MESQUITE TORNILLO** *Prosopis pubescens*

If the pods are long and bean-like, go to next page

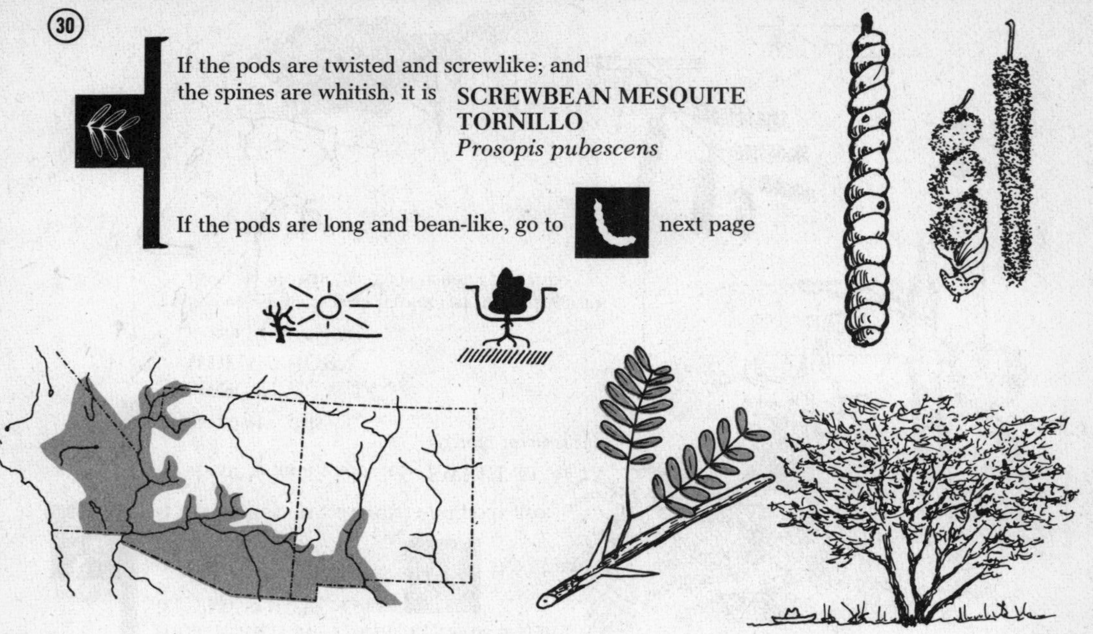

31
If the twigs, leaves and pods are hairless,
it is HONEY MESQUITE
Prosopis juliflora var. *torreyana*
If they're velvety, it is
VELVET MESQUITE
Prosopis juliflora var. *velutina*

(32)

If the leaves are tiny and scale-like, held close against the twig, go to below

If they're not scale-like, go to page 35

If crushed foliage smells resinous, it's a JUNIPER. Go to next page

If it's not resinous, it is

FRENCH TAMARISK
SALT-CEDAR
Tamarix sp.

Tamarisk is usually shrub-shaped, with several long branches rising from the base. Narrow clusters of pink flowers bloom March to August. The first seeds of this Mediterranean tree probably came to America in hay for Spanish horses. It's widely naturalized along rivers, drainage ditches, even enduring alkali flats.

If the trunk bark is deeply furrowed and checkered into squarish plates, it is **ALLIGATOR JUNIPER** *Juniperus deppeana*

If the trunk bark is stringy and fibrous go to  next page

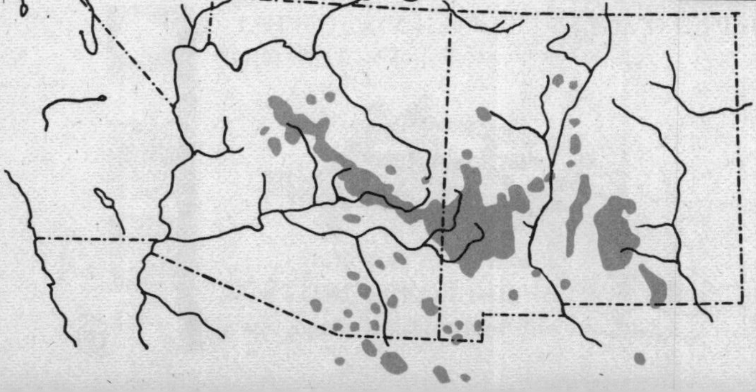

34

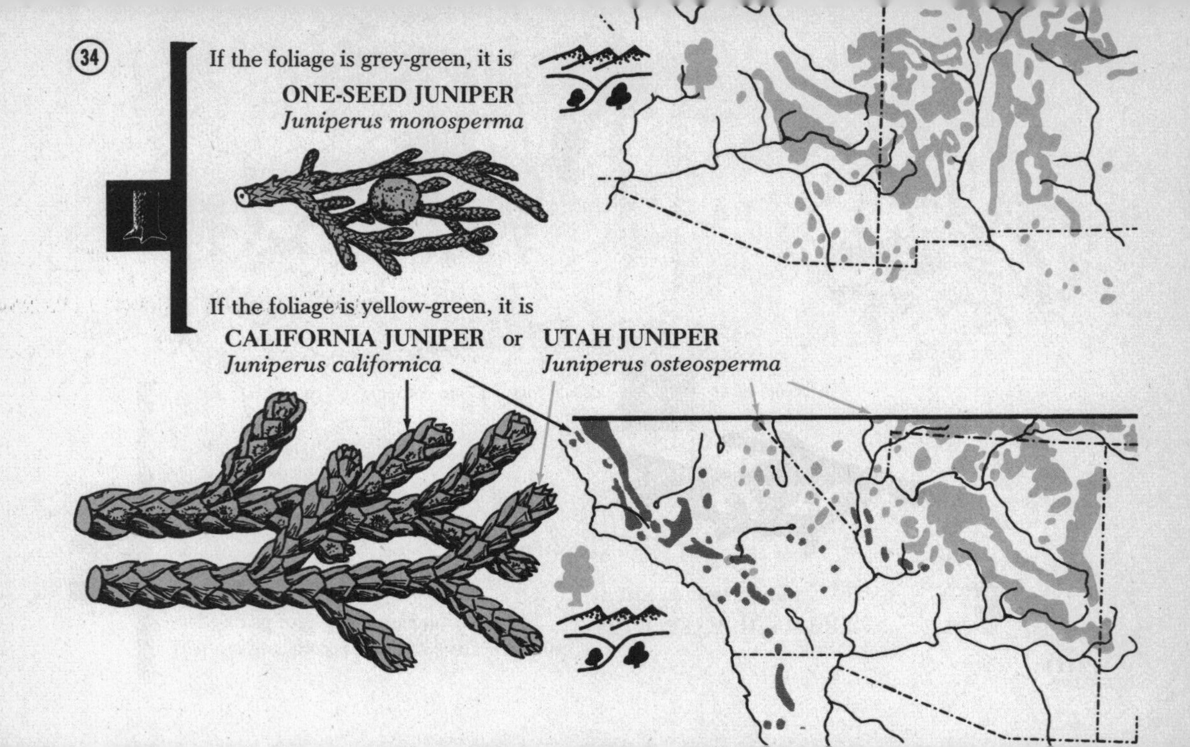

If the foliage is grey-green, it is
ONE-SEED JUNIPER
Juniperus monosperma
If the foliage is yellow-green, it is
CALIFORNIA JUNIPER or UTAH JUNIPER
Juniperus californica
Juniperus osteosperma

(35)

If the leaf surface is about as wide as it is long, being round, triangular, star-shaped, or heart-shaped; with a leaf stem an inch or more long, go to → below

If the leaves are not like that, go to → page 41

If the leaf is triangular, with small rounded teeth, it's a COTTONWOOD. Go to → next page

Cottonwood flowers are borne in drooping catkins—the pollen-bearing catkins more brightly colored and compact than the seed-bearing ones which are on separate trees.

If the leaves are not triangular, go to → page 38

36

If you can find seed capsules on stalks longer than half an inch; or if buds on the twigs are slightly hairy, it is → **RIO GRANDE COTTONWOOD** *Populus fremonti* var. *wislizeni*

If the stalks of seed capsules are shorter; or if the buds are without hair, it is **FREMONT COTTONWOOD** *Populus fremontii*

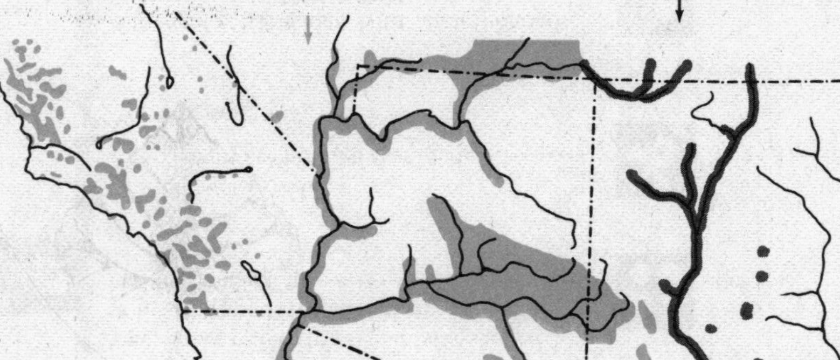

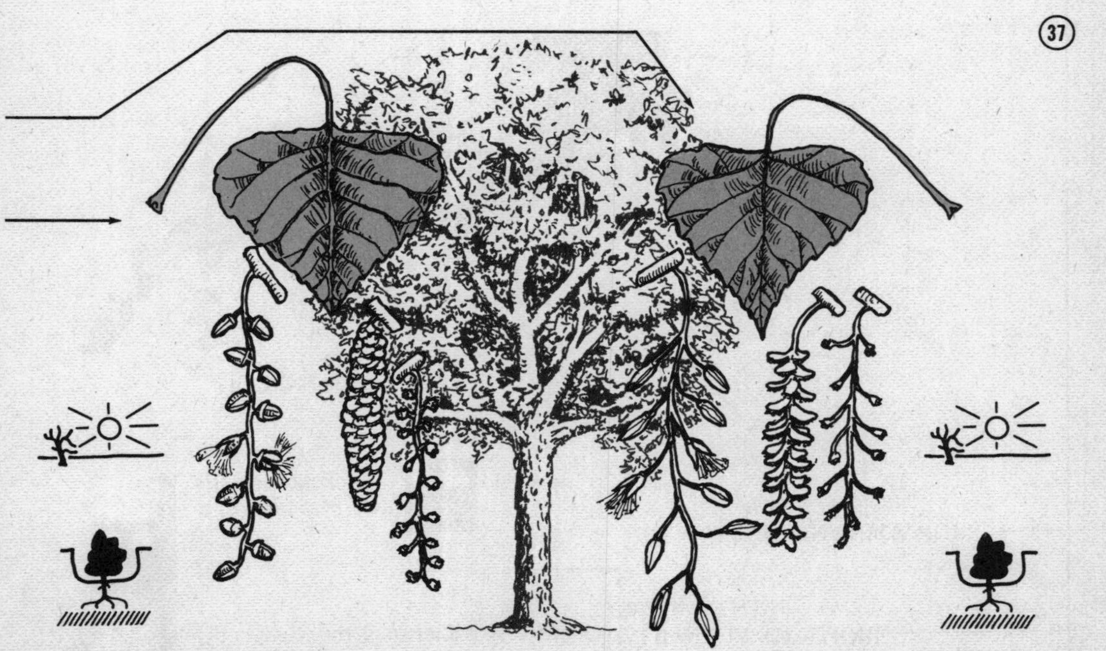
37

38

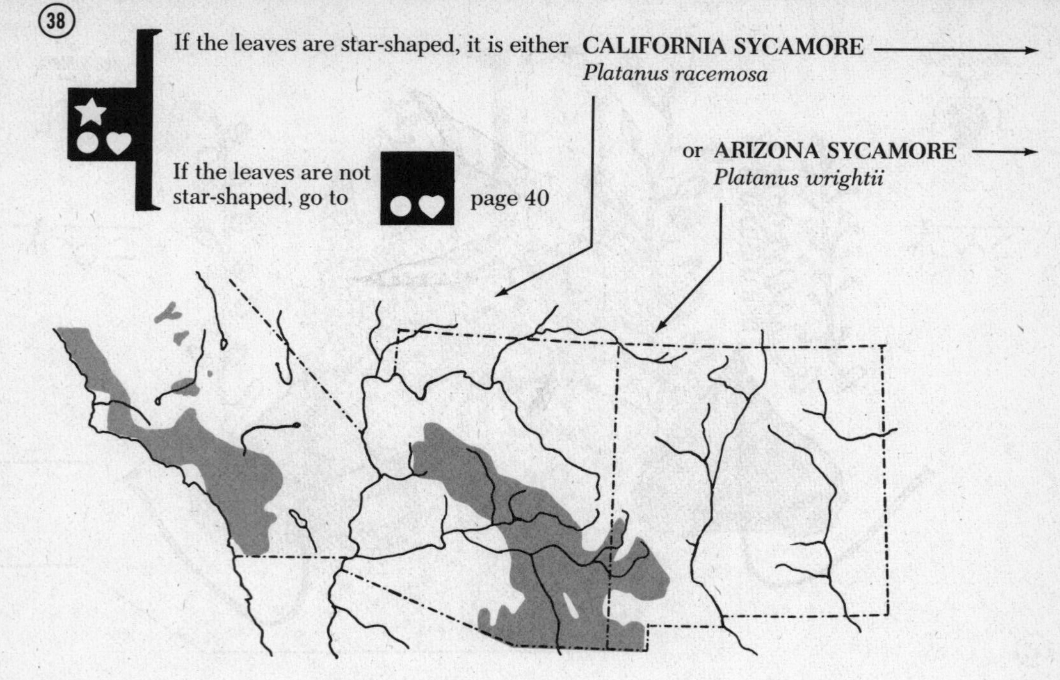

If the leaves are star-shaped, it is either **CALIFORNIA SYCAMORE** → *Platanus racemosa*

or **ARIZONA SYCAMORE** → *Platanus wrightii*

If the leaves are not star-shaped, go to page 40

39

The white young branches later flake off in brown patches, eventually becoming dark grey with thick plates. The canopy is hung with small greenish balls of clustered flowers in March and April, and with brown seed balls later. Sycamores may make displaced easterners homesick.

40

If the leaf is thin, round, with no teeth along the margin, it is **CALIFORNIA REDBUD**
Cercis occidentalis

Redbud trees are covered with pink sweet pea-shaped flowers in spring. Later there are flat, thin pods.

If the leaf is deeply indented, and saw-toothed along the thick, colorful margin, it is **CASTOR-BEAN**
Ricinus communis

The long leafstalk is hollow. The spiny seed capsule splits open showing three extremely poisonous seeds.

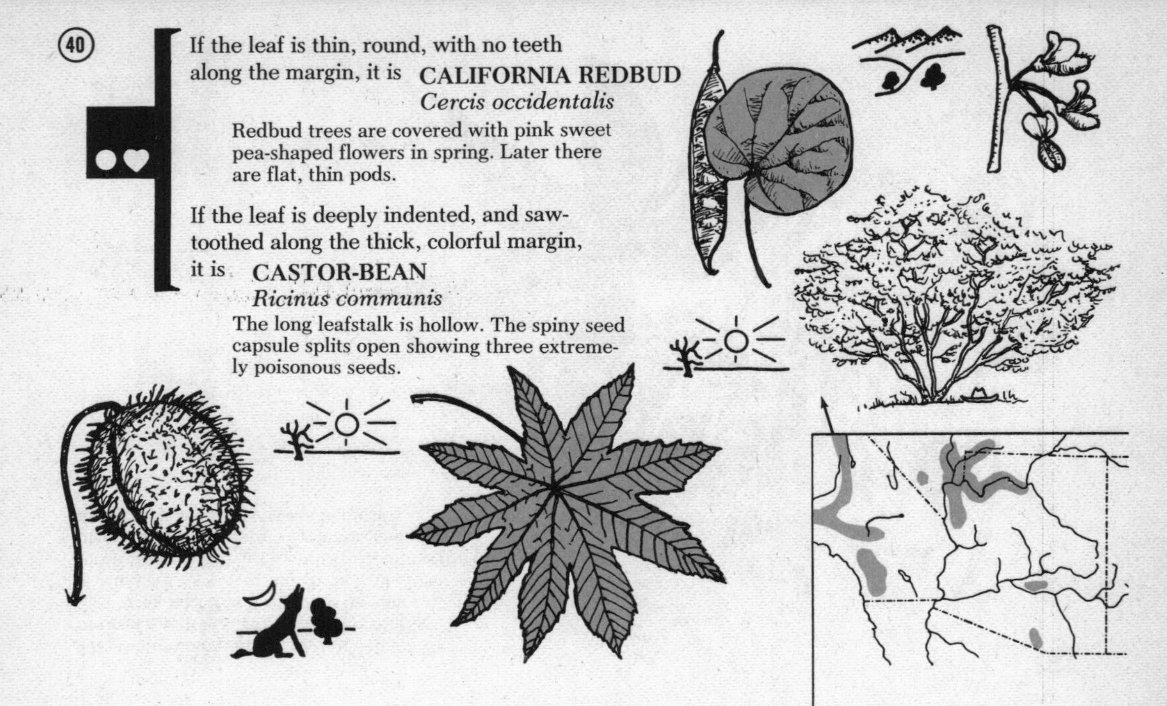

If the leaves are compound, composed of three or more leaflets, like this: go to — below

There's a bud on the twig at the base of a leaf, but not at the base of a leaflet.

If the leaves are not made up of leaflets, go to → below

If the leaves (but not necessarily the leaflets) come out opposite each other, paired, along the twig, go to → next page

If the leaves come out alternately along the twig, not in pairs, go to → page 44

If the leaf is long and narrow (more than three times as long as wide), go to → page 50

If it's wider than that, go to → page 46

42

If the leaves have sharply saw-toothed margins; or if there are flat-topped clusters of yellow-white flowers; or if there are berries, it is

MEXICAN ELDER
Sambucus mexicana

If not, it's an ASH. Go to [saw symbol] below

If the whole leaf—usually only three leaflets—is about 1-1/2 inches long, it is

LITTLELEAF ASH
Fraxinus greggii

This tree is almost evergreen.

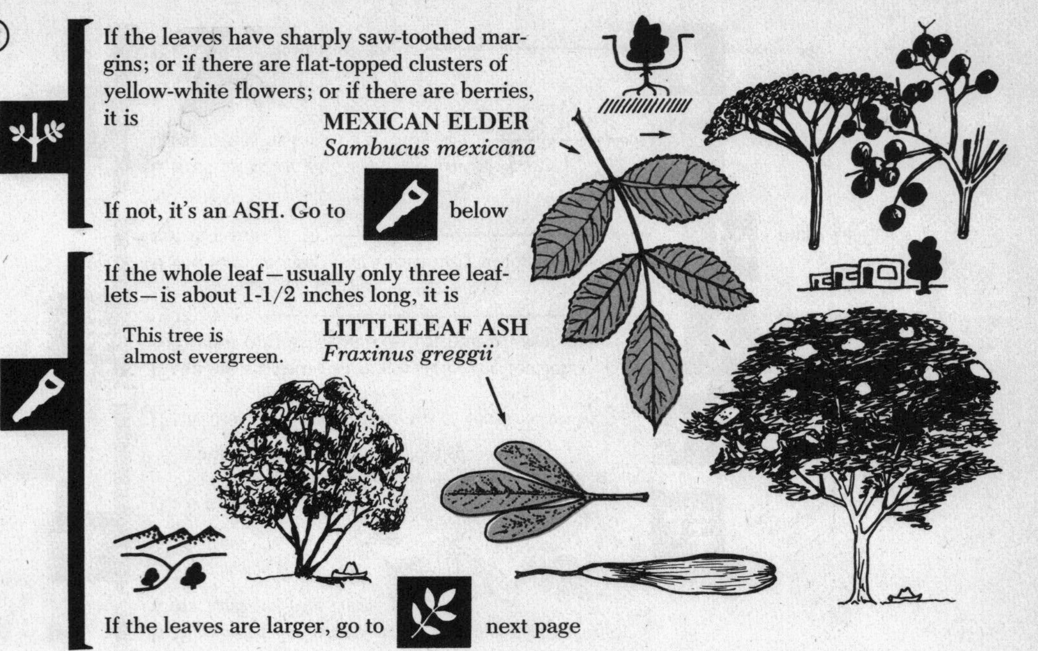

If the leaves are larger, go to [leaf symbol] next page

If the twigs are four-sided and the leaflets oval, it is **LOWELL ASH**
Fraxinus lowellii

If they're not four-sided, go to ● below

If the leaves are all under 4 inches long (sometimes having only one or two leaflets); or if the tree has fragrant flowers with petals, or grows on a dry slope, it is **FRAGRANT ASH**
Fraxinus cuspidata

If the leaves are larger; or if the tree is taller or grows in a watercourse or bottomland, it is **VELVET ASH**
Fraxinus velutina

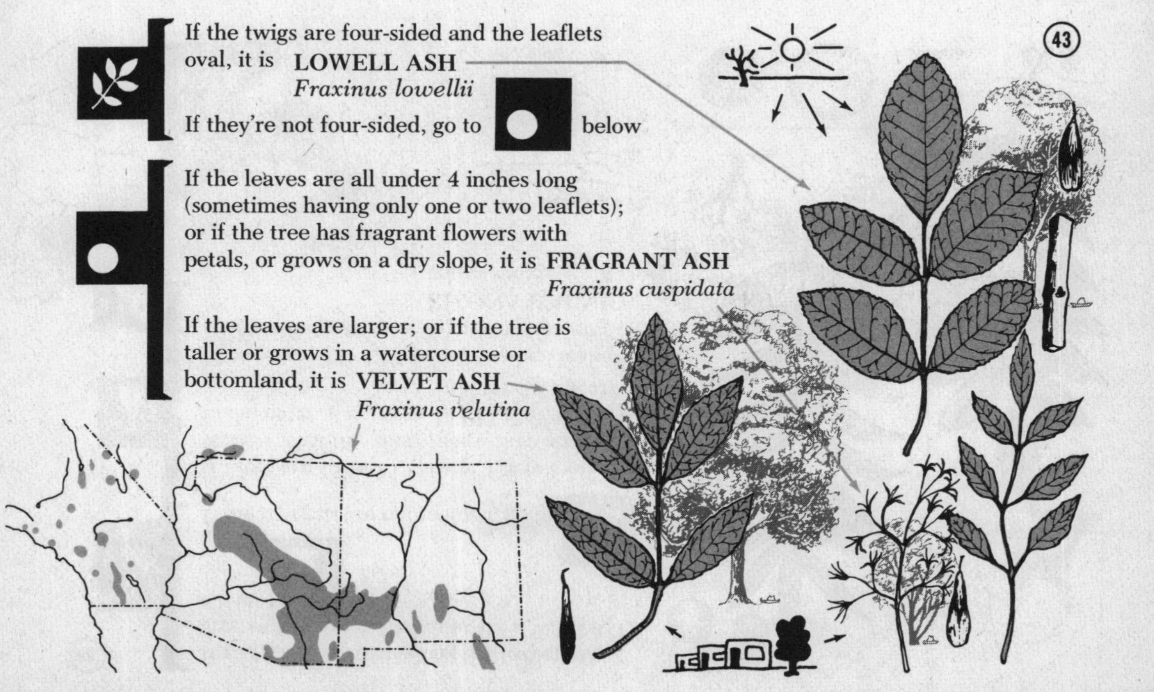

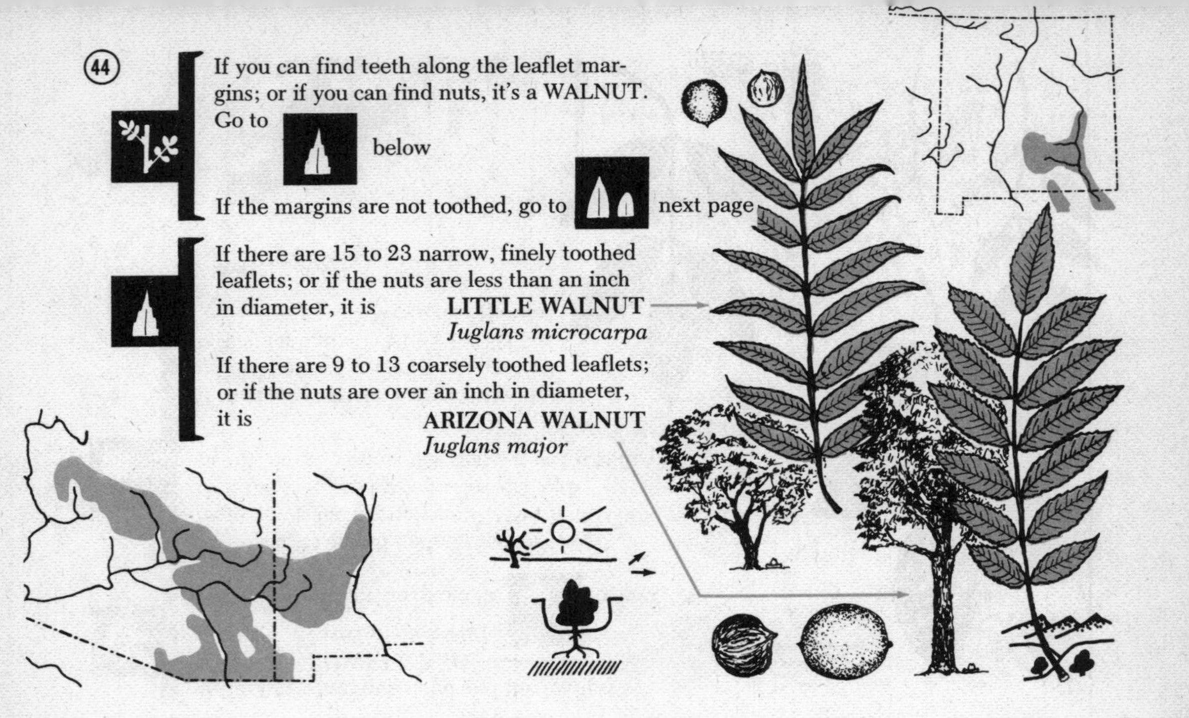
44
If you can find teeth along the leaflet margins; or if you can find nuts, it's a WALNUT. Go to below
If the margins are not toothed, go to next page
If there are 15 to 23 narrow, finely toothed leaflets; or if the nuts are less than an inch in diameter, it is
LITTLE WALNUT
Juglans microcarpa
If there are 9 to 13 coarsely toothed leaflets; or if the nuts are over an inch in diameter, it is
ARIZONA WALNUT
Juglans major

If the leaflets are about 1/4 inch long; and the branches and trunk look thick and swollen, it is **ELEPHANTTREE** →
Bursera microphylla

The tree is leafless except after rain.

If the leaflets are larger, it is
WESTERN SOAPBERRY
WILD CHINA-TREE
Sapindus saponaria drummondi

Flowers are borne in long clusters, May to August. Fruits are yellow, berrylike and translucent.

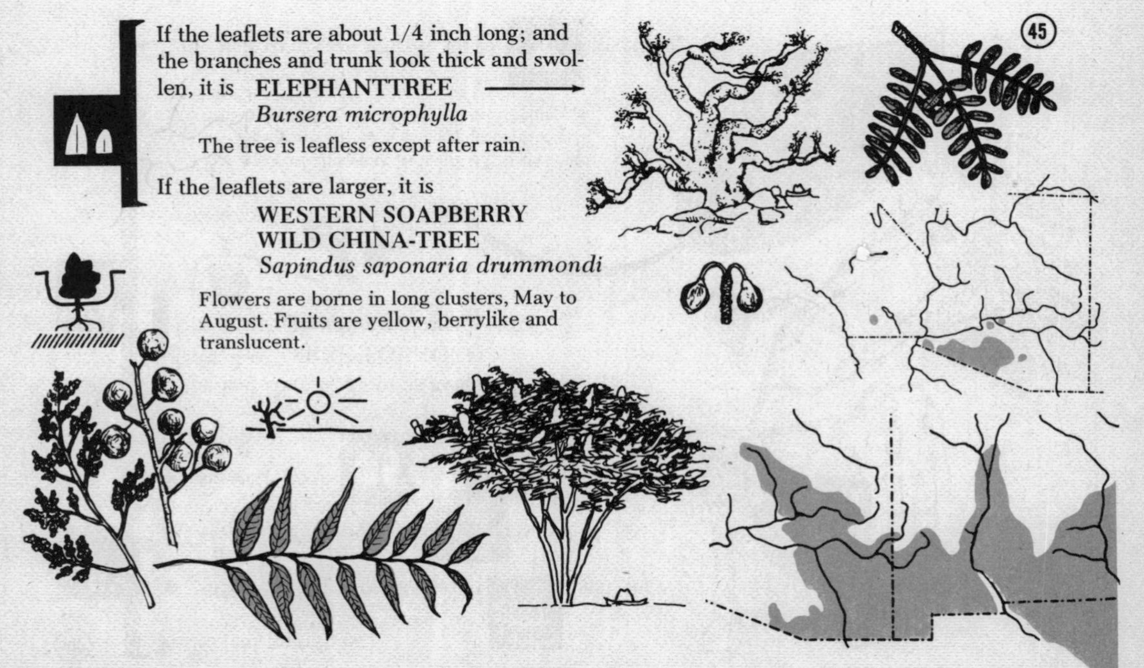

(46) If the leaf margin is:

- stiff, with spiny points, go to next page
- saw-toothed, go to p. 48
- smooth, go to below

If the leaf stem is about as long as the leaf blade, it is **TREE TOBACCO**
Nicotiana glauca

For most of the year there are tubular, yellow, fragrant flowers. The tree is native to South America, but naturalized in the southwestern U.S.

If the leaf stems are shorter, go to page 49

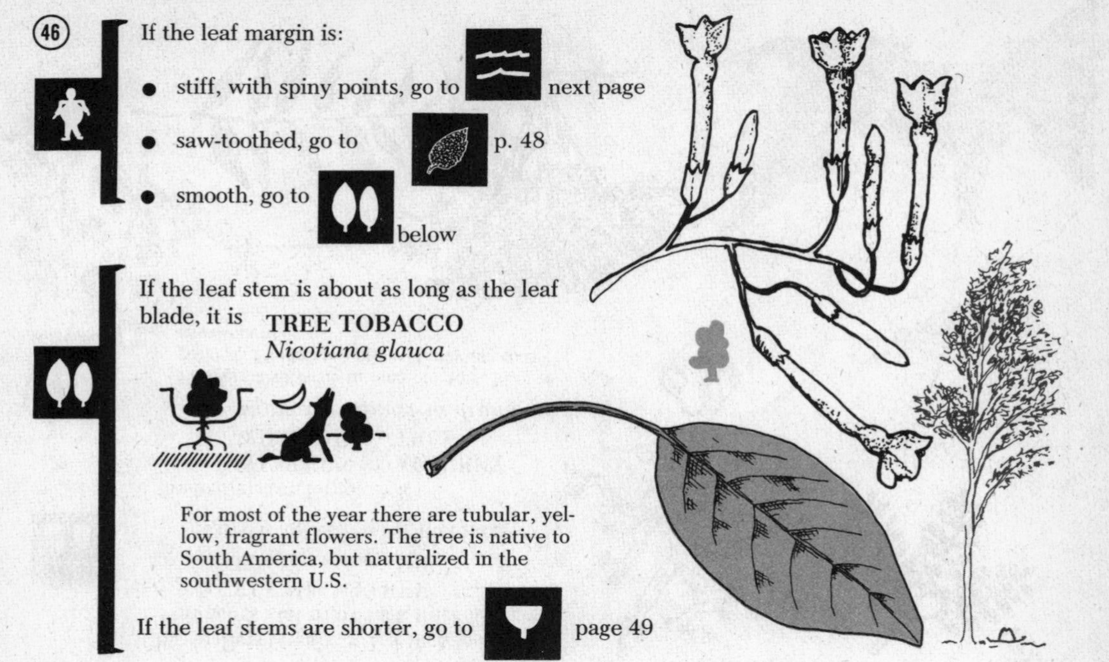

47

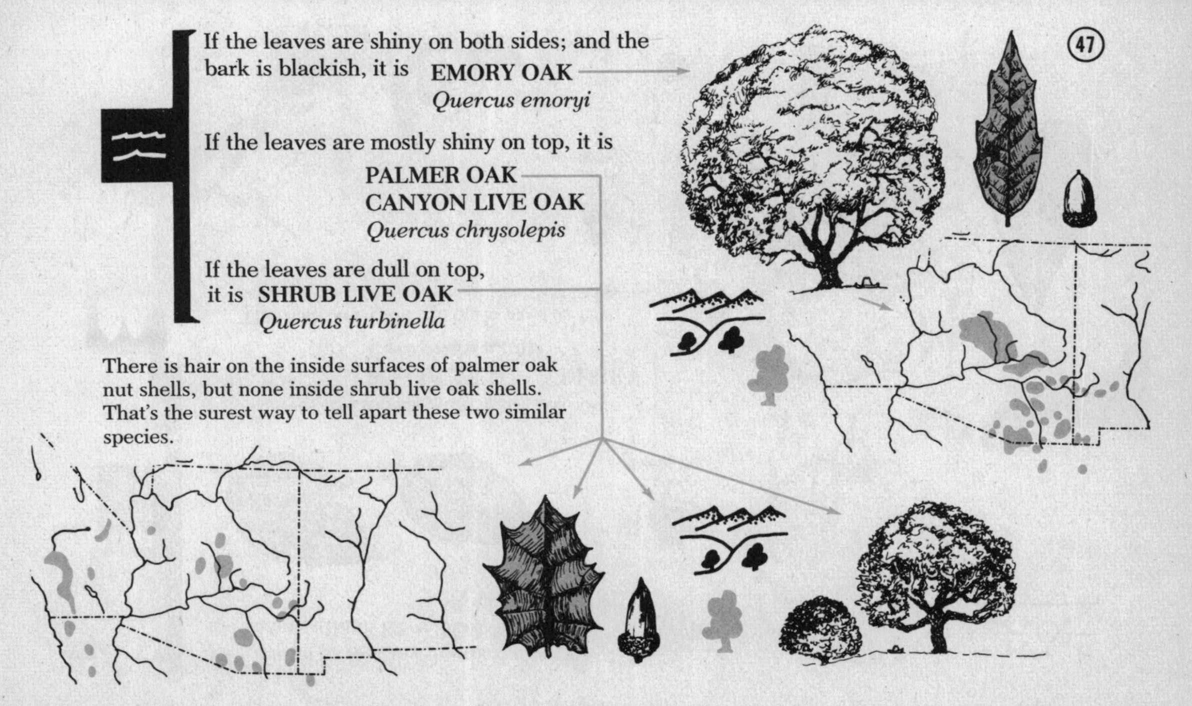

If the leaves are shiny on both sides; and the bark is blackish, it is **EMORY OAK**
Quercus emoryi

If the leaves are mostly shiny on top, it is

PALMER OAK
CANYON LIVE OAK
Quercus chrysolepis

If the leaves are dull on top, it is **SHRUB LIVE OAK**
Quercus turbinella

There is hair on the inside surfaces of palmer oak nut shells, but none inside shrub live oak shells. That's the surest way to tell apart these two similar species.

(48)

If all leaves have a saw-toothed margin, and some of them have lobes, it is

TEXAS MULBERRY
Morus microphylla

If the leaves are lop-sided, usually without teeth, it is

NETLEAF HACKBERRY
Celtis reticulata

There are warts on the bark, galls on the leaves, and often tangles of dwarfed twigs caused by a gall insect.

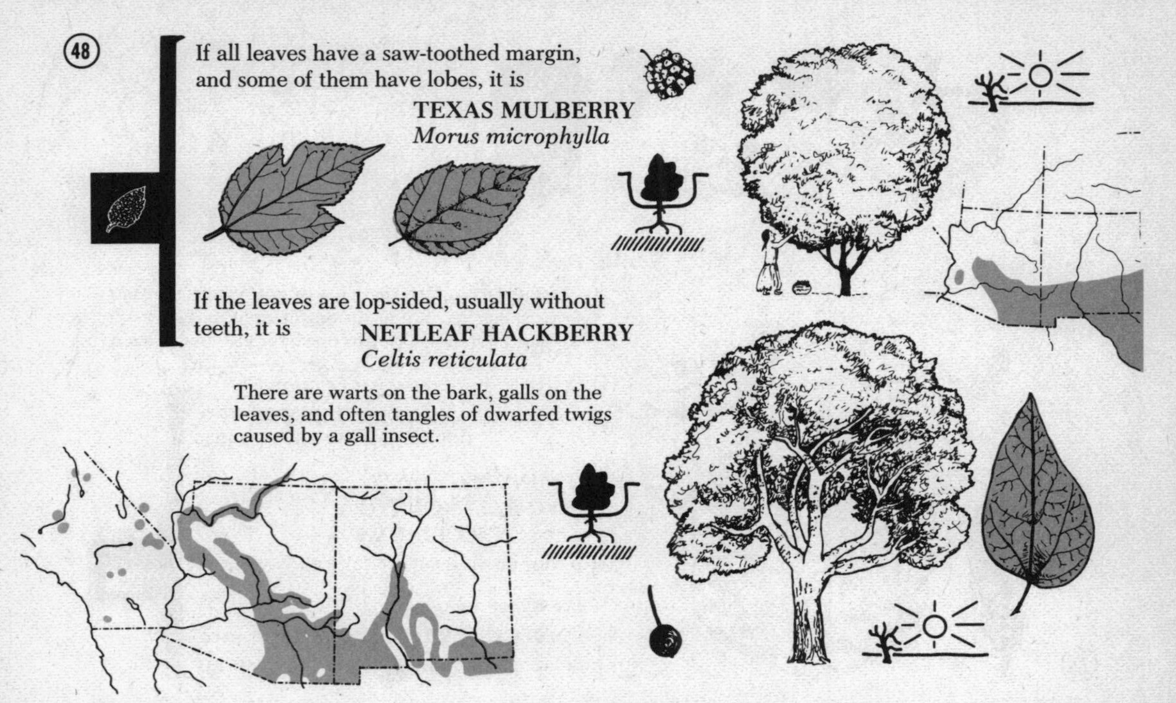

If the leaf tips are rounded, it is **MEXICAN BLUE OAK**
Quercus oblongifolia

If they're pointed, it is
NETLEAF HACKBERRY
Celtis reticulata

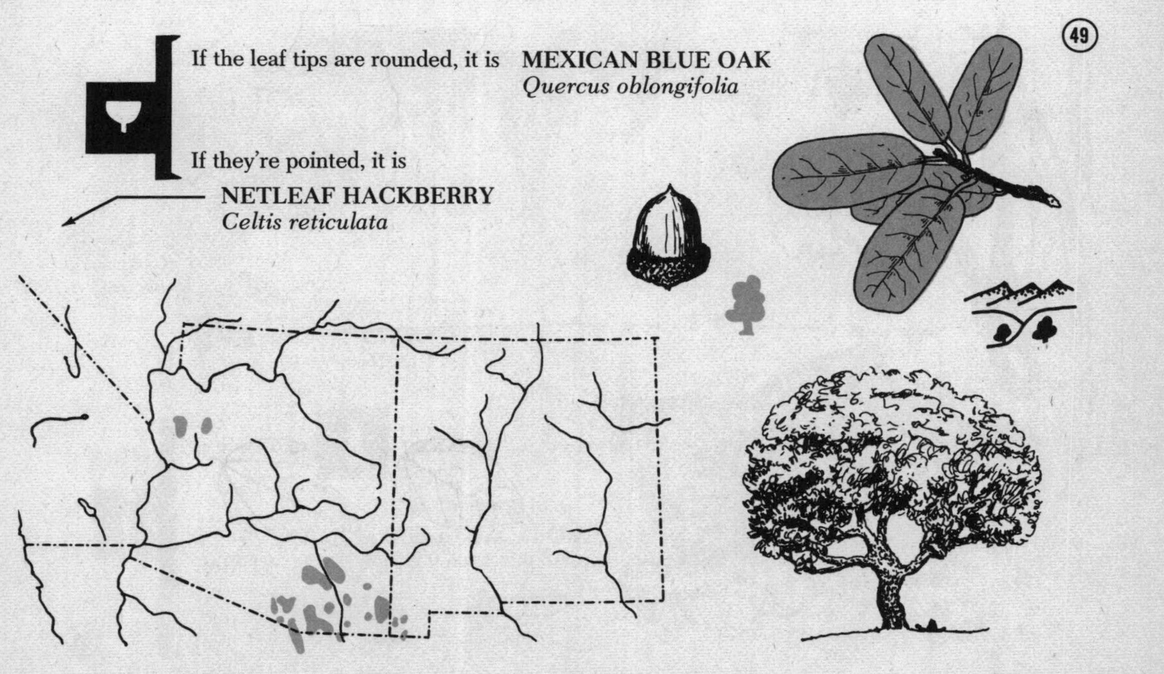

50

If the leaves are 1/4 inch wide and over 3 inches long, it is **DESERTWILLOW** *Chilopsis linearis*

If not, go to next page

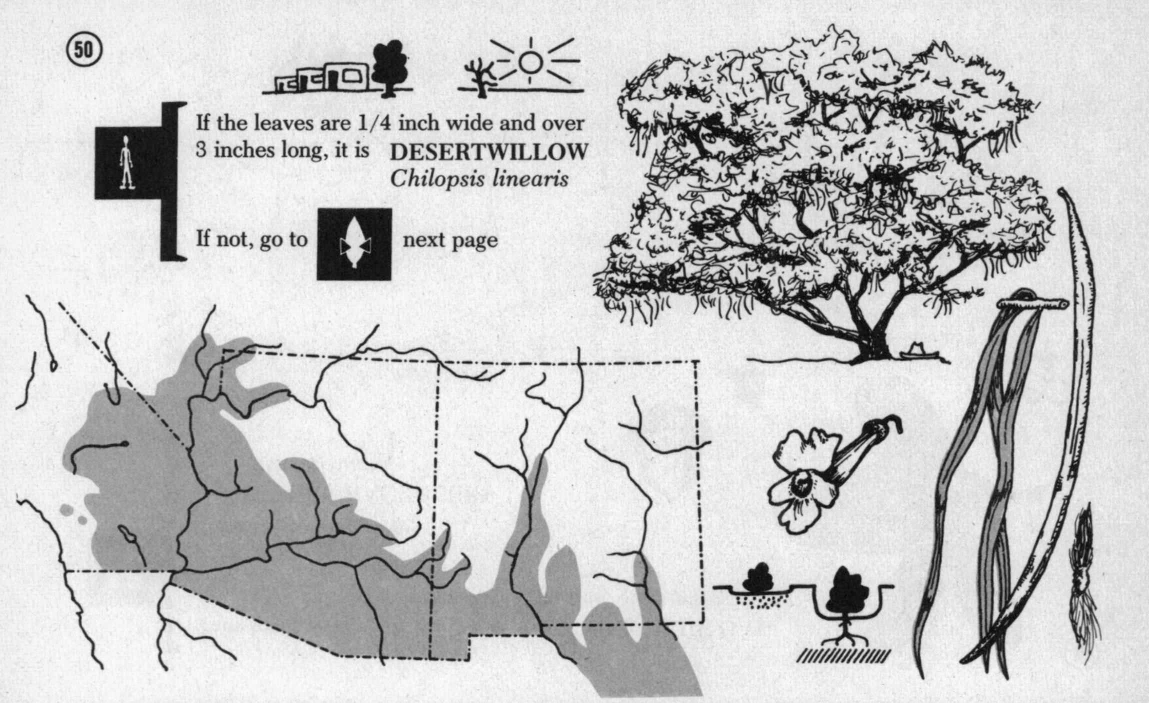

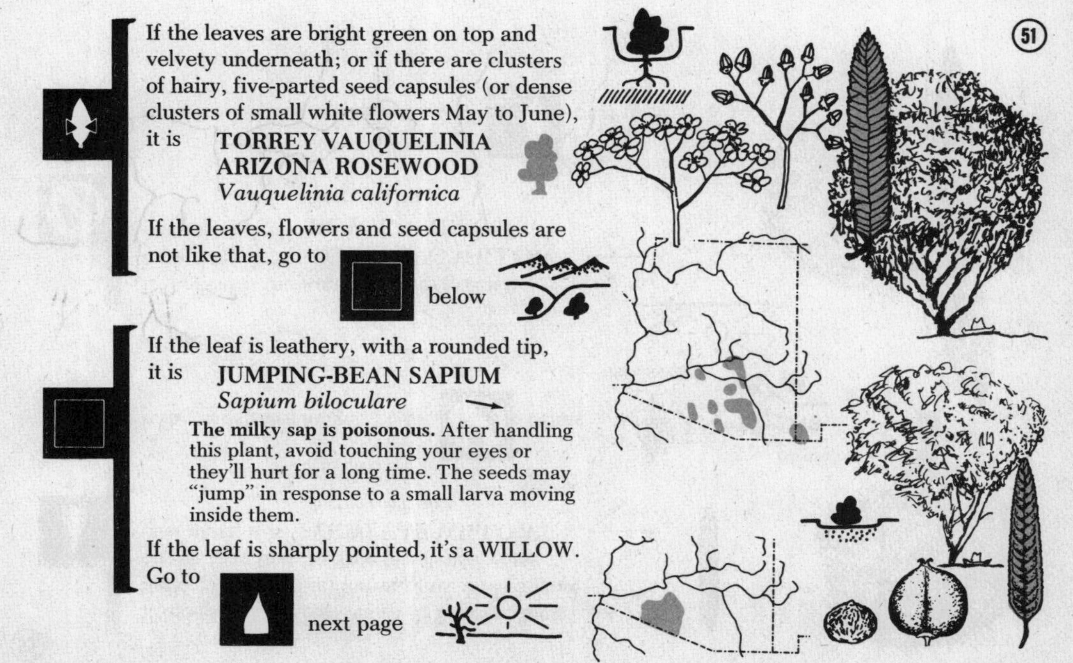

If the leaves are bright green on top and velvety underneath; or if there are clusters of hairy, five-parted seed capsules (or dense clusters of small white flowers May to June), it is **TORREY VAUQUELINIA**
ARIZONA ROSEWOOD
Vauquelinia californica

If the leaves, flowers and seed capsules are not like that, go to below

If the leaf is leathery, with a rounded tip, it is **JUMPING-BEAN SAPIUM**
Sapium biloculare →

The milky sap is poisonous. After handling this plant, avoid touching your eyes or they'll hurt for a long time. The seeds may "jump" in response to a small larva moving inside them.

If the leaf is sharply pointed, it's a WILLOW.
Go to next page

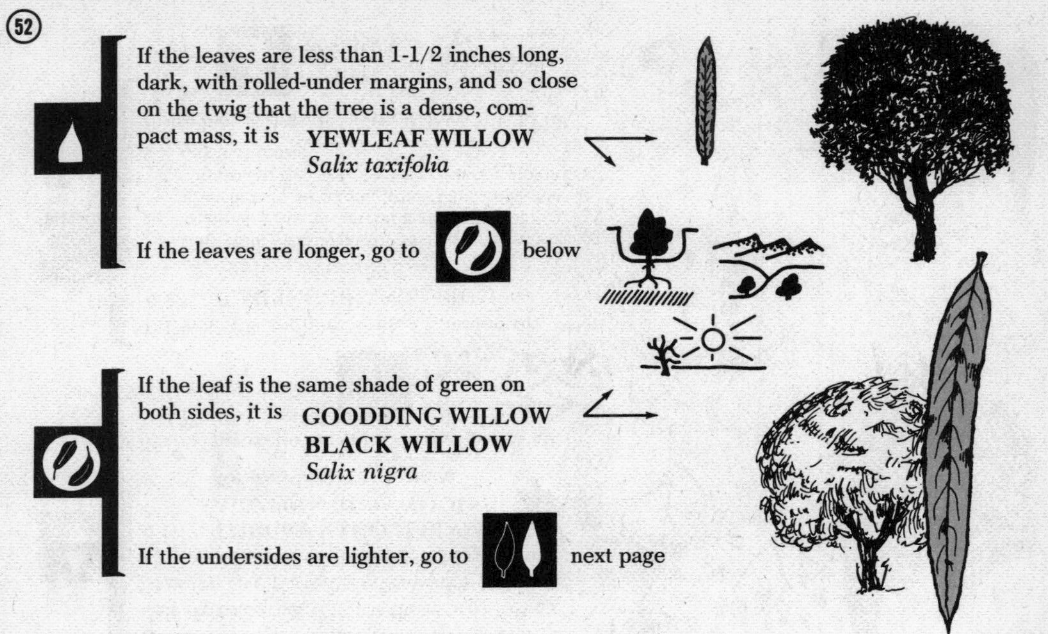

If the leaves are less than 1-1/2 inches long, dark, with rolled-under margins, and so close on the twig that the tree is a dense, compact mass, it is **YEWLEAF WILLOW** *Salix taxifolia*

If the leaves are longer, go to below

If the leaf is the same shade of green on both sides, it is **GOODDING WILLOW** **BLACK WILLOW** *Salix nigra*

If the undersides are lighter, go to next page

If the leaves are widest in the middle; and the trunk is blackish, it is **BONPLAND WILLOW**
Salix bonplandiana

If the leaves are wider toward their bases go to [leaf symbol] below

If the leaves are dark green, with short-pointed tips and edges slightly turned under, it is **RED WILLOW**
Salix laevigata

If they're yellow-green and long-pointed, with flat edges; or if there are grey-barked twigs, it is **PEACHLEAF WILLOW**
Salix amygdaloides

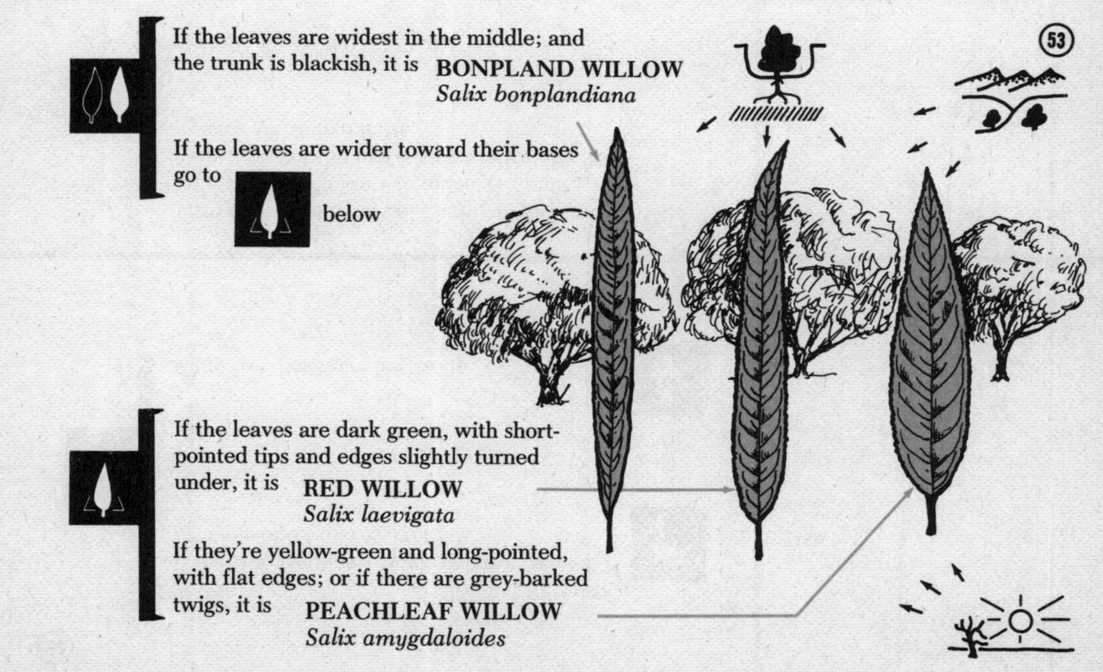

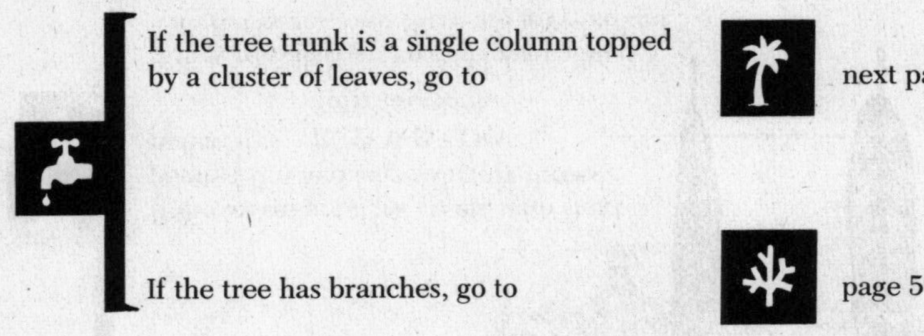

If the tree trunk is a single column topped by a cluster of leaves, go to next page

If the tree has branches, go to page 56

With abundant artificial water, almost any kind of tree will grow in a desert climate. Only a few of the more commonly cultivated species are shown here.

If the trunk is rough with the stubs of old leaf bases; and leaflets are borne along the side of the leaf stems, it is **DATE PALM** *Phoenix dactylifera*

Date palms were brought from Africa.

If the trunk is smoother; and the leaves are fan-like, it is **CALIFORNIA FAN PALM** *Washingtonia filifera*

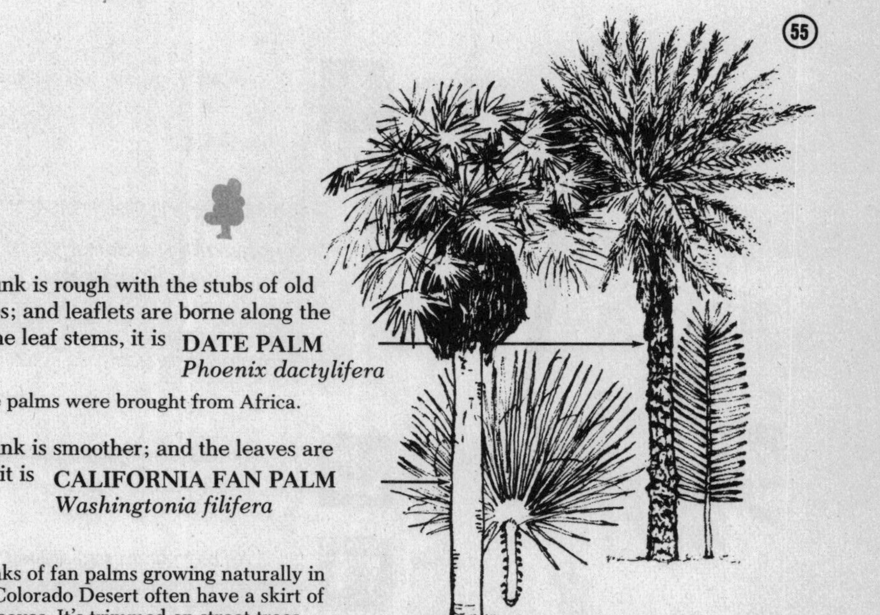

Trunks of fan palms growing naturally in the Colorado Desert often have a skirt of old leaves. It's trimmed on street trees.

(56)

If the tree is dark green with scale-like leaves or needle-like foliage, go to  below

If there are ordinary leaves, go to  next page

If the foliage is feathery, with branches that look like pine needles except that they're jointed, it is **AUSTRALIAN PINE BEEFWOOD**
Casuarina equisetifolia

This Australian tree has cone-like fruits.

If the foliage is not feathery, go to  next page

If there are glossy, oval leaves with winged stems, it is

ORANGE, GRAPEFRUIT, or LEMON
Citrus sp.

These compact, evergreen trees originated in Asia. They have fragrant fruit and flowers present at the same time.

If the leaves are not glossy and oval, go to 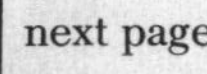 next page

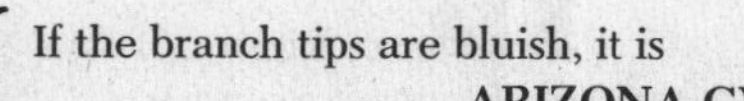

If the branch tips are bluish, it is

ARIZONA CYPRESS
Cupressus arizonica

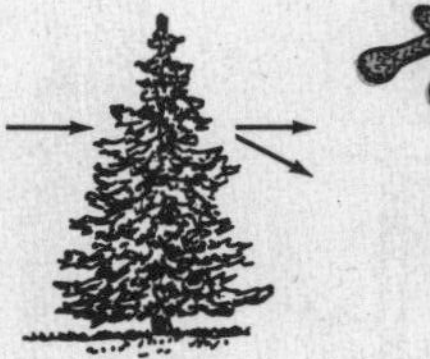

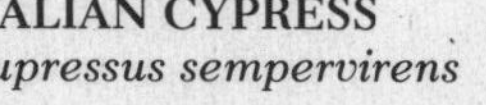

If the tree is columnar, compact, tapering, and dark green, it is **ITALIAN CYPRESS**
Cupressus sempervirens

If the leaves are long, dull green on both sides, sharply pointed, curved, and fragrant, it is

BLUE GUM
Eucalyptus globulus

This widely planted Australian tree sheds bark and flower capsules. Neat people prefer other species of Eucalyptus.

If the leaflets have many divisions into leaflets or lobes, go to

below

If the leaves are fernlike, with rolled-under margins, silky on the undersides, it is

SILK-OAK
Grevillea robusta

This Australian tree has orange flowers and small pods.

If there are separate leaflets, go to

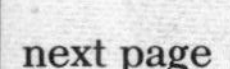

next page

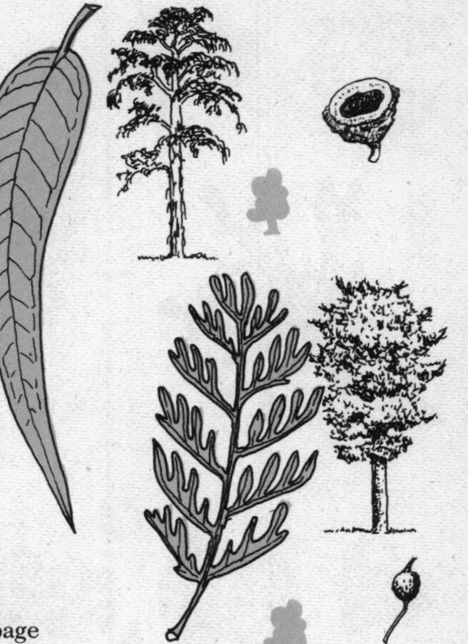

If the foliage is feathery and smells spicy,
it is **CALIFORNIA PEPPER TREE**
Schinus molle

This Peruvian tree bears long clusters of rosy, beadlike fruit (not the pepper Columbus sought).

If the foliage is coarse, foul-smelling; and the tree has thick twigs and few branches,
it is **TREE OF HEAVEN**
Ailanthus altissima

This Chinese tree has followed civilization, growing especially in city grime. Look for massive, rosy culsters of winged seeds.

Index

A Checklist of Trees Found in Rocky Mountains

EVERGREEN OR CONE BEARING TREES

- ☐ Cedar, Western Red
- ☐ Cypress, Arizona
- ☐ Fir, Douglas
- ☐ Fir, Grand
- ☐ Fir, Subalpine
- ☐ Fir, White
- ☐ Hemlock, Mountain
- ☐ Hemlock, Western
- ☐ Juniper, Alligator
- ☐ Juniper, One Seed
- ☐ Juniper, Rocky Mountain
- ☐ Juniper, Utah
- ☐ Larch, Subalpine
- ☐ Larch, Western

Evergreen Oaks

- ☐ Arizona White Oak
- ☐ Canyon Live Oak
- ☐ Emory Oak
- ☐ Mexican Blue Oak
- ☐ Silverleaf Oak

Pines

- ☐ Apache Pine
- ☐ Arizona Pine
- ☐ Bristlecone Pine
- ☐ Chihuahua Pine
- ☐ Colorado Pinyon
- ☐ Limber Pine
- ☐ Lodgepole Pine
- ☐ Mexican Pinyon
- ☐ Ponderosa Pine
- ☐ Singleleaf Pinyon
- ☐ Western White Pine
- ☐ Whitebark Pine

- ☐ Spruce, Colorado Blue
- ☐ Spruce, Engelmann
- ☐ Spruce, White
- ☐ Yew, Pacific

DECIDUOUS TREES

- ☐ Alder, Arizona
- ☐ Alder, Mountain
- ☐ Alder, White
- ☐ Ash, Green
- ☐ Ash, Lowell
- ☐ Ash, Singleleaf
- ☐ Ash, Velvet
- ☐ Aspen, Quaking
- ☐ Birch, Paper
- ☐ Birch, Water
- ☐ Boxelder
- ☐ Buckthorn, Cascara
- ☐ Cherry, Bitter
- ☐ Cherry, Choke
- ☐ Cherry, Pin
- ☐ Cliffrose

Cottonwoods

- ☐ Black Cottonwood
- ☐ Fremont Cottonwood
- ☐ Lanceleaf Cottonwood
- ☐ Narrowleaf Cottonwood
- ☐ Plains Cottonwood
- ☐ Rio Grande Cottonwood

- ☐ Elm, American
- ☐ Hackberry
- ☐ Hackberry, Netleaf
- ☐ Hawthorn, Black
- ☐ Hoptree
- ☐ Hophornbeam, Knowlton
- ☐ Ironwood
- ☐ Locust, New Mexican
- ☐ Maple, Bigtooth
- ☐ Maple, Rocky Mountain
- ☐ Mountainash, Sitka
- ☐ Mountain-mahogany, Curlleaf
- ☐ Mountain-mahogany, Hairy
- ☐ Mulberry, Texas
- ☐ Oak, Bur
- ☐ Oak, Gambel
- ☐ Plum, American
- ☐ Poplar, Balsam
- ☐ Redbud, California
- ☐ Serviceberry, Saskatoon
- ☐ Sycamore, Arizona
- ☐ Walnut, Arizona
- ☐ Willow, Peachleaf

To use this book:

1. Select a typical leaf or some needles from the tree you wish to identify. Avoid freaks.
2. Begin on page 10 and proceed step by step, considering each choice as you come to it.
3. When you've made the final choice, arriving at the name of the tree, compare your leaf with the illustration and check the other features shown.

advice: Look at pages 1-10 before you begin.

area covered by this book

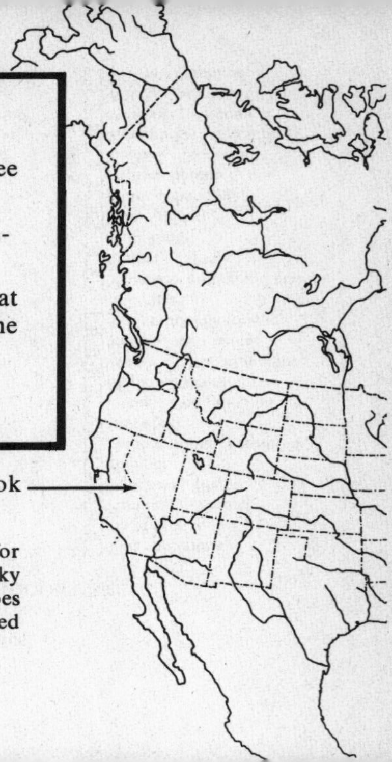

Note: This book is for trees native to the Rocky Mountain area. It does not identify introduced species.

Rocky Mountain Tree Distribution

Maps in this book show the area where each tree species grows naturally:

① Subalpine Fir

Where trees can grow depends on climate. The very things people like about the Rocky Mountain climate - cool mountain summers, deep snow for skiers, year 'round dry sunshine in the low altitudes - are hard on trees. The Rockies have abundant water and abundant warmth, but not in the same places. Trees must be somehow adapted to this adversity.

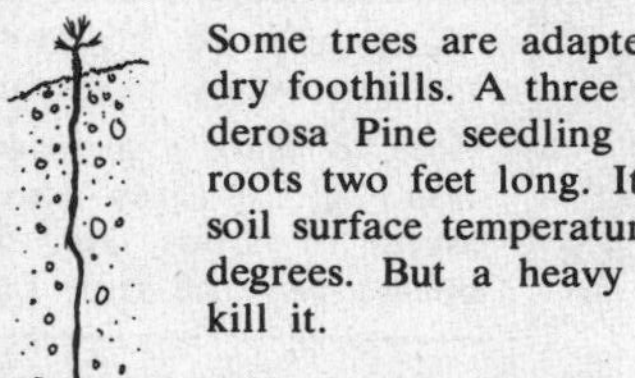

Some trees are adapted to hot, dry foothills. A three inch Ponderosa Pine seedling may have roots two feet long. It can take soil surface temperatures of 180 degrees. But a heavy frost can kill it.

Other trees can survive short summers and bitter winters. The new needles of Subalpine Fir resist frost. Its branches shed heavy snow. But its roots are shallow.

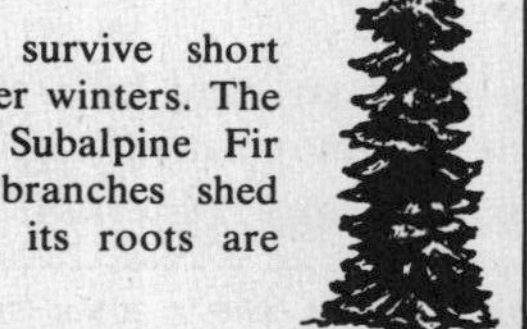

Subalpine Fir

Douglas Fir

Ponderosa Pine

Each tree's range has an upper limit, the altitude where it's too cold for the tree to grow, and a lower limit where it's too dry.

② *The next pages describe five life zones found at different altitudes in the Rocky Mountains. Some trees grow in several zones, but if you know what zone you're in you can usually tell what trees you'll find.*

PLAINS ZONE - *Upper Sonoran Zone* annual rainfall: 10 - 20 inches

Grasses, sagebrush, or dry shrubbery dominate this zone, the dryest in the Rocky Mountains. To survive here trees must have roots that reach moisture.

Small trees grow with wide-spreading roots in loose, porous soil or the cool crevices of a rocky outcrop:

Pinyons Gambel Oak
Junipers Mt. Mahogany

The only large trees are ones rooted in subsurface water along a stream bed:

Cottonwoods Hackberry
Box Elder Willow

FOOTHILLS ZONE - *Transition Zone* annual rainfall: 20 - 25 inches ③

Deep-rooted Ponderosa Pine dominates this zone, except for fine-soiled sagebrush plains in northern Rockies.

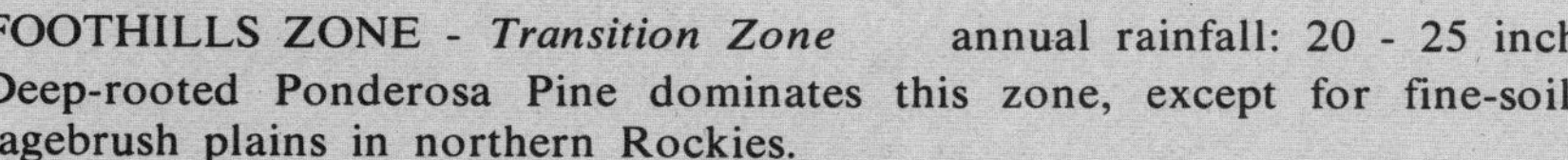

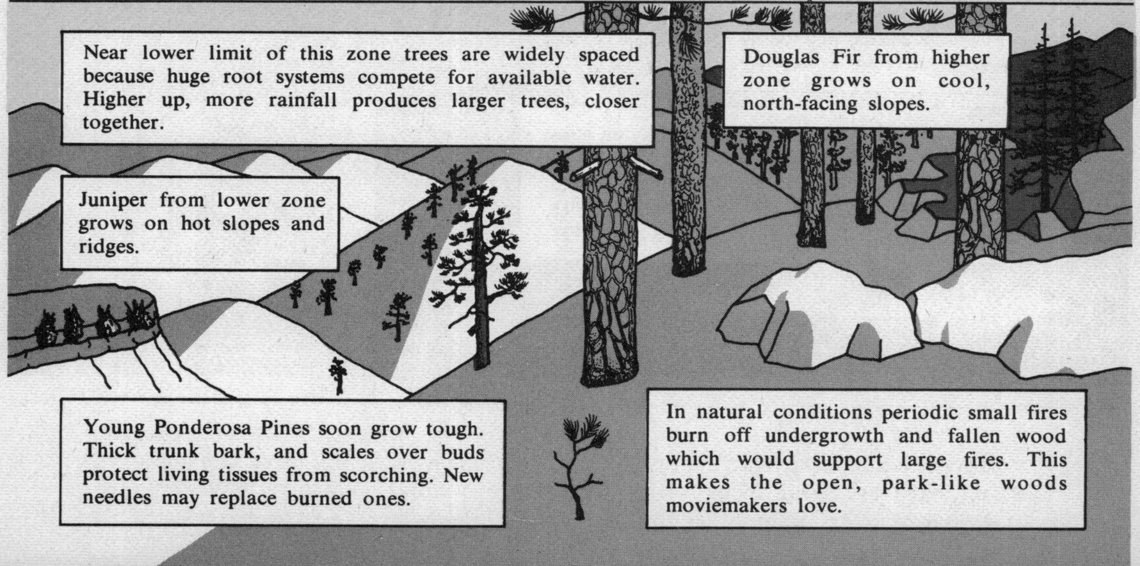

④ MONTANE ZONE - *Canadian Zone* annual rainfall: 25 - 30 inches

This zone has enough rainfall to support a dense, shady forest. Douglas Fir dominates except in areas of repeated burning in the Great Basin and northern Rockies.

Mountain Parks

There are flat, treeless "parks" in this zone where fine, water-deposited soils impede the growth of tree roots. Adjacent slopes with better aerated, porous soils are wooded.

Ponderosa Pine occupies warm slopes and burned areas in lower part of this zone.

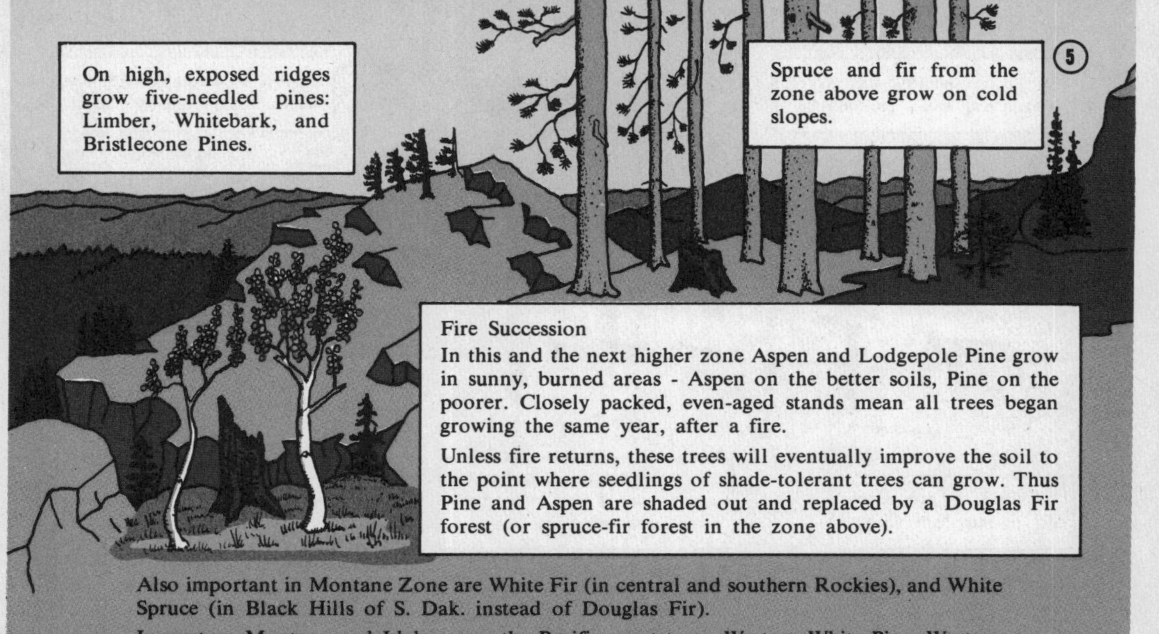

Fire Succession

In this and the next higher zone Aspen and Lodgepole Pine grow in sunny, burned areas - Aspen on the better soils, Pine on the poorer. Closely packed, even-aged stands mean all trees began growing the same year, after a fire.

Unless fire returns, these trees will eventually improve the soil to the point where seedlings of shade-tolerant trees can grow. Thus Pine and Aspen are shaded out and replaced by a Douglas Fir forest (or spruce-fir forest in the zone above).

Also important in Montane Zone are White Fir (in central and southern Rockies), and White Spruce (in Black Hills of S. Dak. instead of Douglas Fir).

In western Montana and Idaho grow the Pacific coast trees: Western White Pine, Western Larch, Western Hemlock, Western Red Cedar, and Grand Fir.

(6) SUBALPINE ZONE- *Hudsonian Zone* annual precipitation: over 30 inches

Englemann Spruce and Subalpine Fir dominate this zone. To survive here trees must resist late and early frost, and mature new growth in a short summer.

Meadows in this zone are kept lush and green by afternoon thunderstorms.

Trees are shaped by exposure to wind.

Bent Aspen trees may mark path of snow slides.

Patches of snow last into July and August.

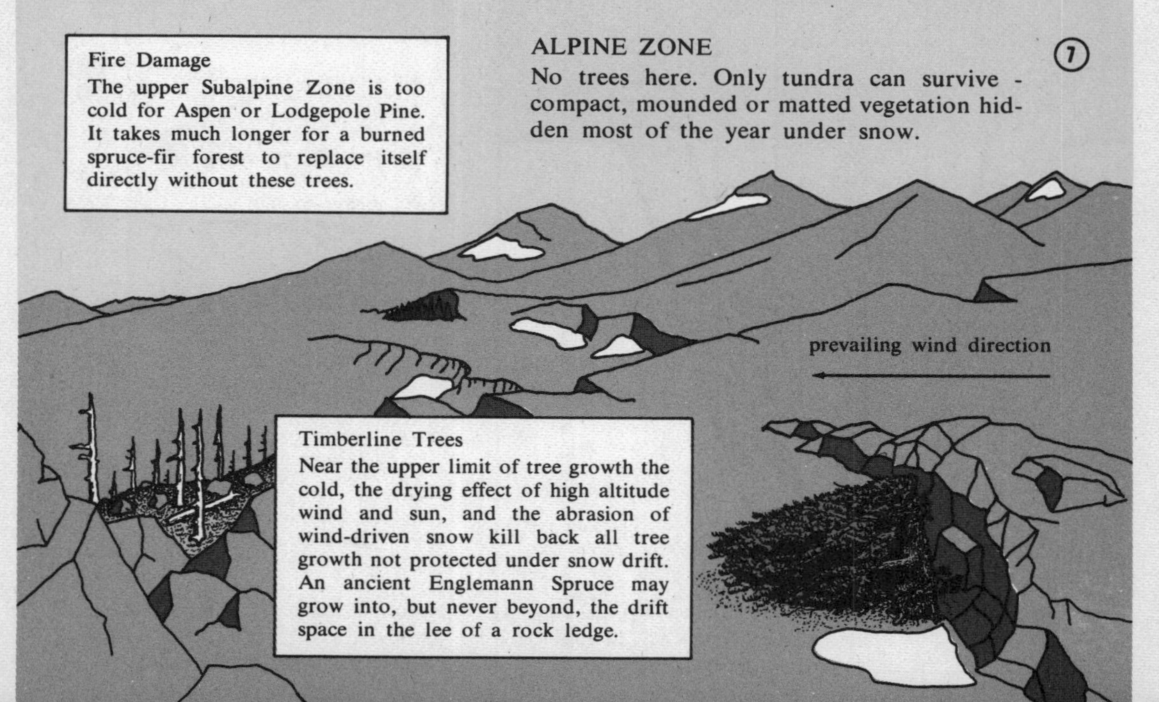

Fire Damage
The upper Subalpine Zone is too cold for Aspen or Lodgepole Pine. It takes much longer for a burned spruce-fir forest to replace itself directly without these trees.
ALPINE ZONE
7
No trees here. Only tundra can survive - compact, mounded or matted vegetation hidden most of the year under snow.
prevailing wind direction
Timberline Trees
Near the upper limit of tree growth the cold, the drying effect of high altitude wind and sun, and the abrasion of wind-driven snow kill back all tree growth not protected under snow drift. An ancient Englemann Spruce may grow into, but never beyond, the drift space in the lee of a rock ledge.

The place you're most likely to find each kind of tree is shown in this book by these symbols:

- Subalpine Zone (with Spruces and firs)
- Montane Zone (with Douglas Firs)
- Foothills Zone (with Ponderosa Pines)
- Plains Zone (among junipers)
- Plains Zone (along stream beds)
- In lowlands or near water
- In burned areas

The altitude of the life zones is higher in the southern Rockies than in the north.

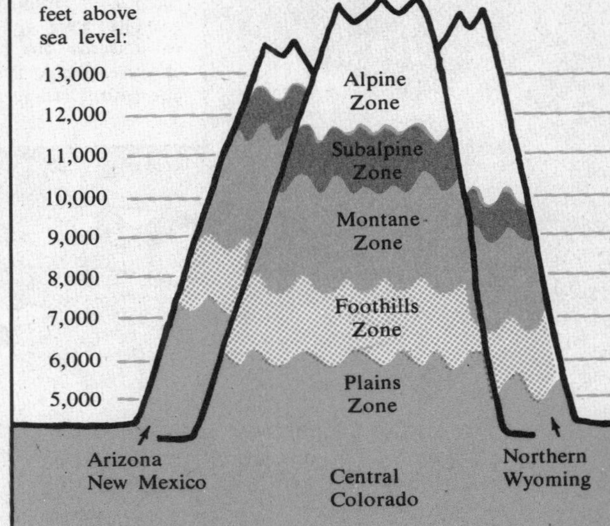

Altitude of the life zones depends also on local climate (microclimate). Southwest-facing canyon slopes and mountainsides are warmed by exposure to full sunlight during the hottest part of the day. Life zones occur at higher elevations there. Northeast-facing slopes are cooler, so life zones extend to lower levels there: (9)

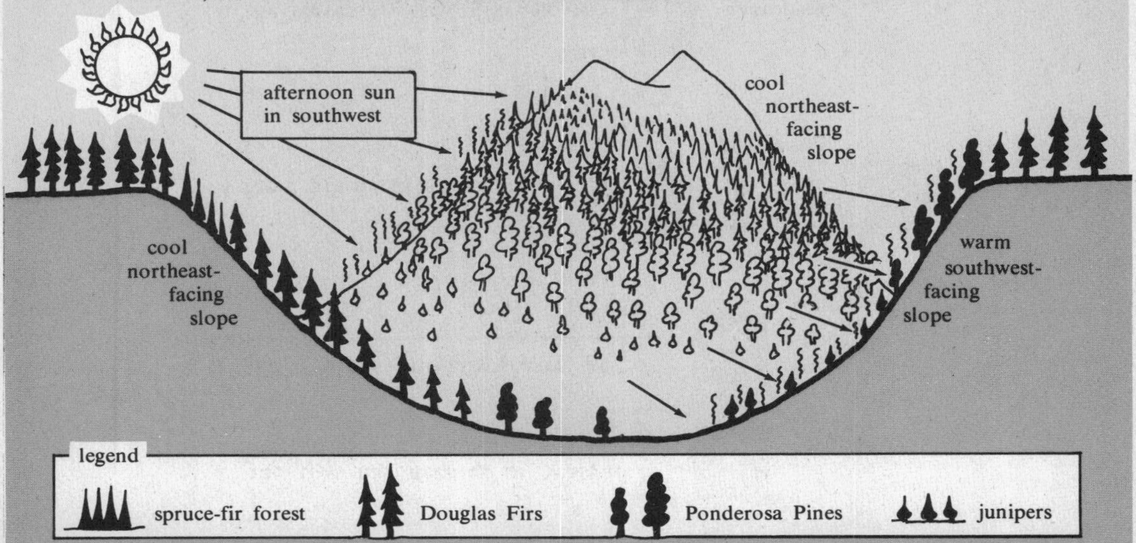

Begin here.

If the tree has needles or scale-like leaves, go to this symbol ——→  below

If the tree has ordinary leaves, go to this symbol ——→ page 30

If there are needles like this: go to  page 14

If the leaves are scale-like, go to next page

11

If the ends of the branches appear flattened as if they had been ironed, it is

WESTERN RED CEDAR
Thuja plicata

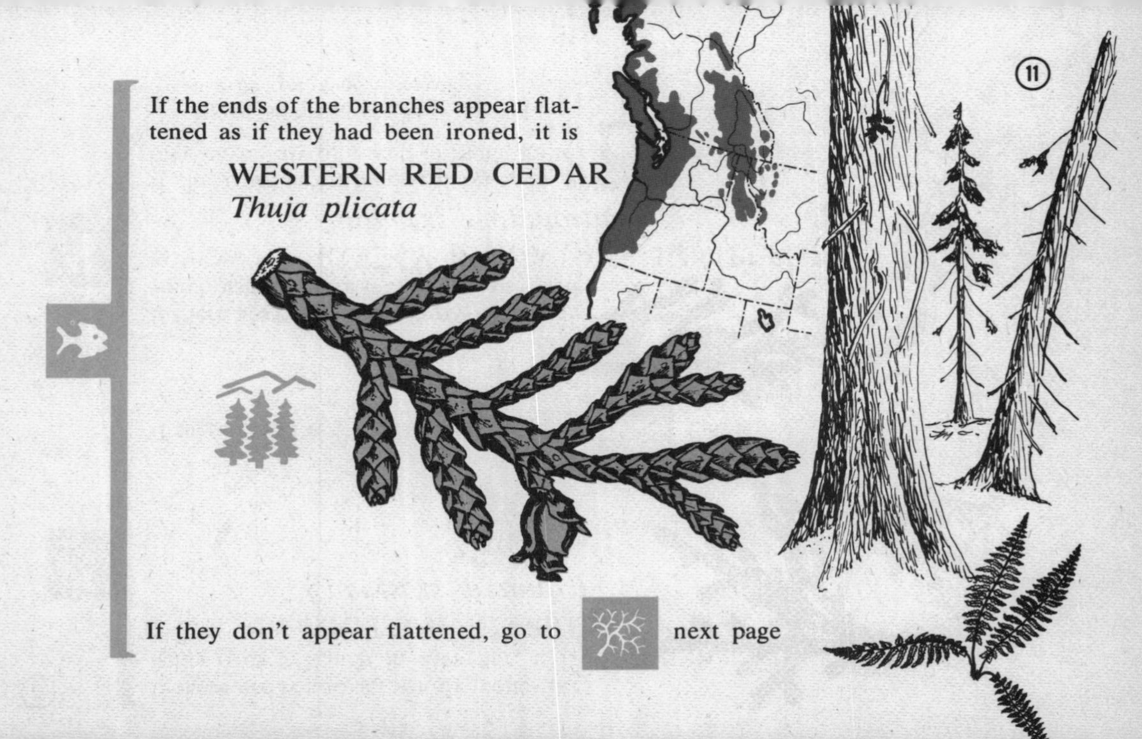

If they don't appear flattened, go to next page

(12)

If there are roundish, woody, cone-like fruits over 1/2 inch in diameter, it is

ARIZONA CYPRESS
Cupressus arizonica

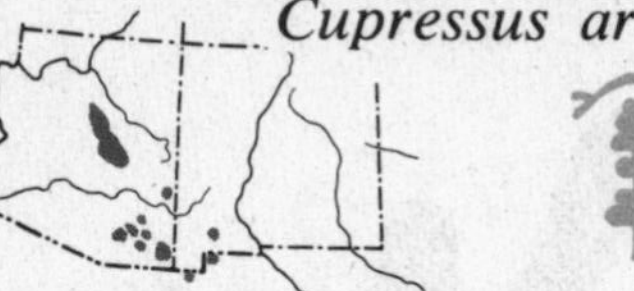

If there aren't any fruits like that, go to below

If there are bright blue, berry-like fruits which usually have more than one seed in them, it is

ROCKY MOUNTAIN JUNIPER
Juniperus scopulorum

If the fruits are not bright blue, or if they have only one seed in them, go to   next page

(If you can't find fruit, you must have a male tree. Find a female.)

8

If the trunk bark is deeply furrowed and checkered into squarish plates, it is

ALLIGATOR JUNIPER
Juniperus deppeana

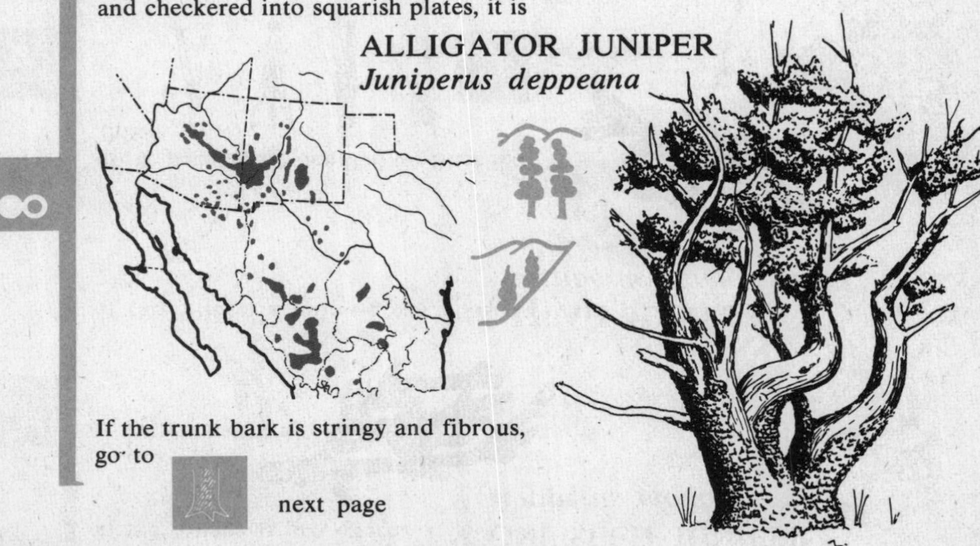

If the trunk bark is stringy and fibrous, go to next page

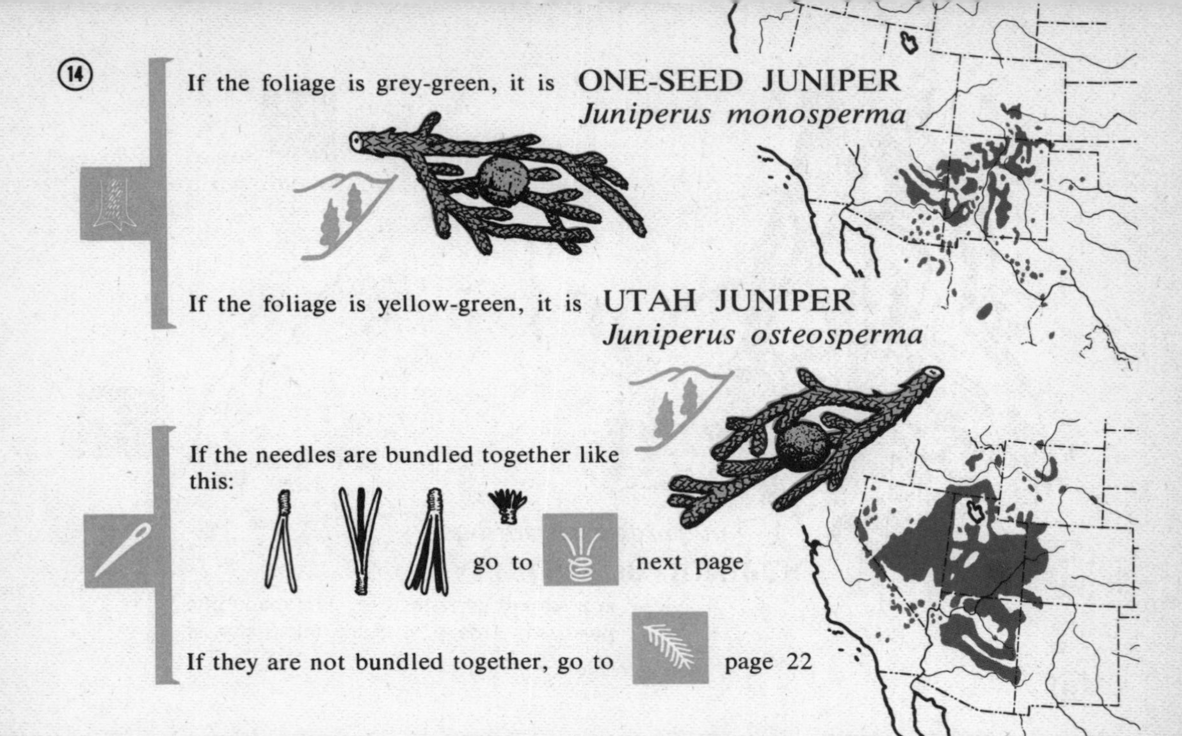

If the foliage is grey-green, it is **ONE-SEED JUNIPER** *Juniperus monosperma*

If the foliage is yellow-green, it is **UTAH JUNIPER** *Juniperus osteosperma*

If the needles are bundled together like this: go to next page

If they are not bundled together, go to page 22

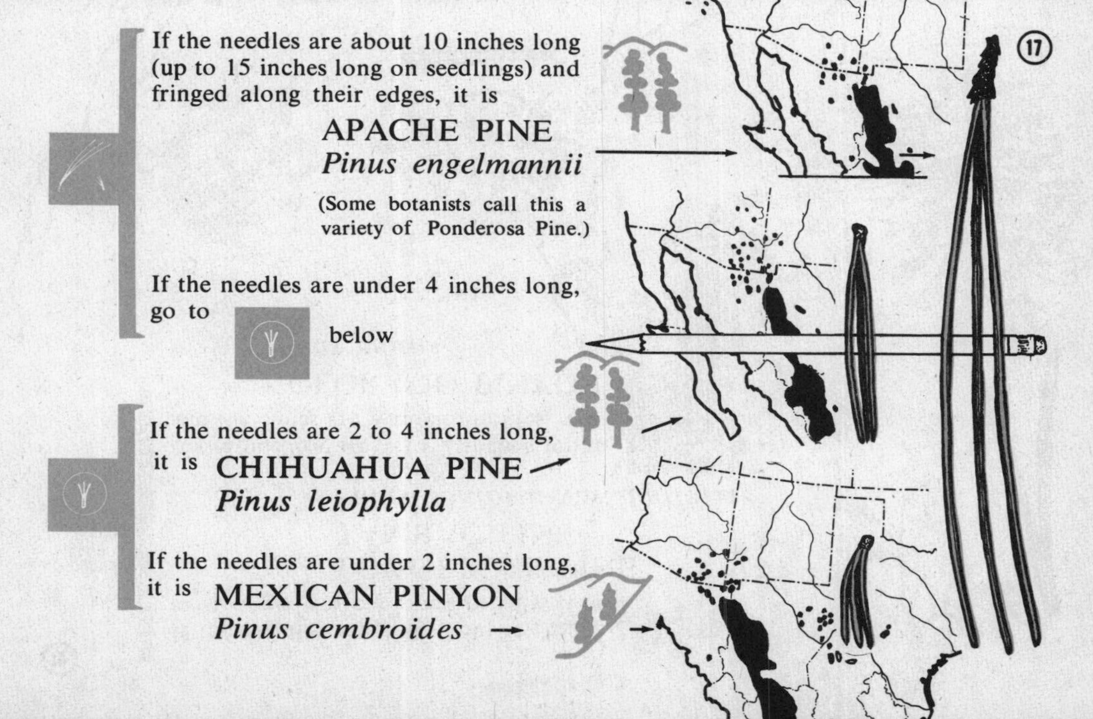

17

If the needles are about 10 inches long (up to 15 inches long on seedlings) and fringed along their edges, it is

APACHE PINE
Pinus engelmannii

(Some botanists call this a variety of Ponderosa Pine.)

If the needles are under 4 inches long, go to [symbol] below

If the needles are 2 to 4 inches long, it is CHIHUAHUA PINE
Pinus leiophylla

If the needles are under 2 inches long, it is MEXICAN PINYON
Pinus cembroides

If the needles are 1 to 3 inches long, twisted; and the cones are prickly, it is

LODGEPOLE PINE
TAMRAC PINE
Pinus contorta var. *latifolia*

If the needles are 1 to 2 inches long; and the cones are without prickles, it is

COLORADO PINYON
Pinus edulis

If the needles are about 1 1/2 inches long it is **BRISTLECONE PINE**
Pinus aristata

If they're longer, go to below

If the outermost twigs are thicker than an ordinary wooden pencil (5/16 in.) go to next page

If they're thinner than a pencil, go to page 21

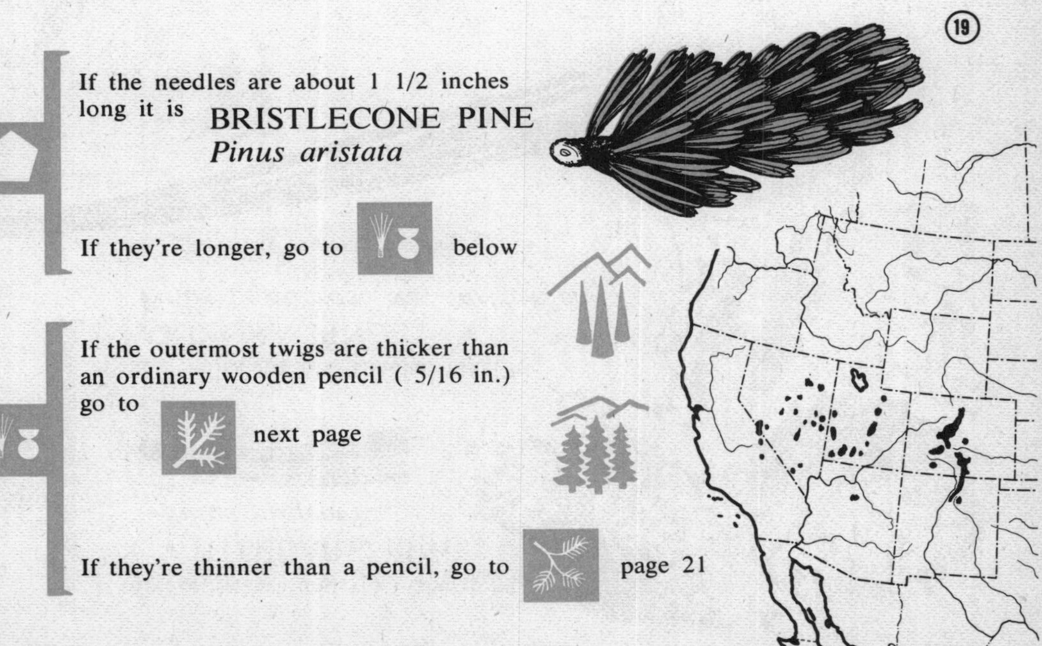

20

If the needles are under 3 inches long, it is
WHITEBARK PINE
Pinus albicaulis

If the needles are 5 to 7 inches long, it is
ARIZONA PINE
Pinus ponderosa var. *arizonica*

(A variety of Ponderosa Pine.)

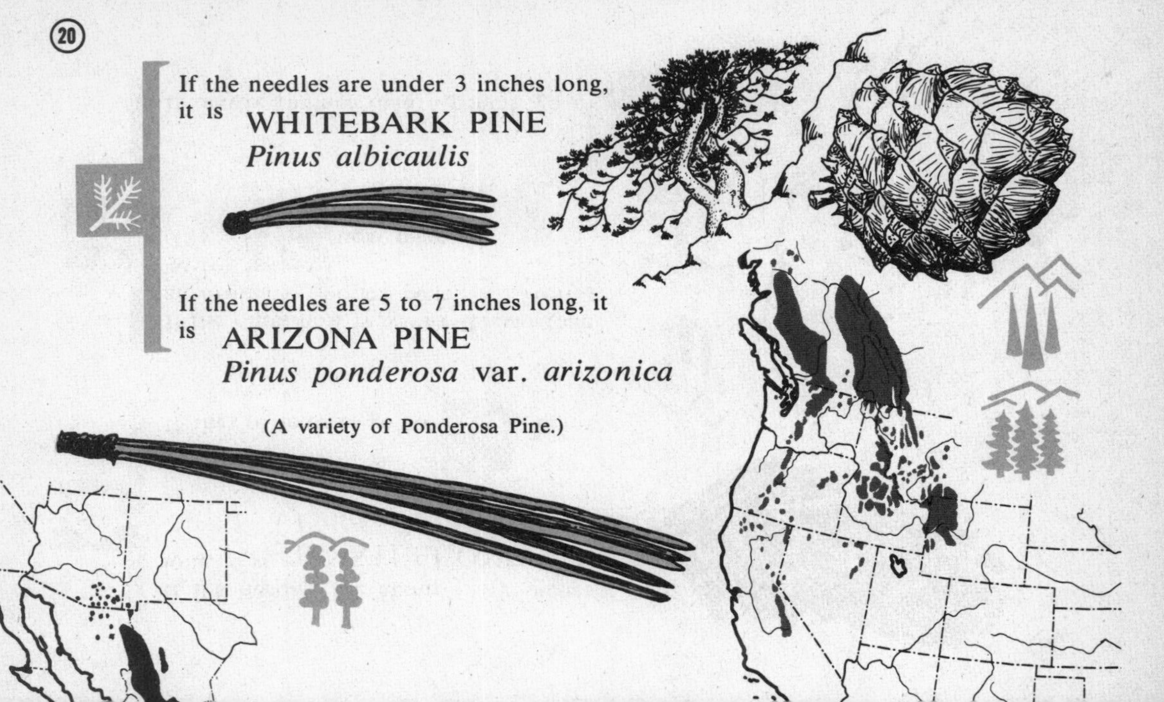

(21)

If the cones have thin scales, it is **WESTERN WHITE PINE** *Pinus monticola*

If the cone scales are thick at their tips, it is **LIMBER PINE** *Pinus flexilis*

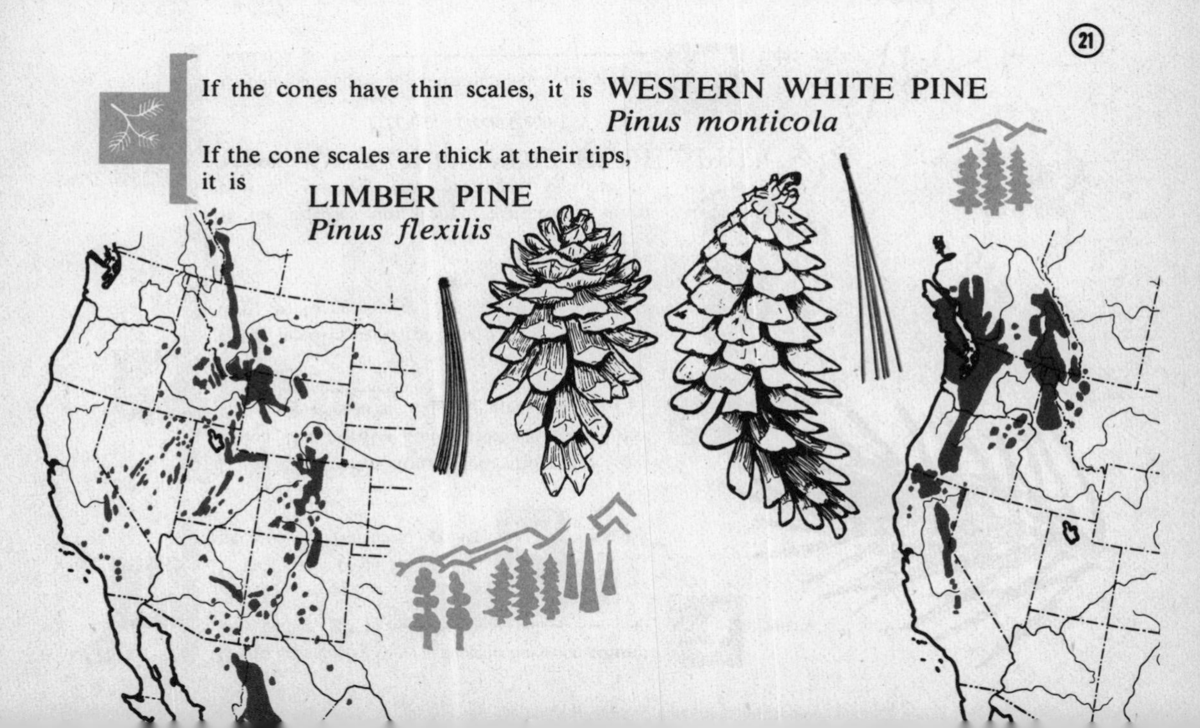

If you can easily twirl a needle between thumb and finger, go to ——→ below

If you can't twirl it, because it's flattened, go to   page 25

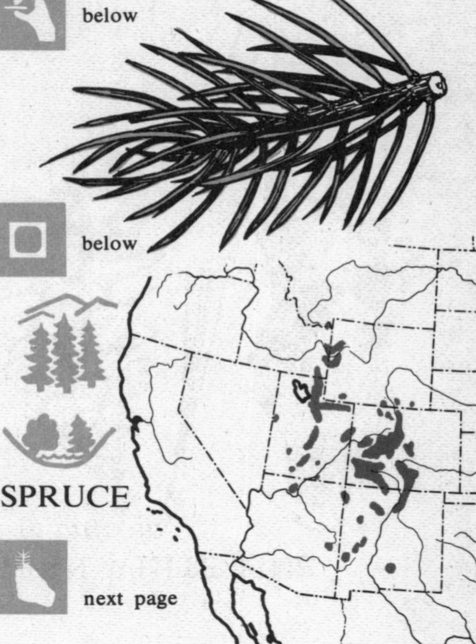

If the needles are four-sided; and twigs from which the needles have fallen are bumpy like this: it's a SPRUCE. Go to below

If the needles are round or oval in cross section, go to  page 24

If the needles are tipped with hard, sharp points, making the branches painful to squeeze, it is **COLORADO BLUE SPRUCE** *Picea pungens*

If you can squeeze a branch without saying "ouch!" go to ——→ next page

(23)

If the tips of the cone scales are toothed, notched, or pointed, it is

ENGLEMANN SPRUCE
Picea engelmannii

If the cone scales have smooth tips, it is

WHITE SPRUCE
Picea glauca

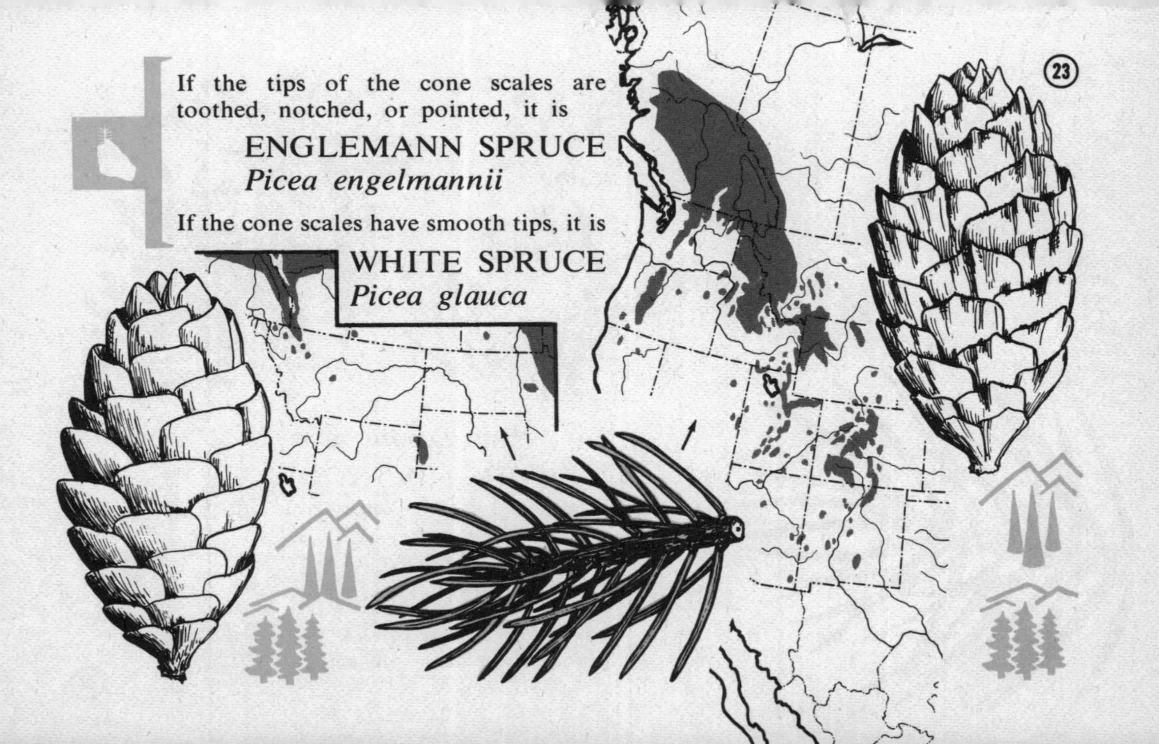

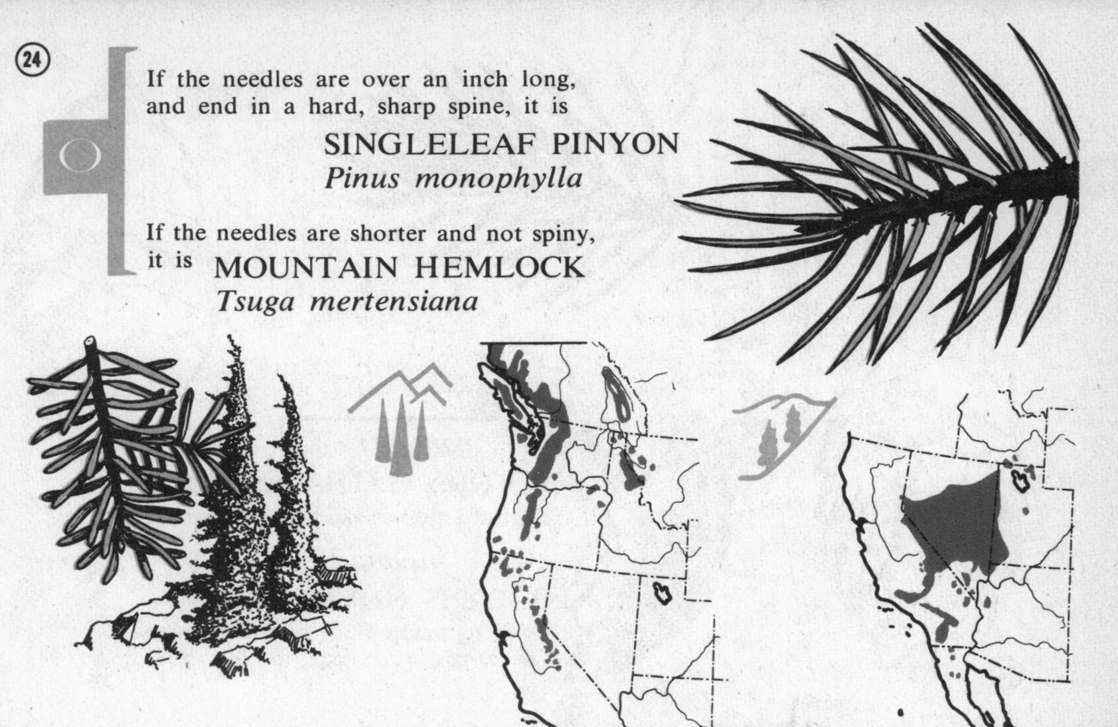

If the needles are over an inch long, and end in a hard, sharp spine, it is

SINGLELEAF PINYON
Pinus monophylla

If the needles are shorter and not spiny, it is MOUNTAIN HEMLOCK
Tsuga mertensiana

If the needles are thick at the base, it is

SUBALPINE FIR
Abies lasiocarpa

If the needles narrow to a stalk at the base, go to next page

In the southern Rocky Mountains you may find a variety of Subalpine Fir with gray, rough, corky trunk bark called **CORKBARK FIR**
Abies lasiocarpa var. *arizonica*

26

If the needles are mostly notched at their tips, like this: it is **GRAND FIR**
Abies grandis

If the tips are rounded or pointed, go to
next page

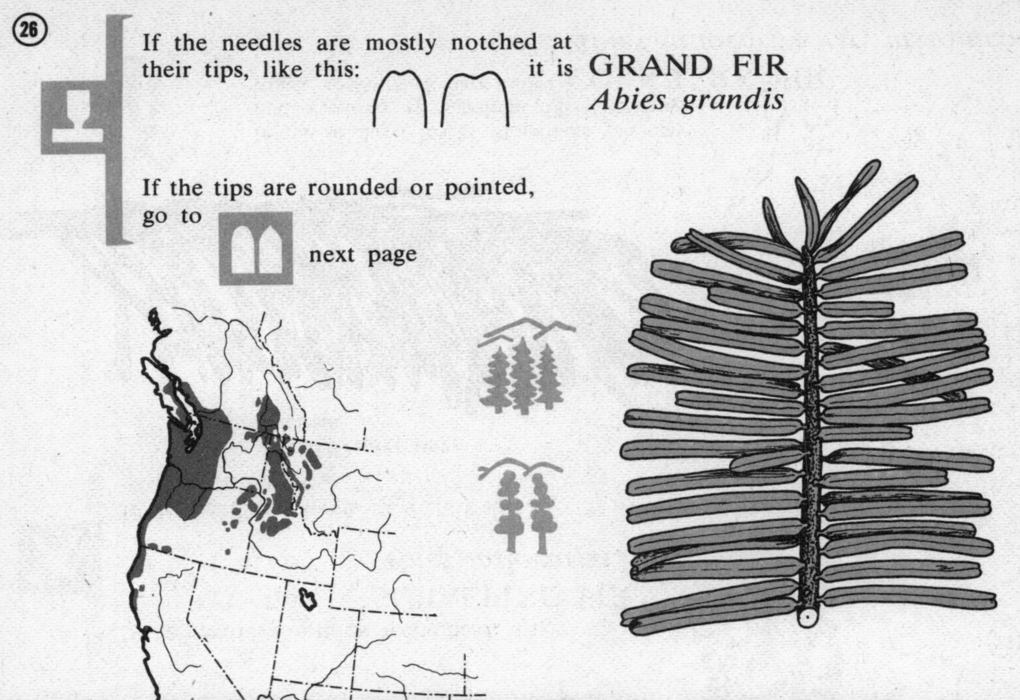

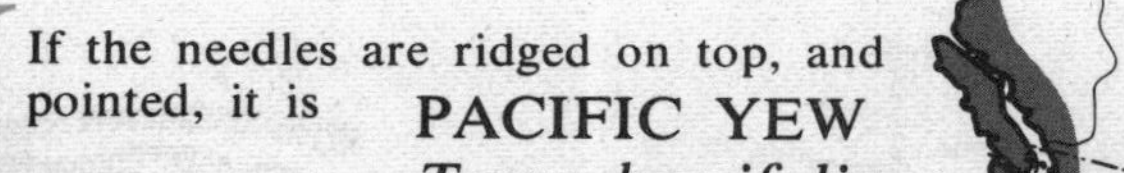

If the needles are ridged on top, and pointed, it is **PACIFIC YEW** *Taxus brevifolia*

If the needles are flat on top, or grooved, and rounded or blunt at the tip, go to 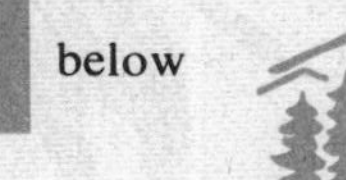 below

If the needles are about 1/2 inch long, and stand on a short, thread-like stalk, it is **WESTERN HEMLOCK** *Tsuga heterophylla*

If the needles are longer, go to next page

28

If the topsides of the needles have a delicate, whitish band, and if their bases resemble tiny, green suction cups; and the cones do not drop whole, but fall apart on the tree, it is **WHITE FIR**

Abies concolor

If the topsides of the needles have a single small groove instead of a band; and pulled-off needles have a bit of twig bark hanging on; or if the tree has dropped cones, it is

DOUGLAS FIR
Pseudotsuga menziesii

If the leaves are compound, composed of several leaflets, go to →  below

(You can tell leaves from leaflets because there is no bud at the base of a leaflet.)

If the leaves are simple, not made up of several leaflets, go to → page 35

If the compound leaves grow opposite each other on the twig, like this: go to next page

If the compound leaves grow alternately like this: go to page 33

If the leaflet margins are jagged, it is BOXELDER
Acer negundo

If the margins are saw-toothed, go to [saw icon] below

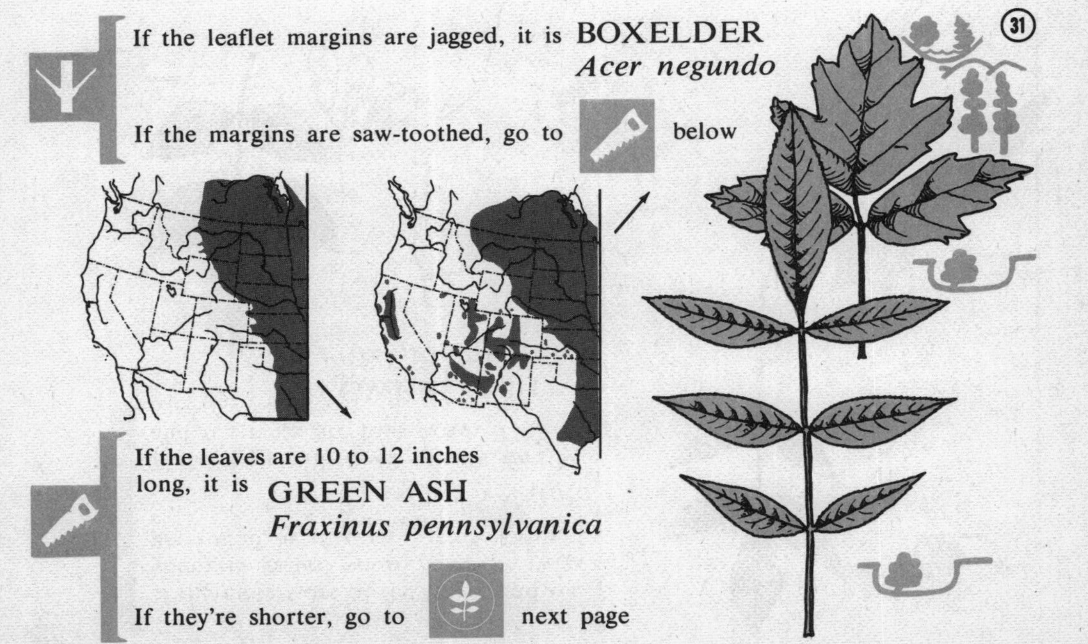

If the leaves are 10 to 12 inches long, it is GREEN ASH
Fraxinus pennsylvanica

If they're shorter, go to [leaf icon] next page

If the undersides of the leaves and the young twigs are woolly, and the twigs are round, it is VELVET ASH

Fraxinus velutina

If the twigs and leaves are not woolly, and the twigs are four-sided, it is

LOWELL ASH

Fraxinus lowellii

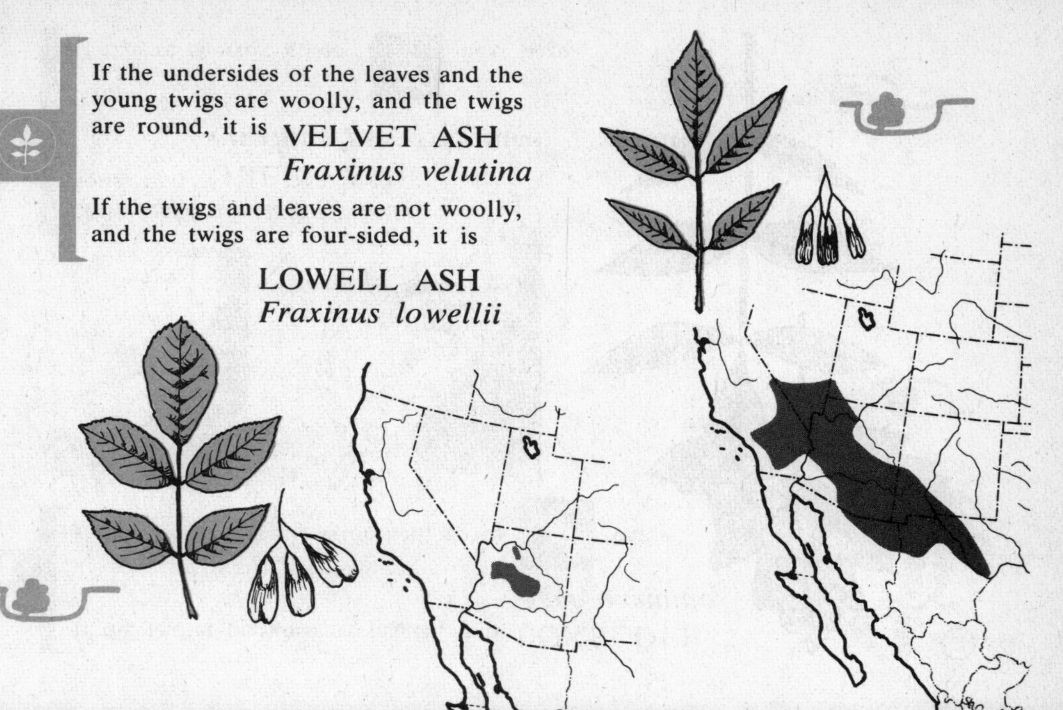

If the twigs are spiny, it is **NEW MEXICAN LOCUST**
Robinia neomexicana

If the twigs are without spines, go to [symbol] below

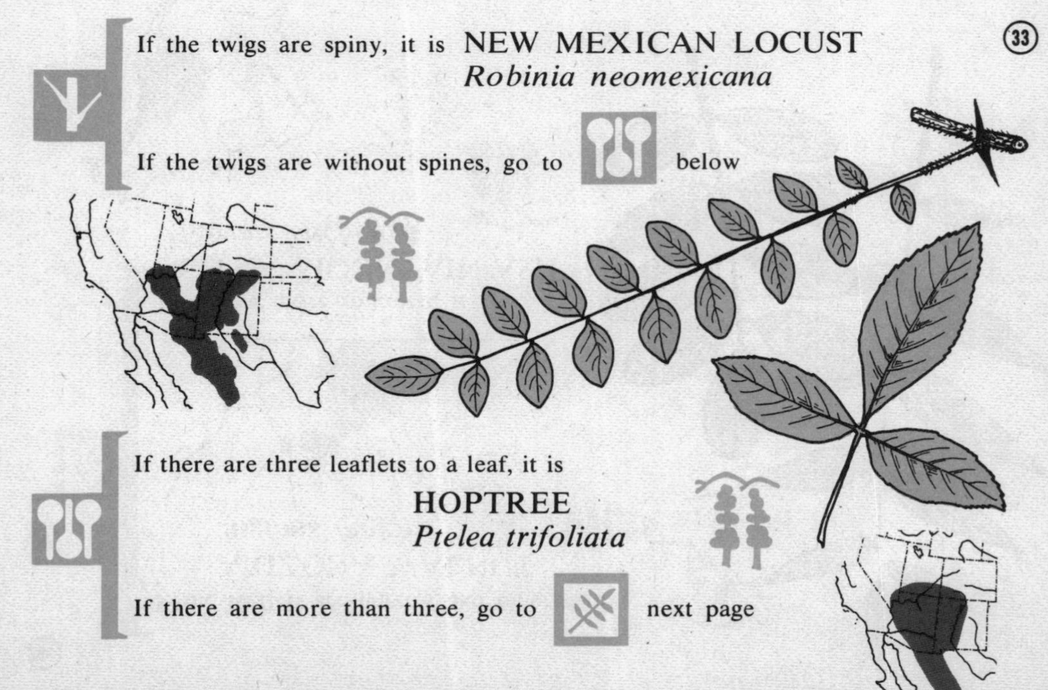

If there are three leaflets to a leaf, it is

HOPTREE
Ptelea trifoliata

If there are more than three, go to [symbol] next page

(34)

If the leaflets are narrow and tapered, it is **ARIZONA WALNUT** *Juglans major*

If they're more rounded, it is **SITKA MOUNTAIN-ASH** *Sorbus sitchensis*

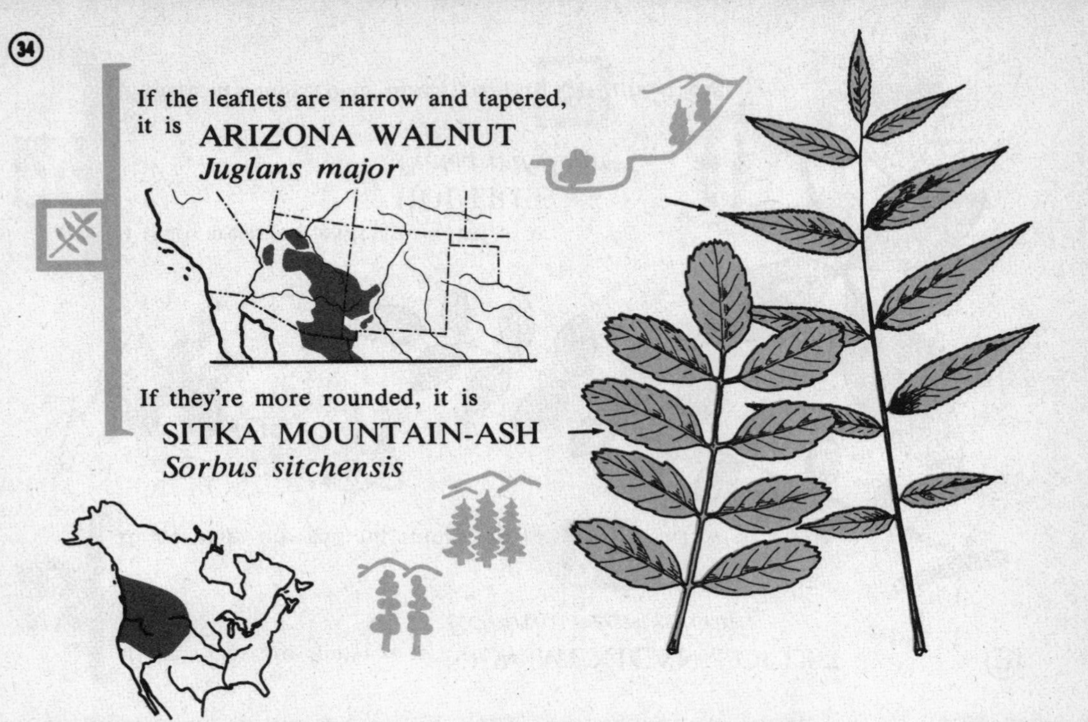

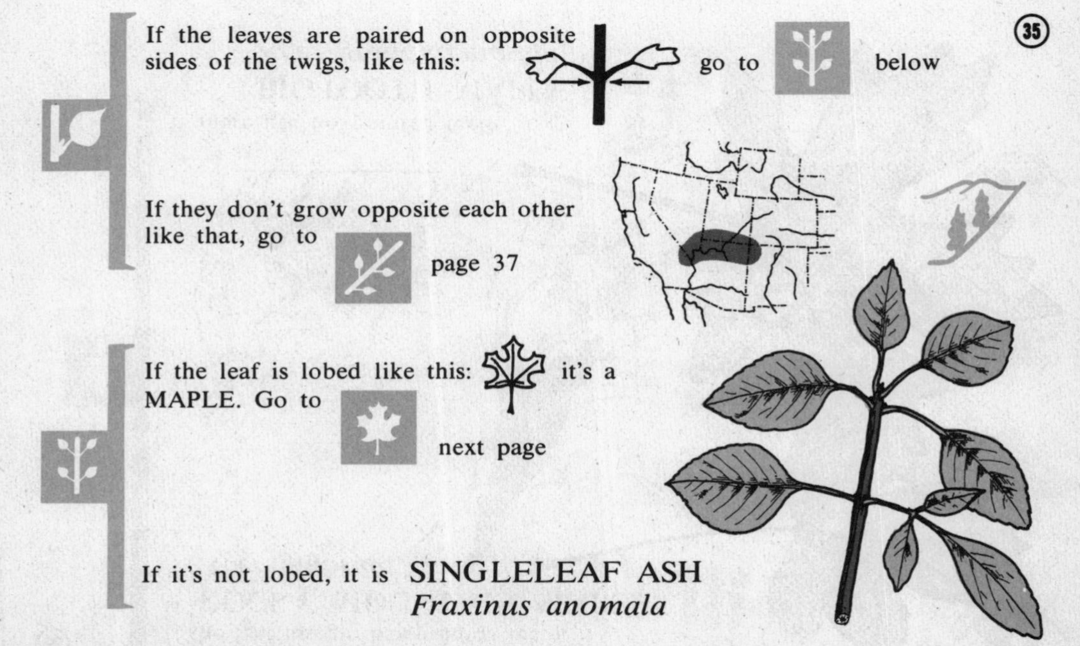

If the leaves are paired on opposite sides of the twigs, like this: go to below

If they don't grow opposite each other like that, go to page 37

If the leaf is lobed like this: it's a MAPLE. Go to next page

If it's not lobed, it is SINGLELEAF ASH
Fraxinus anomala

If the leaf margin has pointed teeth, it is ROCKY MOUNTAIN MAPLE
Acer glabrum

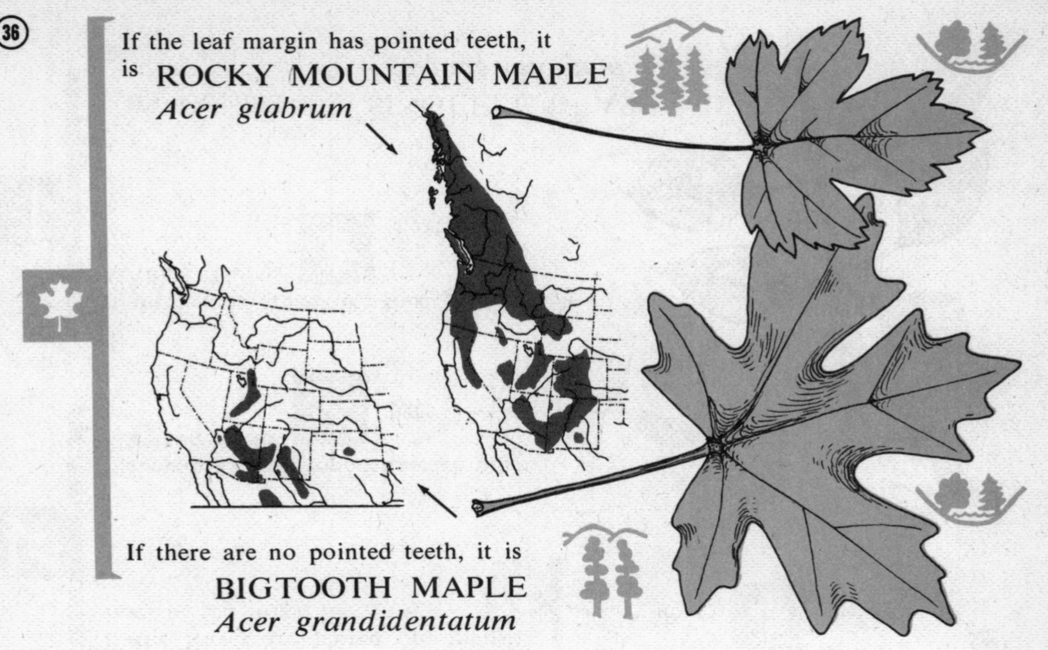

If there are no pointed teeth, it is
BIGTOOTH MAPLE
Acer grandidentatum

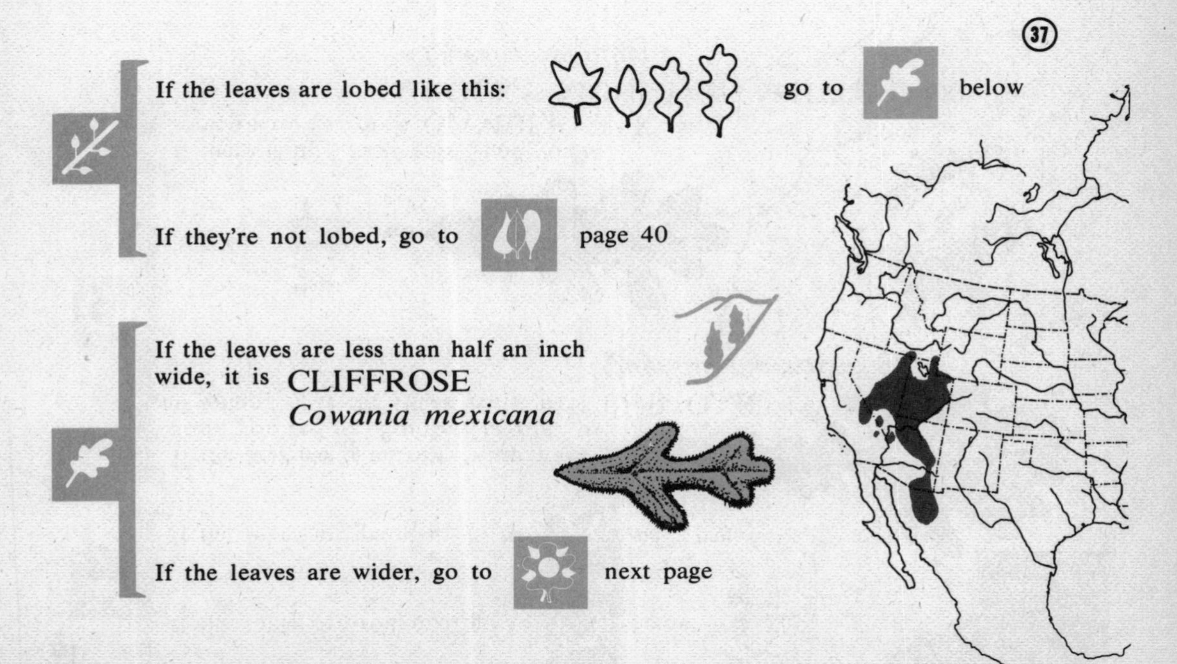

If the leaves are lobed like this: go to below

If they're not lobed, go to page 40

If the leaves are less than half an inch wide, it is CLIFFROSE *Cowania mexicana*

If the leaves are wider, go to next page

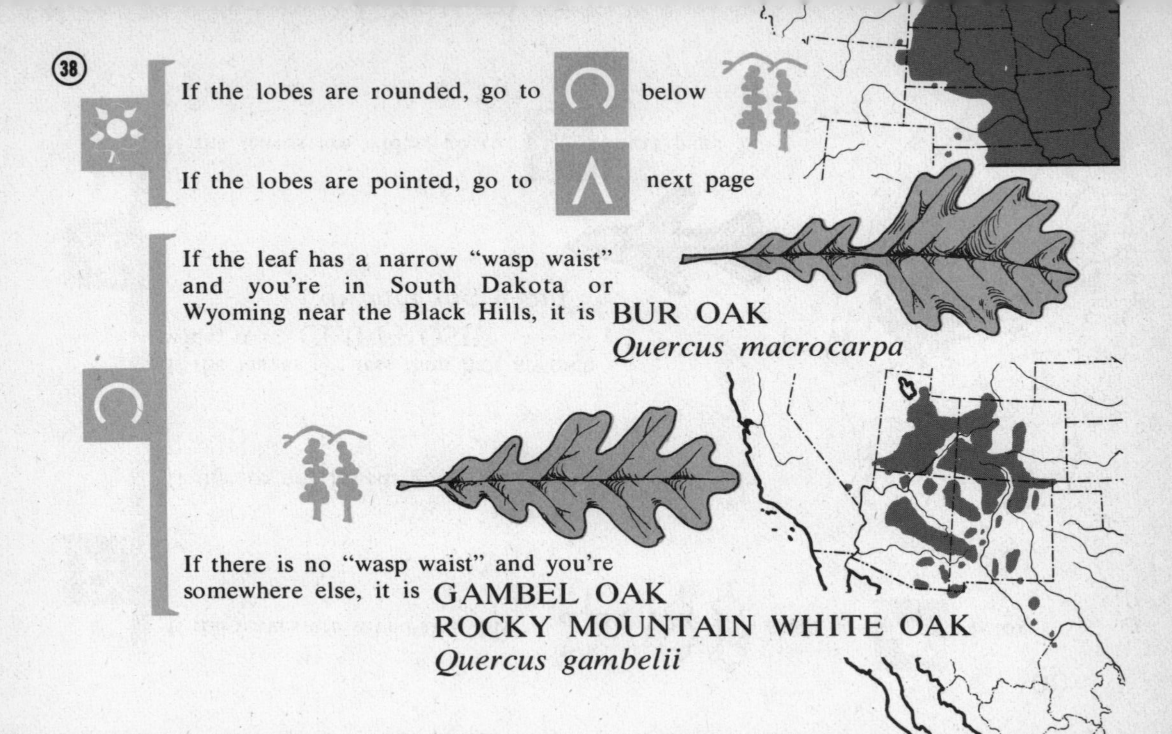

If the lobes are rounded, go to ◠ below

If the lobes are pointed, go to ∧ next page

If the leaf has a narrow "wasp waist" and you're in South Dakota or Wyoming near the Black Hills, it is BUR OAK
Quercus macrocarpa

If there is no "wasp waist" and you're somewhere else, it is GAMBEL OAK
ROCKY MOUNTAIN WHITE OAK
Quercus gambelii

If the leaf margin is saw-toothed, it is

TEXAS MULBERRY
Morus microphylla

If the margin is not saw-toothed, it is

ARIZONA SYCAMORE
Platanus wrightii

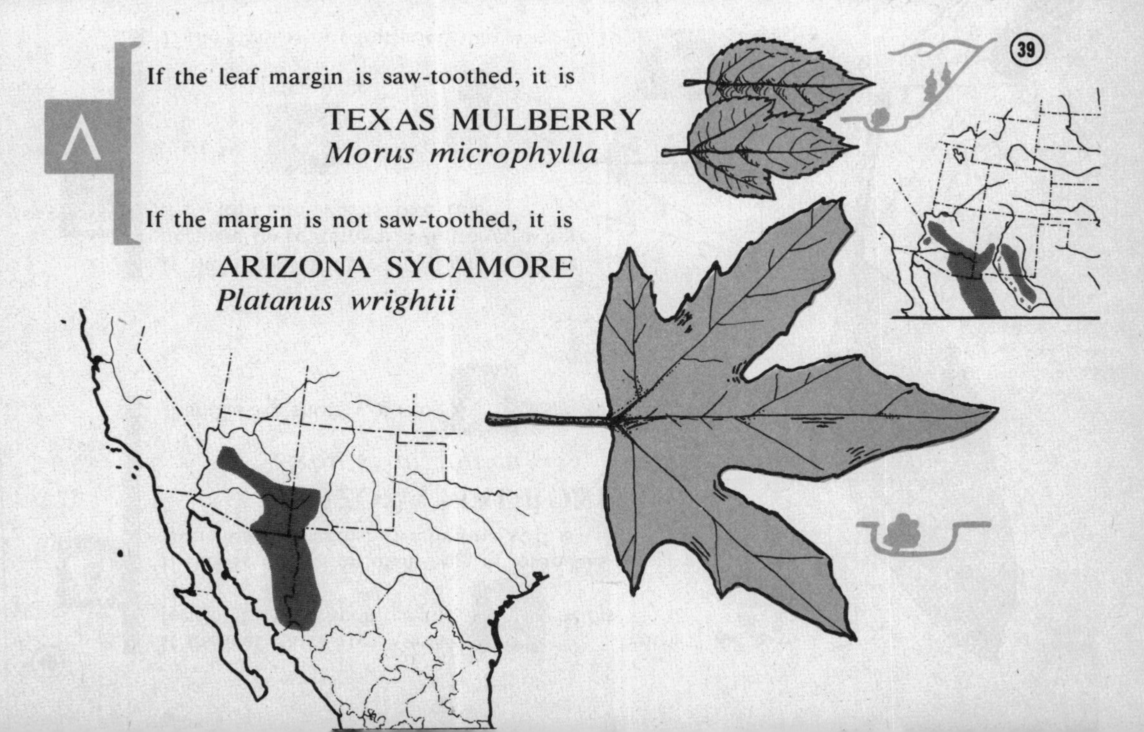

If the leaf stalks are longer than one inch, go to 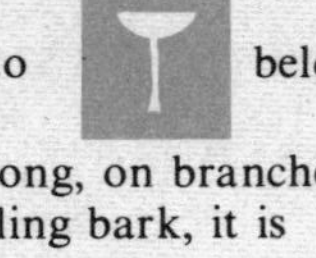 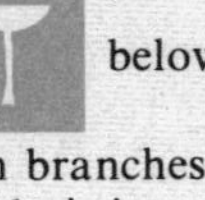 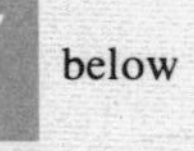 below

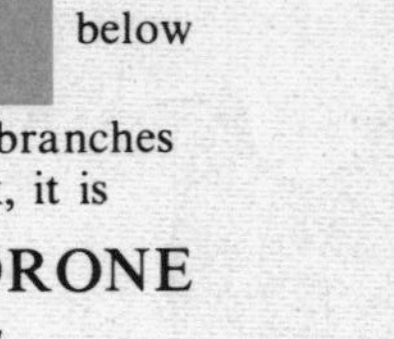

If they're almost an inch long, on branches with smooth, reddish, peeling bark, it is

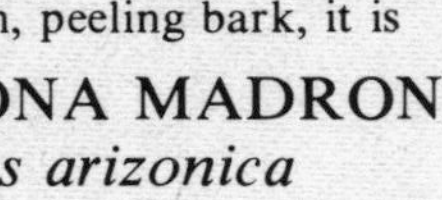

ARIZONA MADRONE
Arbutus arizonica

If stalks are shorter, go to   page 46

If the leaves flutter in a gentle breeze because their stems are flattened where they join the leaves like this:

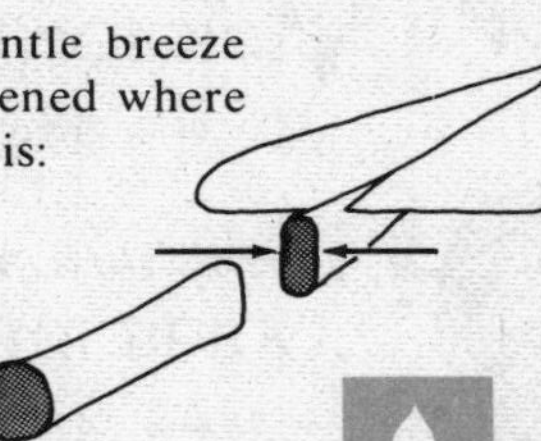

go to next page

If the stem is not flattened that way, go to   page 44

If the leaf is almost round, it is

QUAKING ASPEN
Populus tremuloides

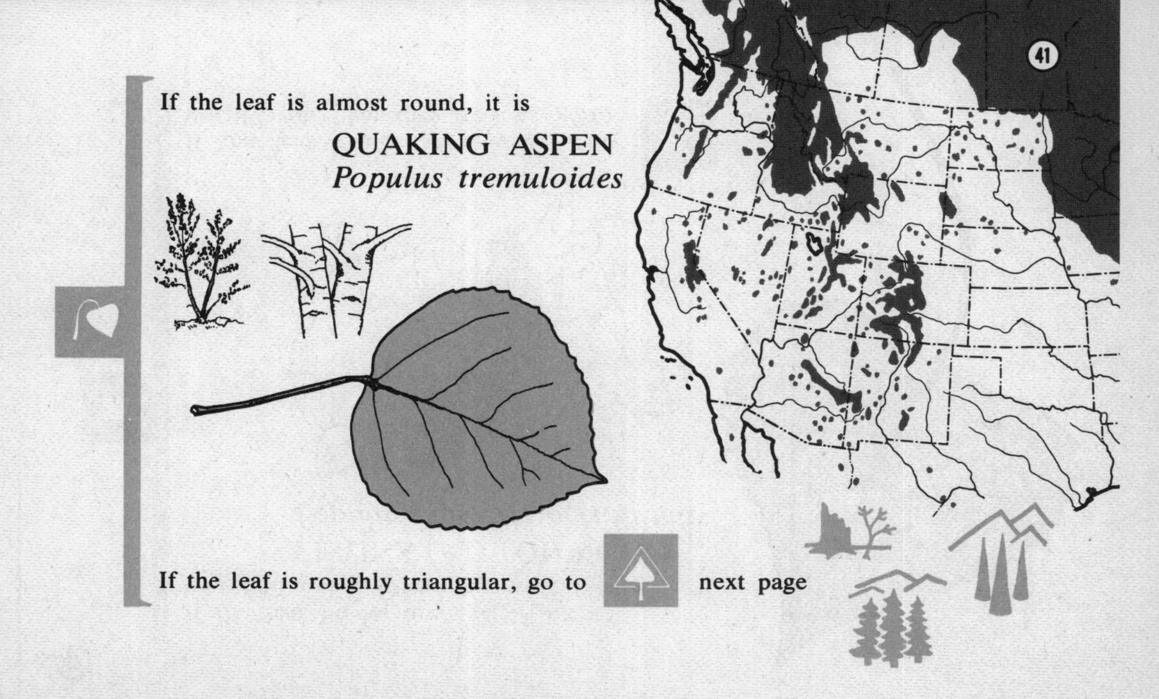

If the leaf is roughly triangular, go to next page

42

If the leaf blades are over 3 inches long, and usually longer than wide, it is

PLAINS COTTONWOOD

Populus deltoides occidentalis

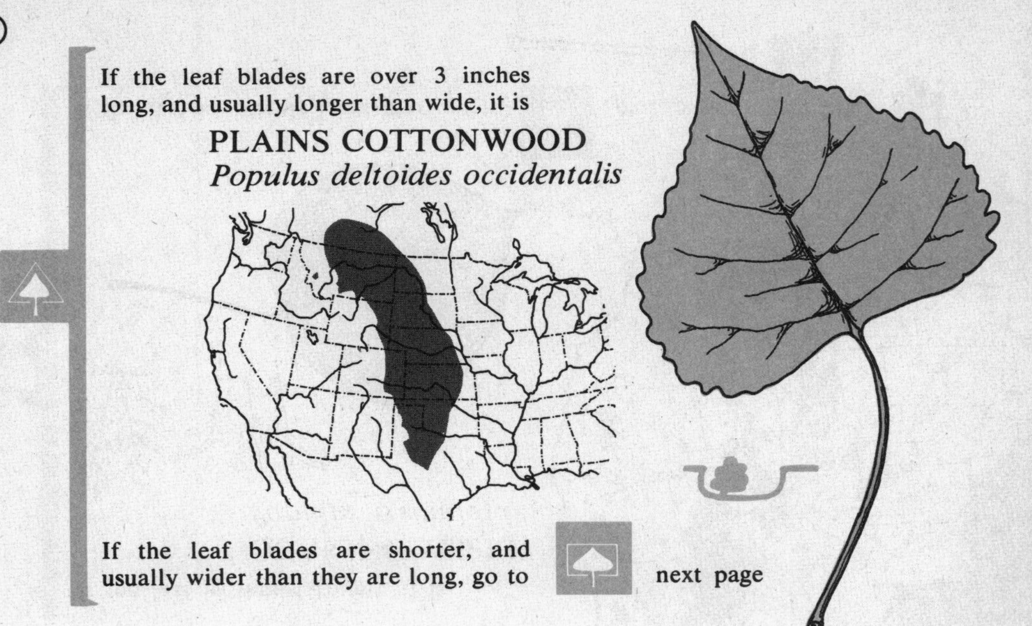

If the leaf blades are shorter, and usually wider than they are long, go to next page

(43)

If you can find seed capsules on stalks longer than half an inch; or if buds on the twigs are slightly hairy, it is

RIO GRANDE COTTONWOOD

Populus fremonti var. *wislizenii*

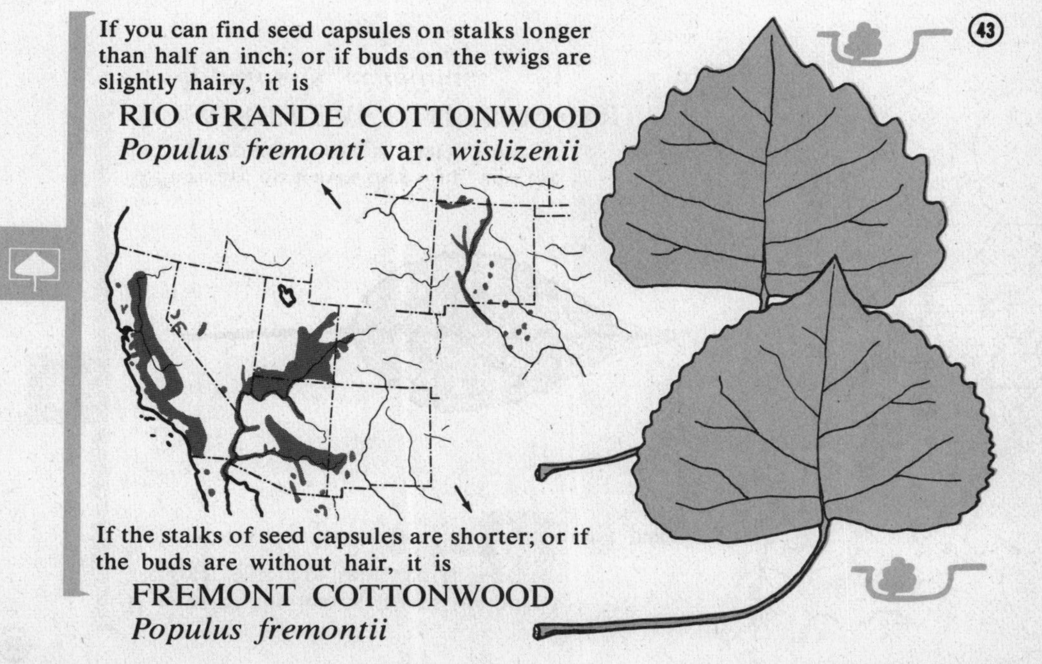

If the stalks of seed capsules are shorter; or if the buds are without hair, it is

FREMONT COTTONWOOD

Populus fremontii

44

If some of the leaves (stems included) are over 4 inches long, go to next page

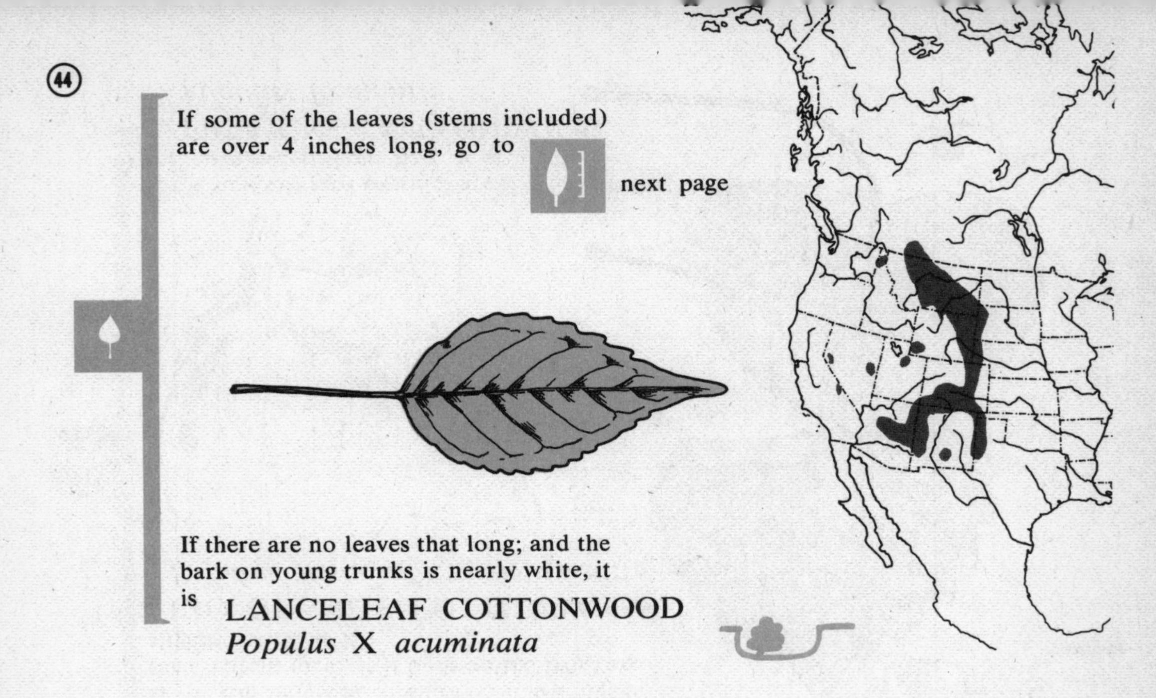

If there are no leaves that long; and the bark on young trunks is nearly white, it is

LANCELEAF COTTONWOOD
Populus X *acuminata*

If the leaf stems are over 2 inches long, it is **BALSAM POPLAR** *Populus balsamifera*

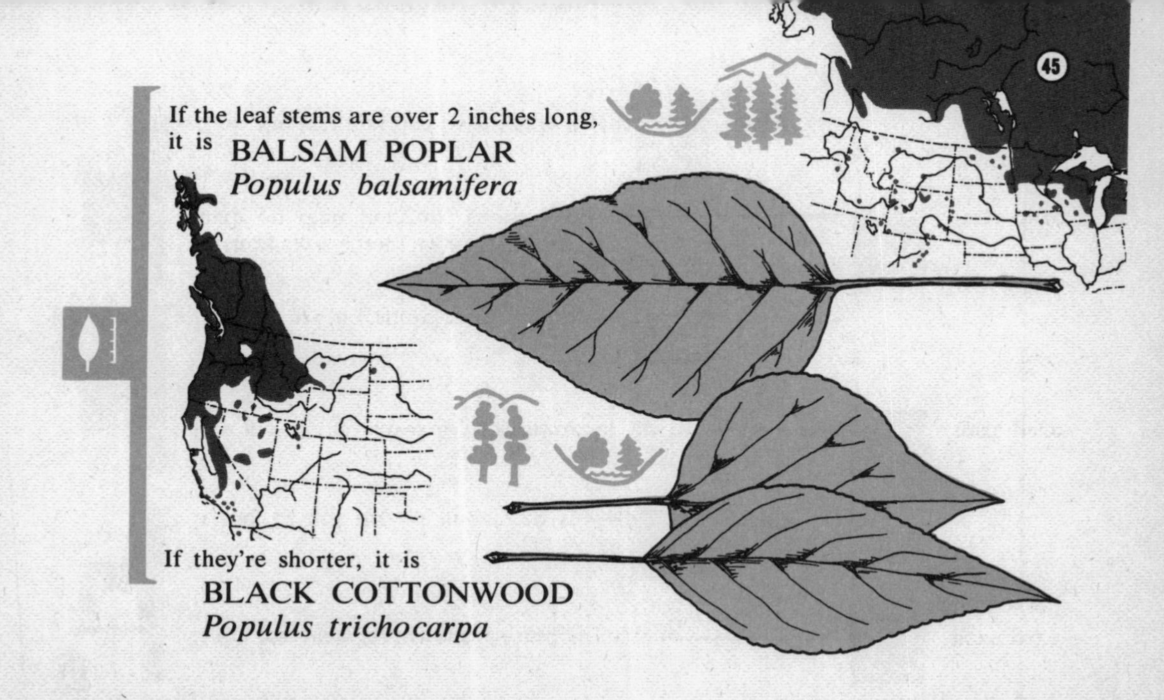

If they're shorter, it is **BLACK COTTONWOOD** *Populus trichocarpa*

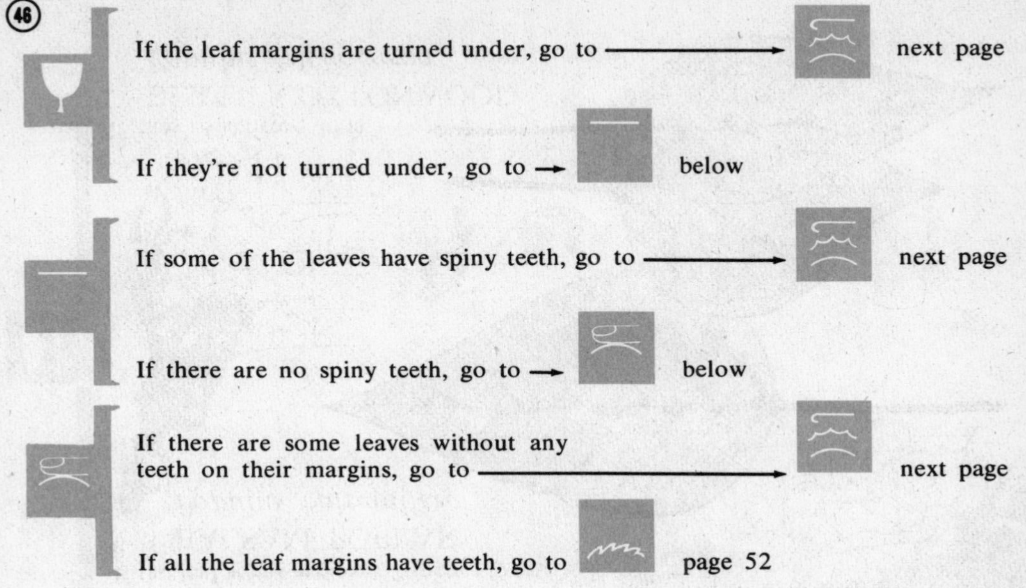

If the leaf margins are turned under, go to → next page

If they're not turned under, go to → below

If some of the leaves have spiny teeth, go to → next page

If there are no spiny teeth, go to → below

If there are some leaves without any teeth on their margins, go to → next page

If all the leaf margins have teeth, go to page 52

If the leaf is roughly triangular, with conspicuous, netted veins on the underside, it is NETLEAF HACKBERRY *Celtis reticulata*

If not, go to ☐ below

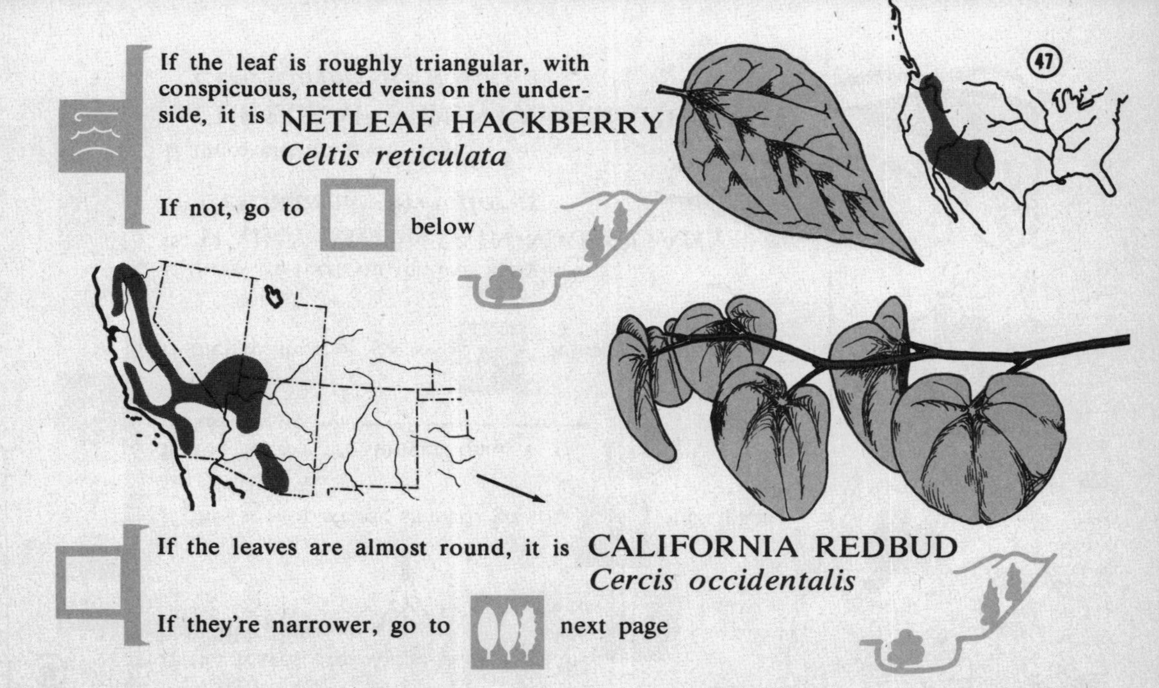

If the leaves are almost round, it is CALIFORNIA REDBUD *Cercis occidentalis*

If they're narrower, go to ☐ next page

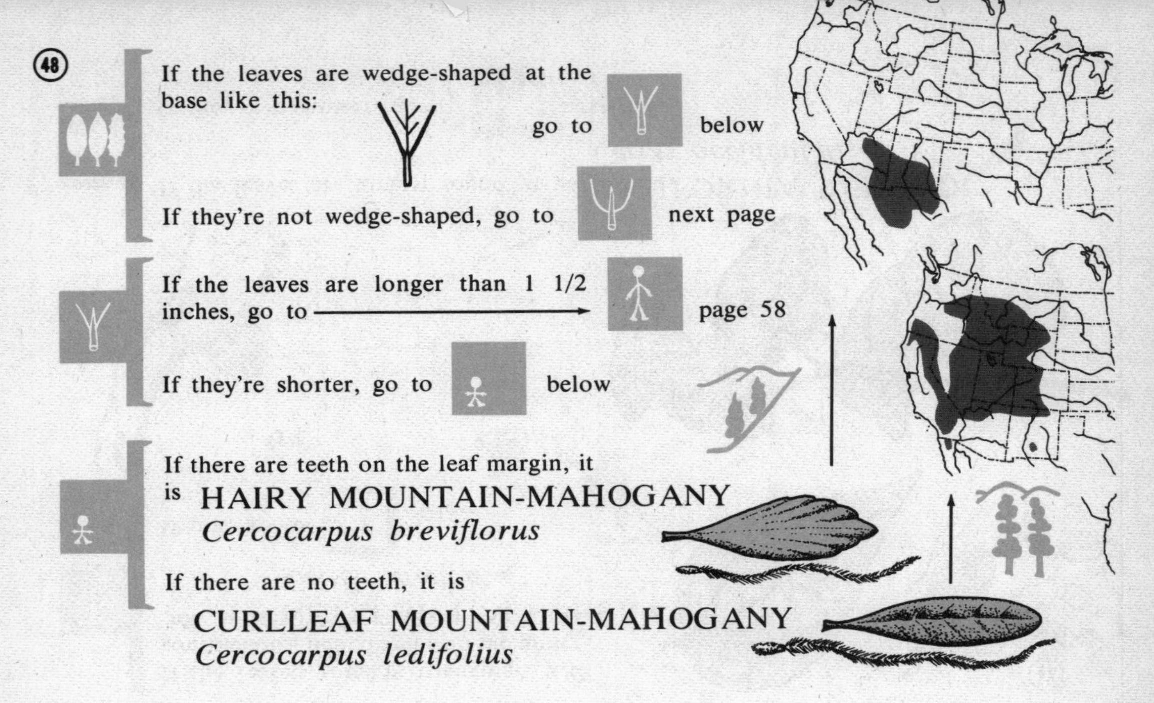

If the leaves are wedge-shaped at the base like this: go to below

If they're not wedge-shaped, go to next page

If the leaves are longer than 1 1/2 inches, go to page 58

If they're shorter, go to below

If there are teeth on the leaf margin, it is HAIRY MOUNTAIN-MAHOGANY
Cercocarpus breviflorus

If there are no teeth, it is
CURLLEAF MOUNTAIN-MAHOGANY
Cercocarpus ledifolius

If the leaves are shiny yellow-green on both sides, it is **EMORY OAK** *Quercus emoryi*

(Trunk bark is dark brown or black)

If they're not shiny on both sides, go to below

If the margins of some or all of the leaves are toothed, go to page 51

If the leaf margins are without teeth (except for a rare leaf with one or two teeth), go to next page

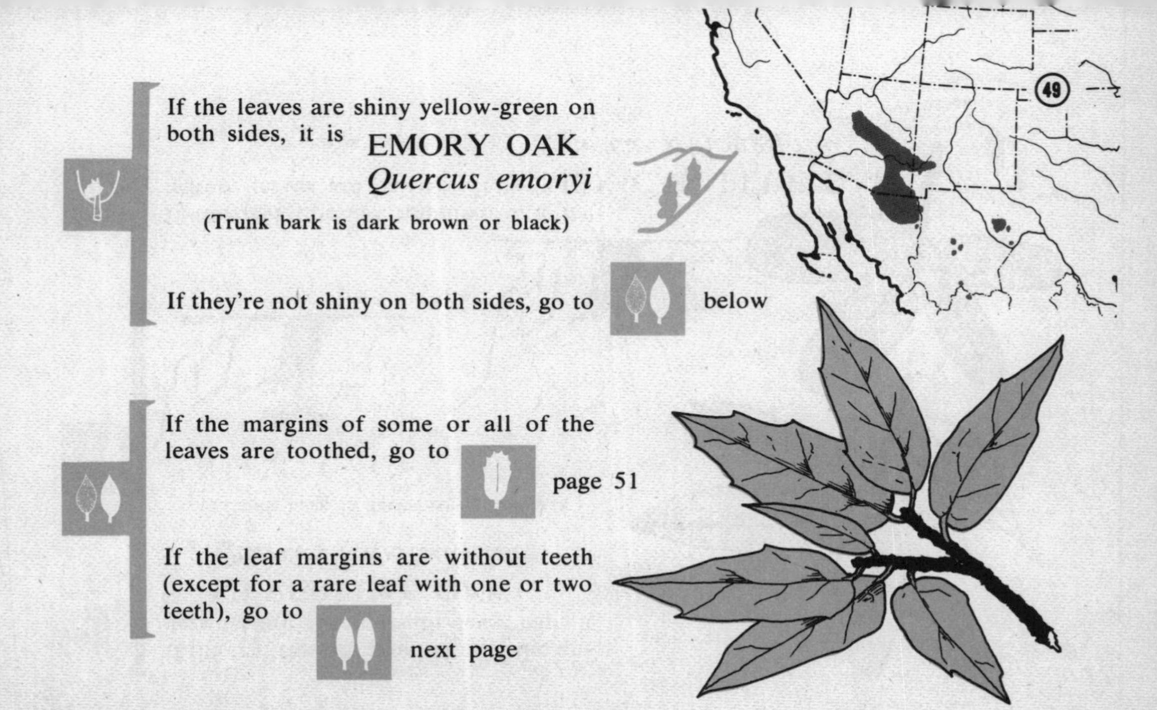

If the leaf tips are pointed, and the undersides are covered with dense hair, it is **SILVERLEAF OAK**
Quercus hypoleucoides

(Trunk bark is dark brown or black.)

If the leaf tips are rounded, and the mature leaves are hairless, it is **MEXICAN BLUE OAK**
Quercus oblongifolia

(Trunk is greyish.)

51

If foliage has yellow or whitish wooly hair you can rub off; or if some leaves are prickly, holly-like, it is

CANYON LIVE OAK
Quercus chrysolepis

If leaves are dull blue-green on top, it is

ARIZONA WHITE OAK
Quercus arizonica

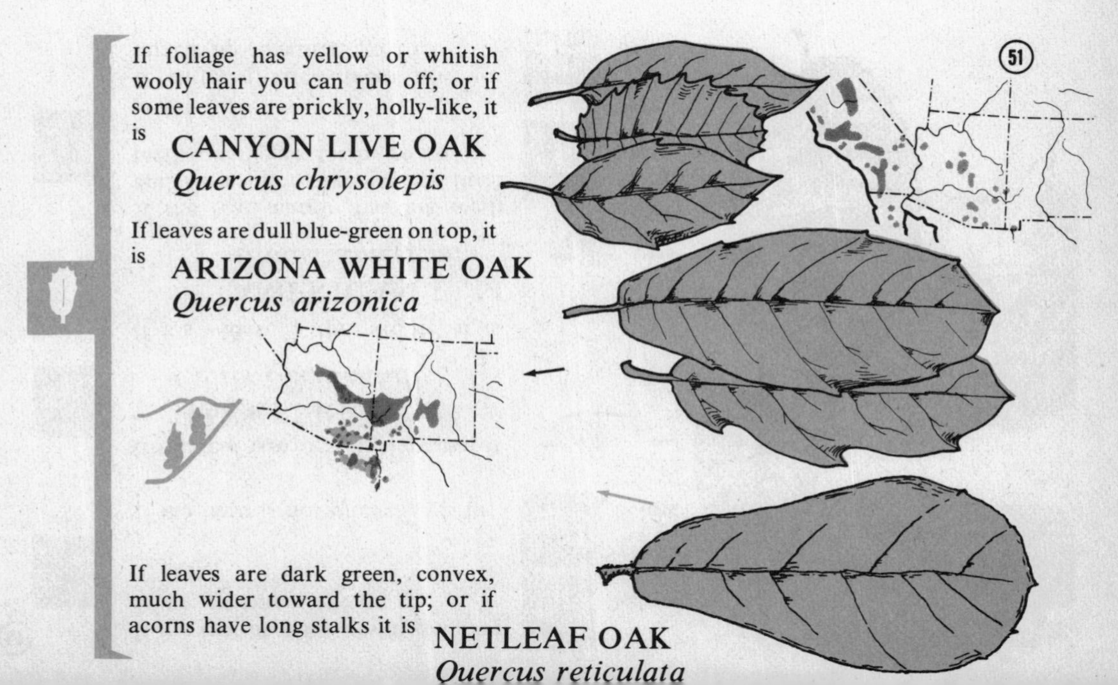

If leaves are dark green, convex, much wider toward the tip; or if acorns have long stalks it is

NETLEAF OAK
Quercus reticulata

If the leaf base is uneven, bulging down on one side, go to below

If the base is not uneven, go to below

If the leaf is widest at the base, it is **HACKBERRY**
Celtis occidentalis

If it's widest in the middle, it is **AMERICAN ELM**
Ulmus americana

If the leaf margin has big teeth and little ones together, or little teeth on bigger teeth, go to next page

If different-sized teeth are not mixed up together, go to page 56

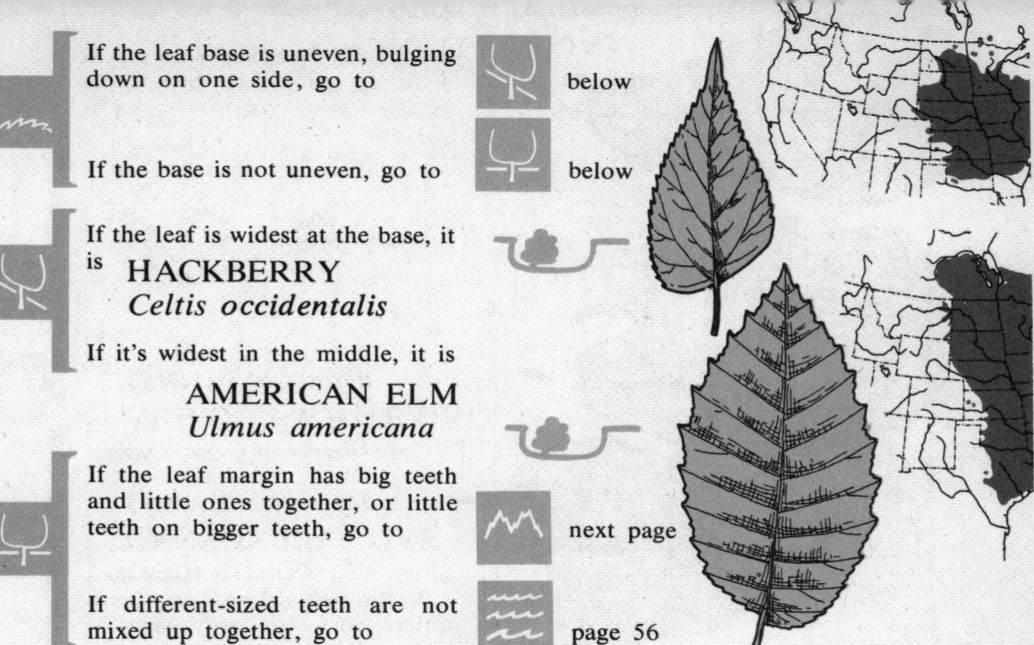

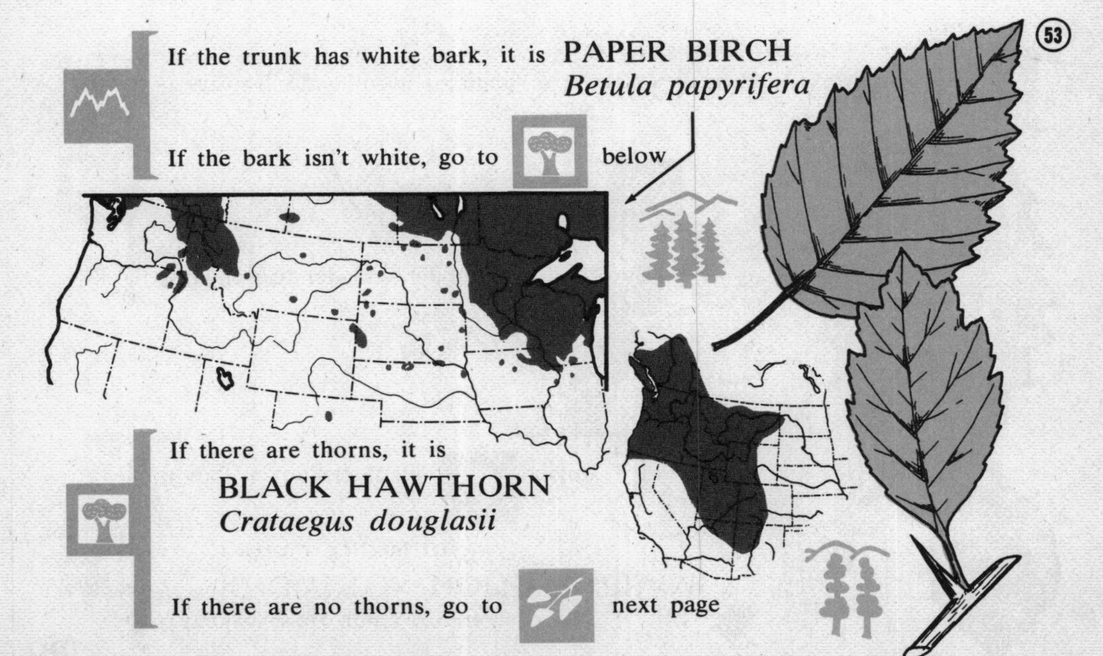

If the trunk has white bark, it is PAPER BIRCH *Betula papyrifera*

If the bark isn't white, go to below

If there are thorns, it is

BLACK HAWTHORN
Crataegus douglasii

If there are no thorns, go to next page

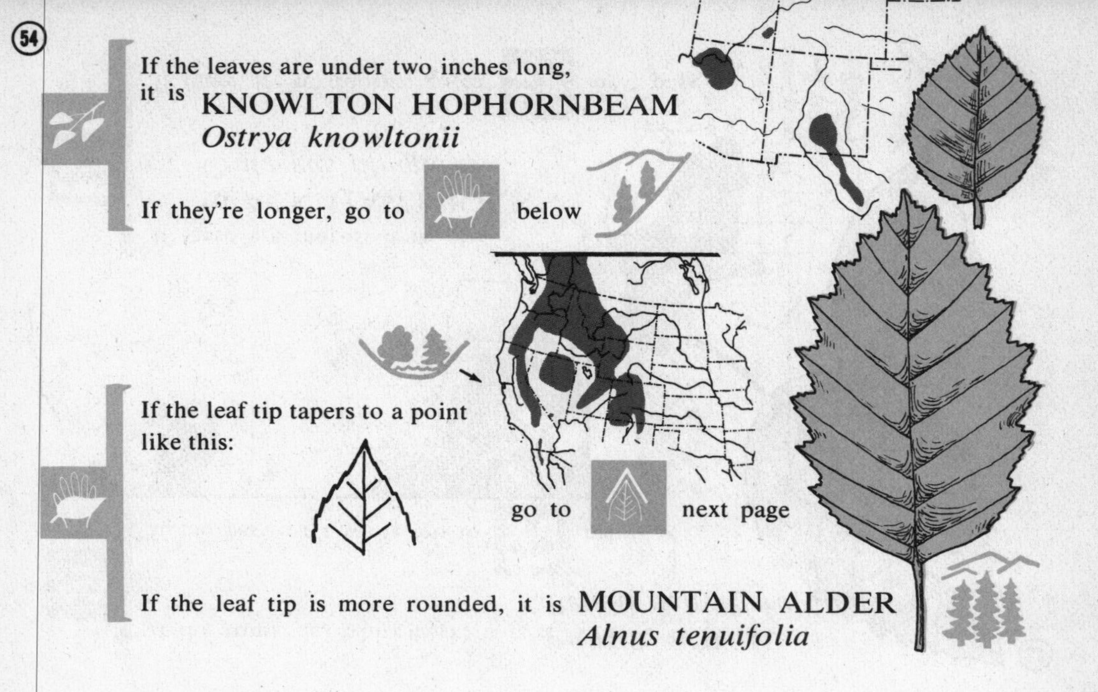

If the leaves are under two inches long, it is **KNOWLTON HOPHORNBEAM** *Ostrya knowltonii*

If they're longer, go to below

If the leaf tip tapers to a point like this:

go to next page

If the leaf tip is more rounded, it is **MOUNTAIN ALDER** *Alnus tenuifolia*

(55)

If you're in New Mexico or Arizona it is **ARIZONA ALDER**
Alnus oblongifolia

If you're in the Black Hills of South Dakota, it is **HOPHORNBEAM IRONWOOD**
Ostrya virginiana

If the main veins on the underside of the leaf go straight to the edge of the leaf without breaking up into smaller veins or turning away from the edge, go to → below

If the veins are not like that, go to → below

If the leaves are under 2 inches long, it is WATER BIRCH →
Betula occidentalis

If they're longer, it is WHITE ALDER →
Alnus rhombifolia

If the end of the leaf is rounded like this: go to → next page

If it tapers to a point, go to → page 58

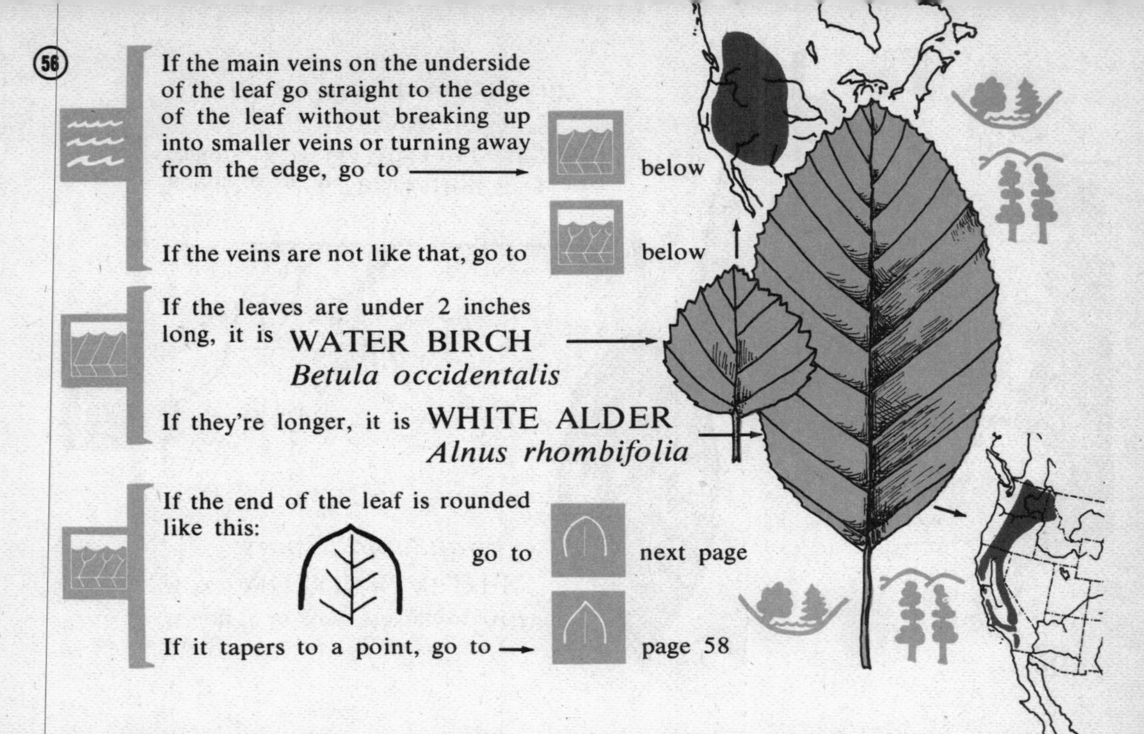

If the leaf base is wedge-shaped, it is

BITTER CHERRY
Prunus emarginata

If it's rounded, go to below

If the leaf margins have fine teeth; or if any of the leaves are longer than 3 inches, it is

CASCARA BUCKTHORN
Rhamnus purshiana

If the margins have coarse teeth; and none of the leaves are longer than 3 inches, it is

SASKATOON SERVICEBERRY
Amelanchier alnifolia

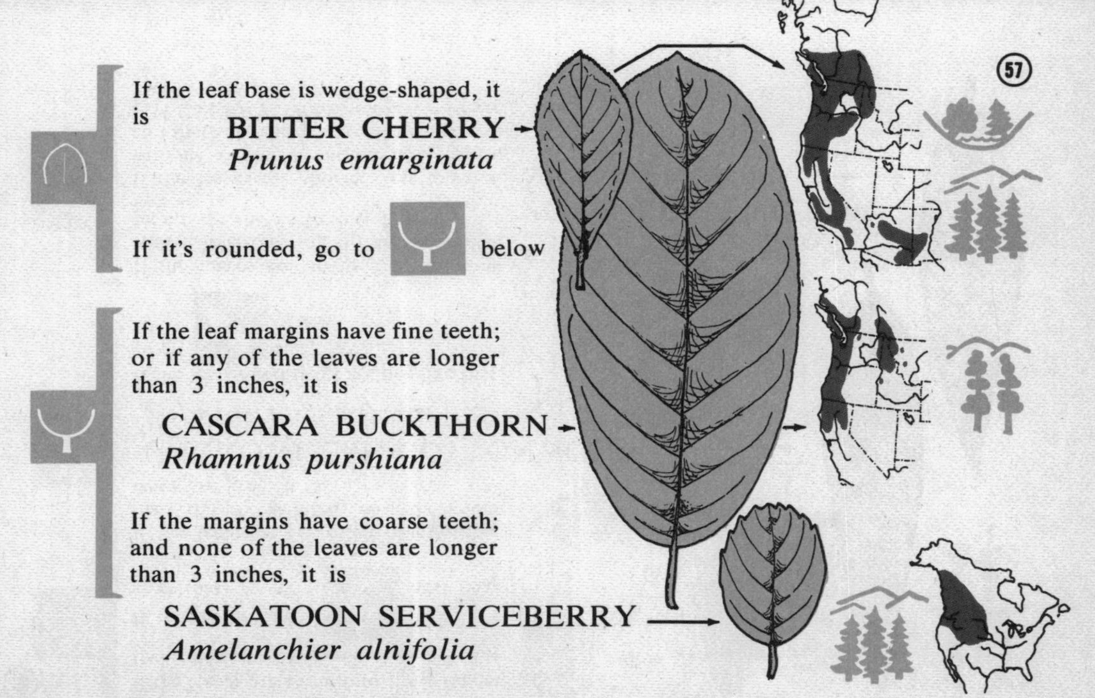

If the leaves are about four times longer than wide, go to ⟶ below

If they're broader than that, go to next page

If the leaf tips are often blunt rather than sharply pointed; and the older twigs are grey, it is

NARROWLEAF COTTONWOOD
Populus angustifolia

If the leaves and twigs are not like that, go to  below

If the leaves are up to 5 inches long with a long-tapering tip and a whitish bloom on the underside, it is

PEACHLEAF WILLOW
Salix amygdaloides

If the leaves are shorter, less tapered, without a whitish bloom underneath; and there are short, spur-like twigs, it is PIN CHERRY. *(Illustration is on page 59.)*

If the leaf is soft; and the veinlets on the underside form a dense network; and the tree has thorn-like twigs and shaggy bark, it is

AMERICAN PLUM
Prunus americana

If the leaves, twigs, and bark are not like that, go to [tree symbol] below

If the the leaves are under two inches long and widest at the base, it is TEXAS MULBERRY. *(Illustration is on page 39.)*

If the leaves are longer, go to [leaf symbol] below

If leaf shape is oval, and teeth on margin are:

- curved outward, it is CHOKE CHERRY *Prunus virginiana*
- curved inward, in Ariz., or New Mex., it is BLACK CHERRY *Prunus serotina*

If leaf is narrower, it is PIN CHERRY *Prunus pensylvanica*

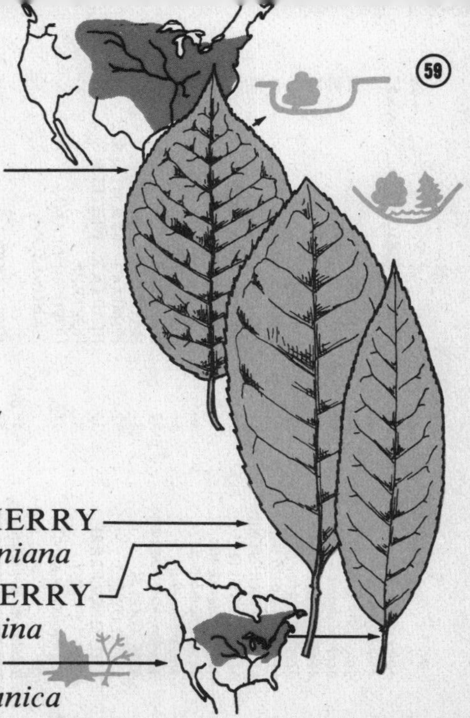

INDEX

PACIFIC COAST TREE FINDER

a pocket manual for identifying Pacific Coast trees

by Tom Watts

To identify a tree:

- Select some typical leaves or needles and turn to page 6.

- Make the first choice, either  or 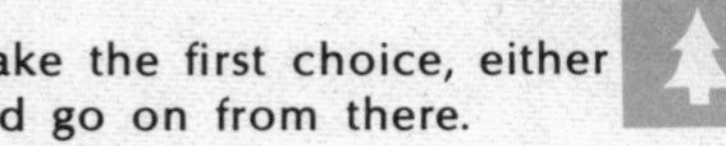 and go on from there.

- After a few more choices you'll come to a drawing and the name of your tree.

Advice: See pages 1 - 5 before you begin.

Note: **This book is for trees that grow naturally in this area.**

It does not identify introduced trees except for a few widely-planted species which have become somewhat naturalized in the area.

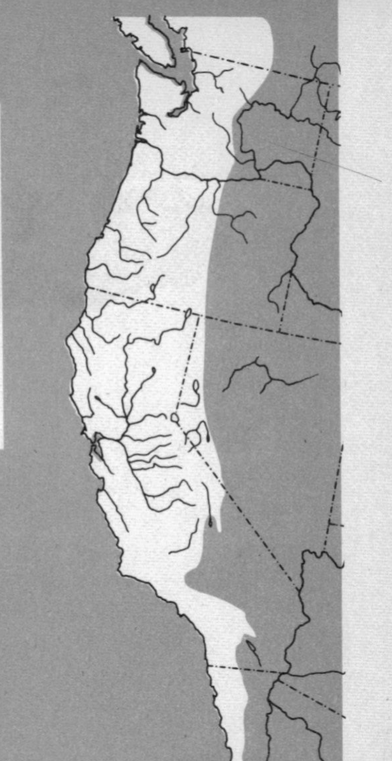

Maps in this book show the natural ranges of trees.

Symbols show the place within its range where you're likely to find each tree growing:

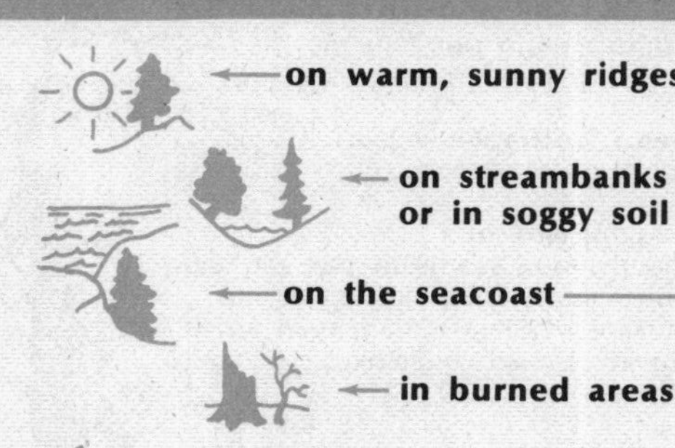

on warm, sunny ridges	These trees grow slowly with roots in dry, rocky soil, where wind blows away the snow and shapes their resinous foliage. Among them you'll find lairs and lizards.
on streambanks or in soggy soil	These trees grow fast, have shiny, pliable foliage, easily broken twigs, soft wood, and birds.
on the seacoast	These are often trees which grow only on windy slopes facing the sea, usually in sandy soil.
in burned areas	Unless fire returns, these trees will eventually be replaced by more shade-tolerant species.
in abandoned farmyards, old settlements	These trees grow so well on the Pacific coast they may seem to be native species, but they or their ancestors were planted here.

other symbols: *(more on pages 2 - 5)*

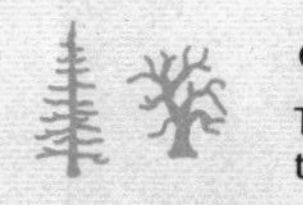

deciduous trees

These are leafless in winter or the dry season.

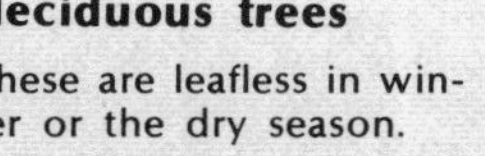

shrubby trees

These are trees that often grow as shrubs and become trees only on sheltered slopes and canyons.

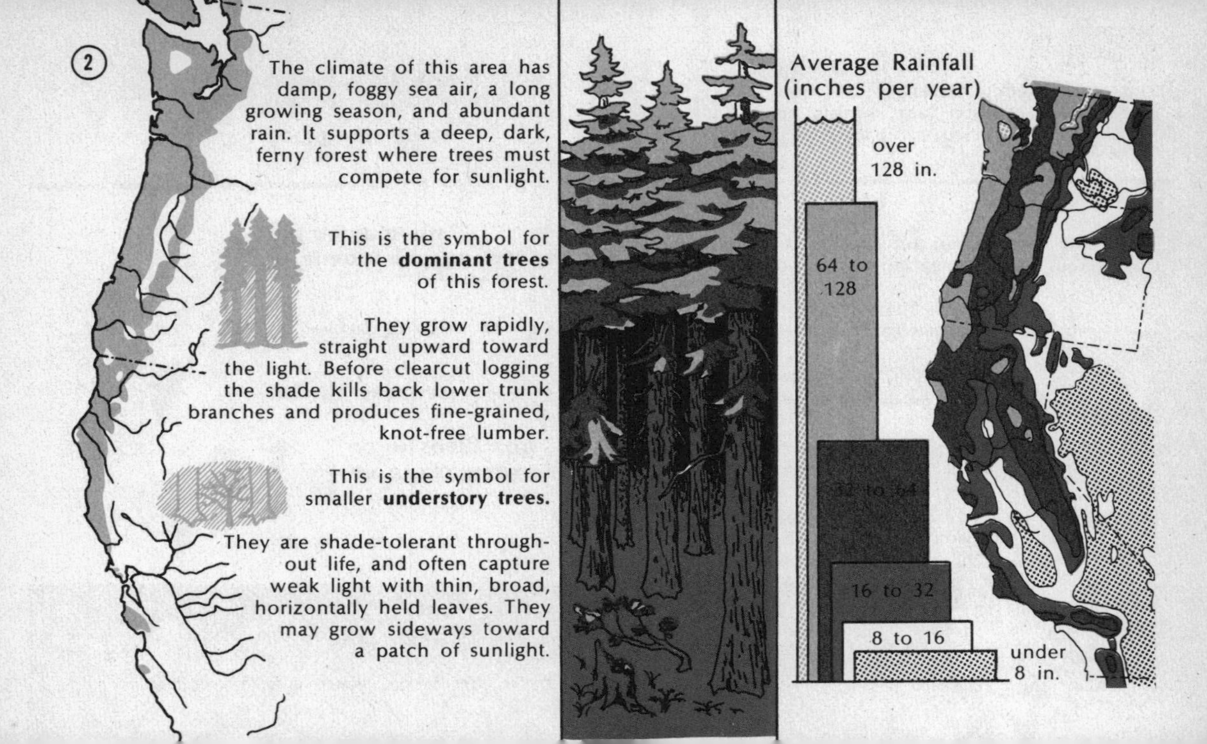

The climate of this area has damp, foggy sea air, a long growing season, and abundant rain. It supports a deep, dark, ferny forest where trees must compete for sunlight.

This is the symbol for the **dominant trees** of this forest.

They grow rapidly, straight upward toward the light. Before clearcut logging the shade kills back lower trunk branches and produces fine-grained, knot-free lumber.

This is the symbol for smaller **understory trees.**

They are shade-tolerant throughout life, and often capture weak light with thin, broad, horizontally held leaves. They may grow sideways toward a patch of sunlight.

The Pacific coast climate is dryer toward the south and in the low-altitude inland valleys:

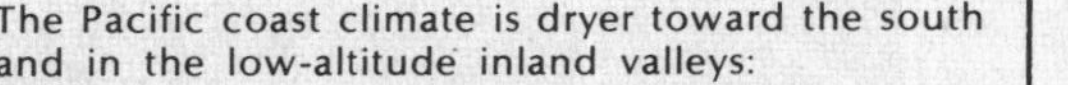

This is the symbol for trees of the **mixed-evergreen forest** of the coast ranges. No big redwoods or hemlocks here. Small Douglas-firs dominate. Leaves here are often thick, leathery, and evergreen. This slows evaporation of moisture during dry summers and takes advantage of mild, wet winters.

This symbol is for trees of the **California oakwoods** where short, muscular-looking, deep-rooted trees with small, bristly leaves stand far apart, or else cluster along canyons and north-facing slopes. Even the pines here look stunted.

Much of this area is a mosaic of woods, grassland, and chaparral (stiff, dry, evergreen shrubbery) on hot slopes.

Acorns from California oaks were a staple food for Indians. They still support woodpeckers.

Average Growing Season (frost-free days)

③

This map shows why coast-range forests differ from higher-altitude forests of the Sierras and Cascades.
(see next page)

over 300 days
240 to 300
180 to 240
120 to 180
60 to 120
under 60 days

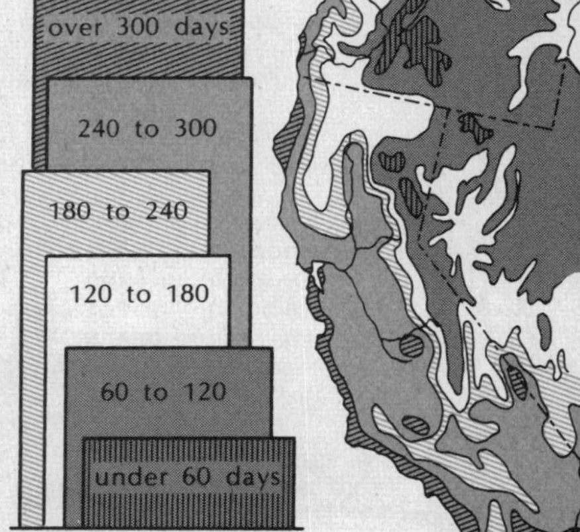

4

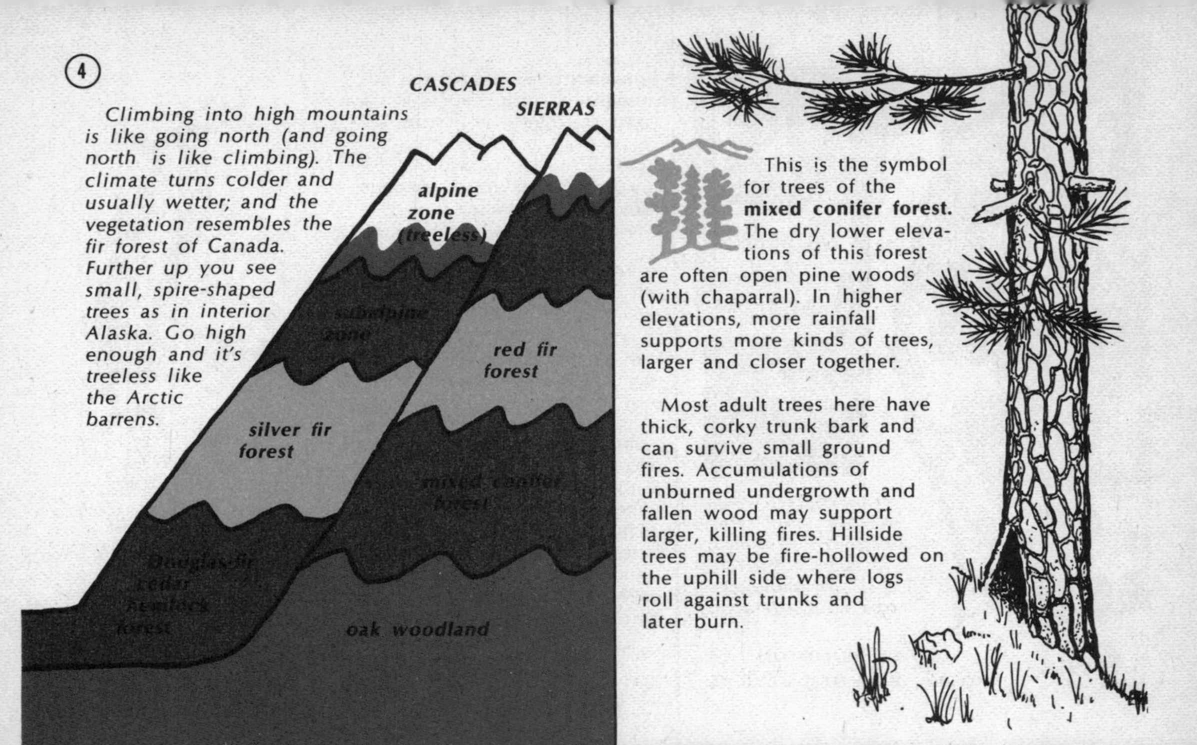

Climbing into high mountains is like going north (and going north is like climbing). The climate turns colder and usually wetter; and the vegetation resembles the fir forest of Canada. Further up you see small, spire-shaped trees as in interior Alaska. Go high enough and it's treeless like the Arctic barrens.

This is the symbol for trees of the **mixed conifer forest.** The dry lower elevations of this forest are often open pine woods (with chaparral). In higher elevations, more rainfall supports more kinds of trees, larger and closer together.

Most adult trees here have thick, corky trunk bark and can survive small ground fires. Accumulations of unburned undergrowth and fallen wood may support larger, killing fires. Hillside trees may be fire-hollowed on the uphill side where logs roll against trunks and later burn.

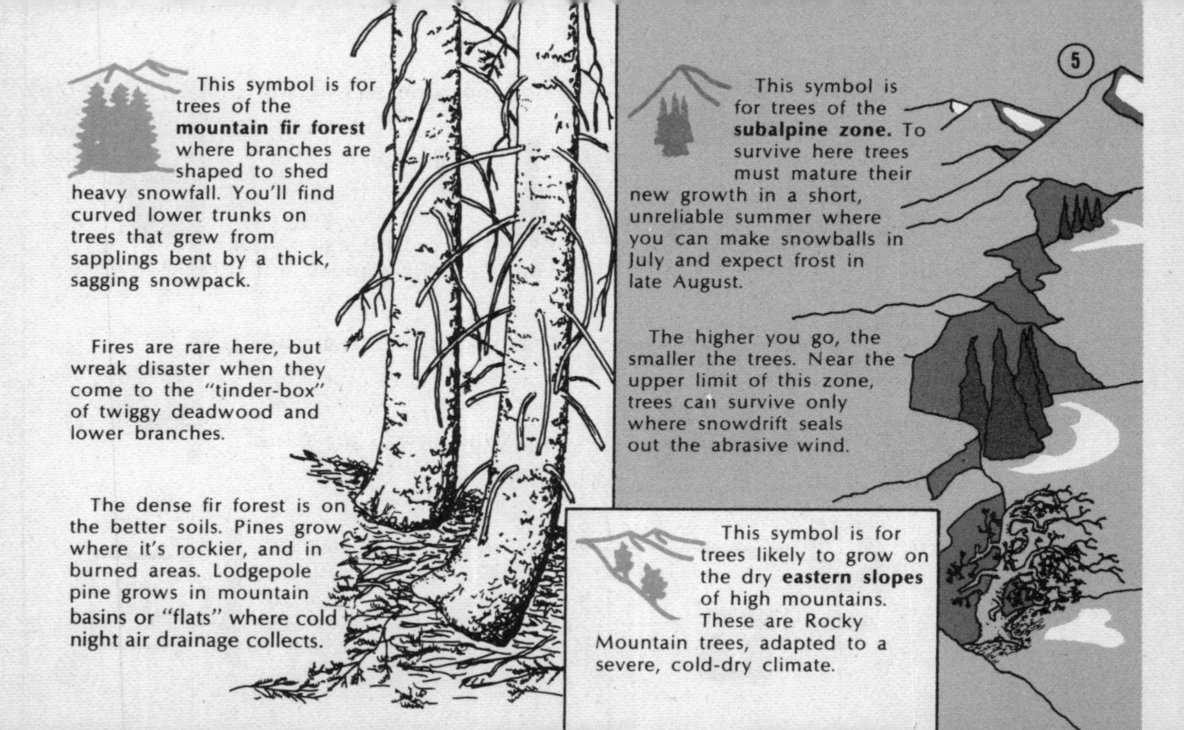

This symbol is for trees of the **mountain fir forest** where branches are shaped to shed heavy snowfall. You'll find curved lower trunks on trees that grew from sapplings bent by a thick, sagging snowpack.

Fires are rare here, but wreak disaster when they come to the "tinder-box" of twiggy deadwood and lower branches.

The dense fir forest is on the better soils. Pines grow where it's rockier, and in burned areas. Lodgepole pine grows in mountain basins or "flats" where cold night air drainage collects.

This symbol is for trees of the **subalpine zone.** To survive here trees must mature their new growth in a short, unreliable summer where you can make snowballs in July and expect frost in late August.

The higher you go, the smaller the trees. Near the upper limit of this zone, trees can survive only where snowdrift seals out the abrasive wind.

This symbol is for trees likely to grow on the dry **eastern slopes** of high mountains. These are Rocky Mountain trees, adapted to a severe, cold-dry climate.

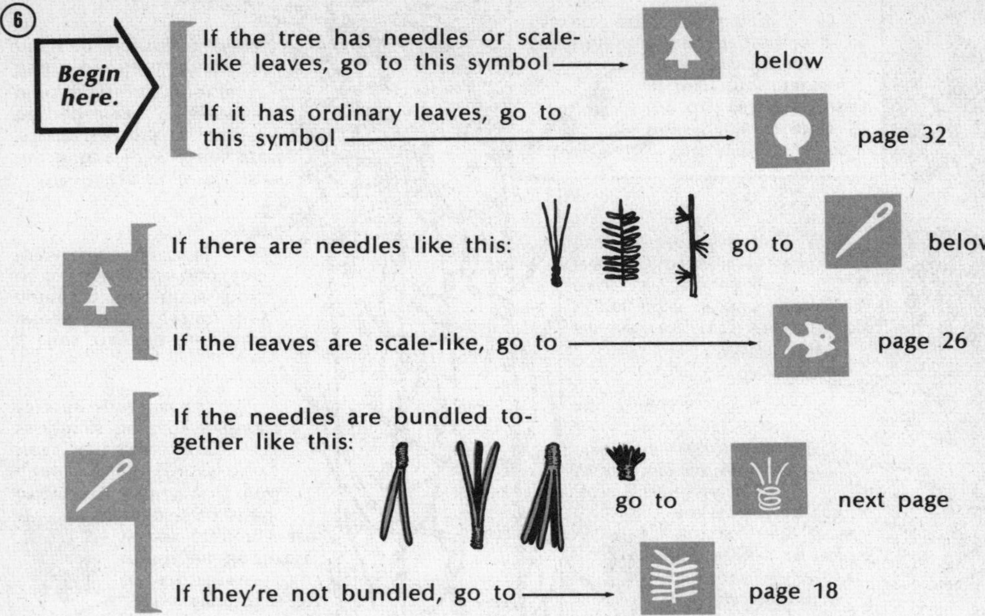

Begin here.

If the tree has needles or scale-like leaves, go to this symbol → below

If it has ordinary leaves, go to this symbol → page 32

If there are needles like this: go to below

If the leaves are scale-like, go to → page 26

If the needles are bundled together like this: go to next page

If they're not bundled, go to → page 18

(7)

If the bundles have fewer than six needles, it's a **PINE.** Go to [icon] next page

If they have more than six, it's a **LARCH.** Go to [icon] below

If the needles are three-sided, it is

WESTERN LARCH
Larix occidentalis

If they're four-sided, it is

SUBALPINE LARCH
Larix lyallii

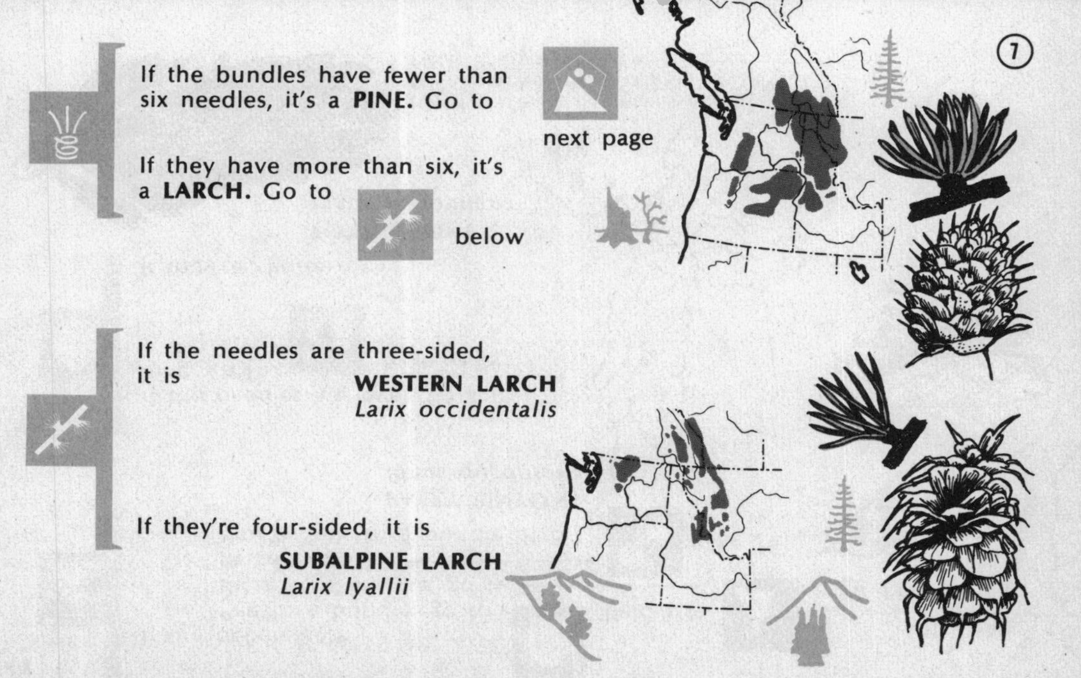

8

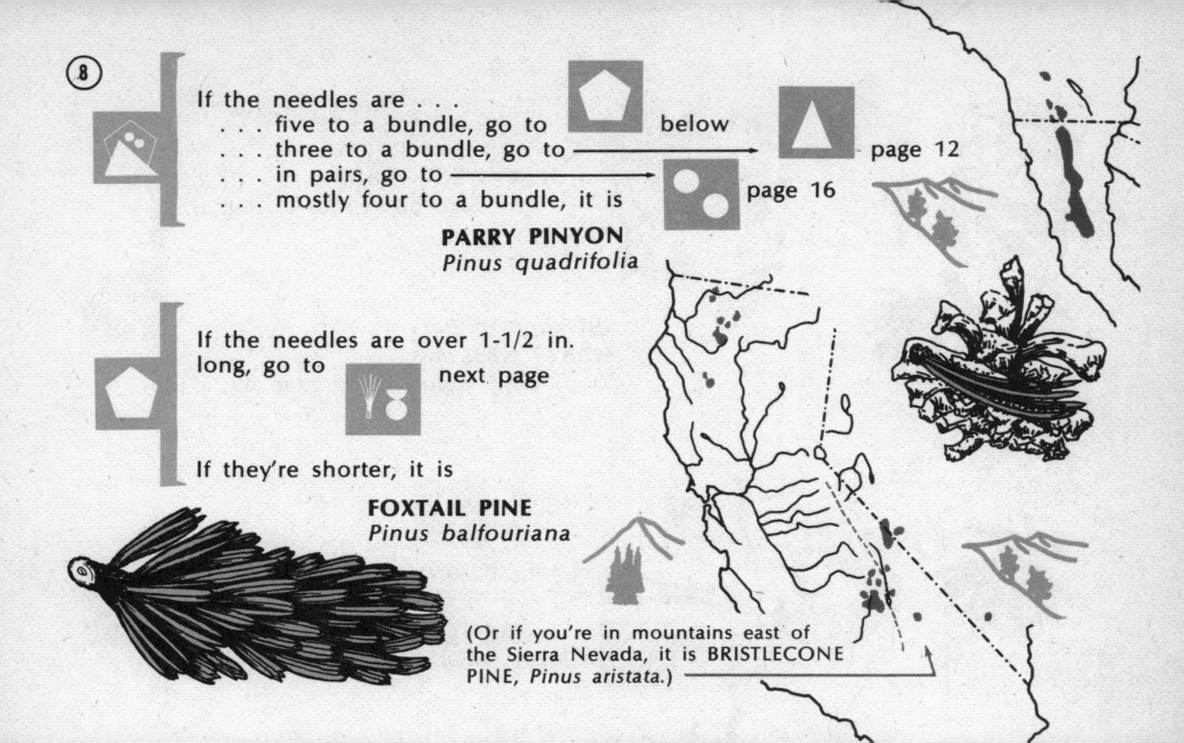

If the needles are . . .
. . . five to a bundle, go to [pentagon symbol] below
. . . three to a bundle, go to → [triangle symbol] page 12
. . . in pairs, go to → [two-circle symbol] page 16
. . . mostly four to a bundle, it is

PARRY PINYON
Pinus quadrifolia

If the needles are over 1-1/2 in. long, go to [symbol] next page

If they're shorter, it is

FOXTAIL PINE
Pinus balfouriana

(Or if you're in mountains east of the Sierra Nevada, it is BRISTLECONE PINE, *Pinus aristata.*)

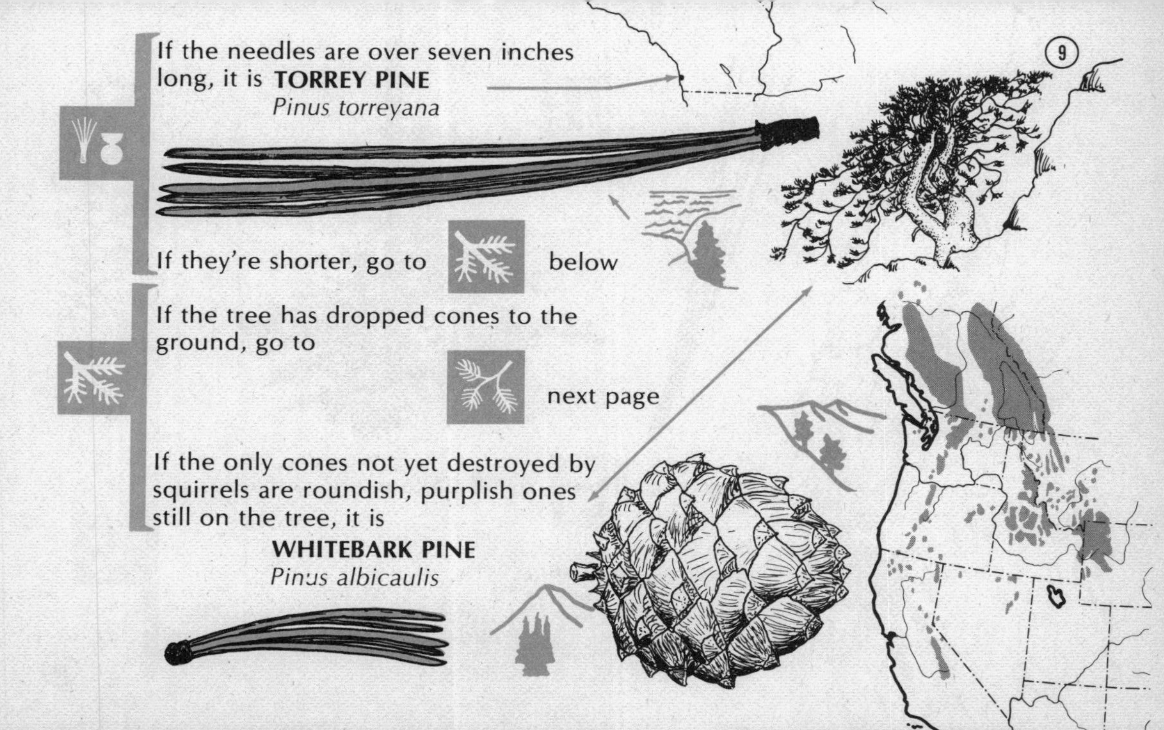

9

If the needles are over seven inches long, it is **TORREY PINE**

Pinus torreyana

If they're shorter, go to [symbol] below

If the tree has dropped cones to the ground, go to [symbol] next page

If the only cones not yet destroyed by squirrels are roundish, purplish ones still on the tree, it is

WHITEBARK PINE

Pinus albicaulis

⑩

If there are cones over one foot long, it is

SUGAR PINE
Pinus lambertiana

If the cones are shorter, go to next page

(11)

If the cones have thin scales, it is **WESTERN WHITE PINE** *Pinus monticola*

If the cone scales are thick at their tips, it is **LIMBER PINE** *Pinus flexilis*

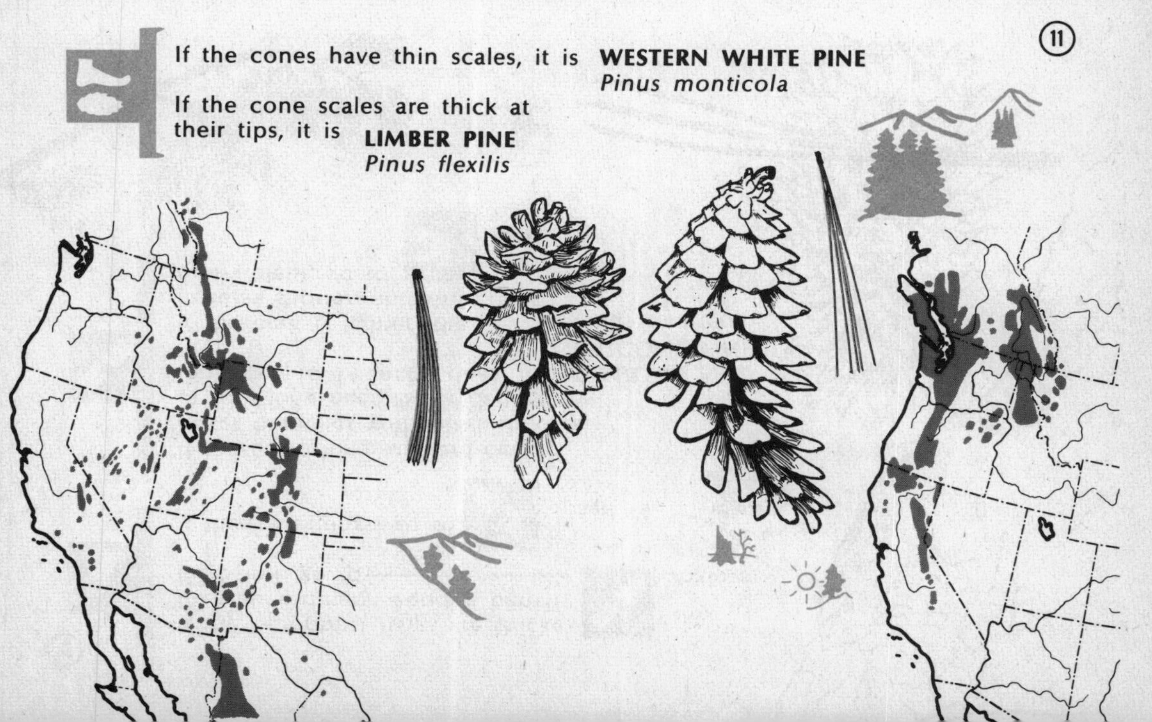

(12)

If the outermost twigs are thicker than an ordinary wooden pencil (5/16 in.), go to → below

If they're thinner, go to page 14

If there are long, upward-curved lower branches with blackish bark, or foot-long needles, or dangerous-looking 9 to 14 inch cones, it is **COULTER PINE** **BIGCONE PINE** *Pinus coulteri*

If the bark is lighter, the needles shorter, and the cones non-violent, go to next page

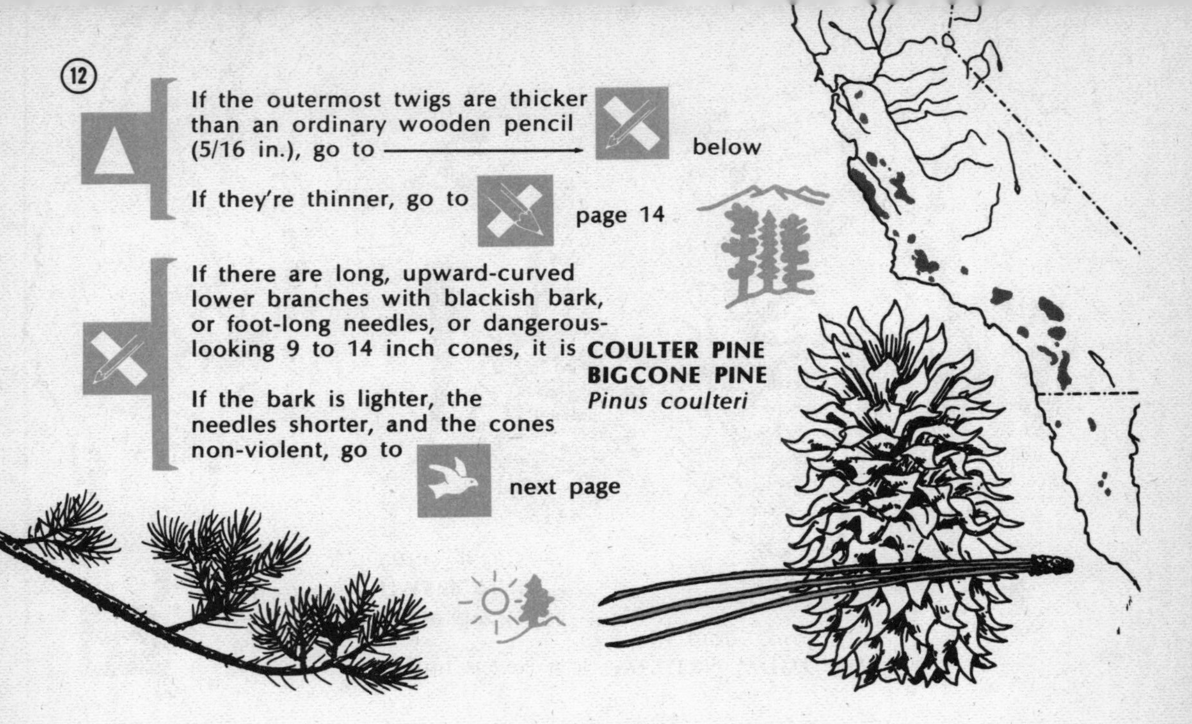

If the cones feel prickly, and if bark flakes broken off the trunk are yellow on the inside, it is

PONDEROSA PINE
Pinus ponderosa

If the cones are not prickly, and if the bark flakes are grey inside, and if the tree trunk smells like pineapple, it is

JEFFREY PINE
Pinus jeffreyi

14

If the needles are 7 to 13 inches long, it is

DIGGER PINE
Pinus sabiniana

If they're shorter, go to next page

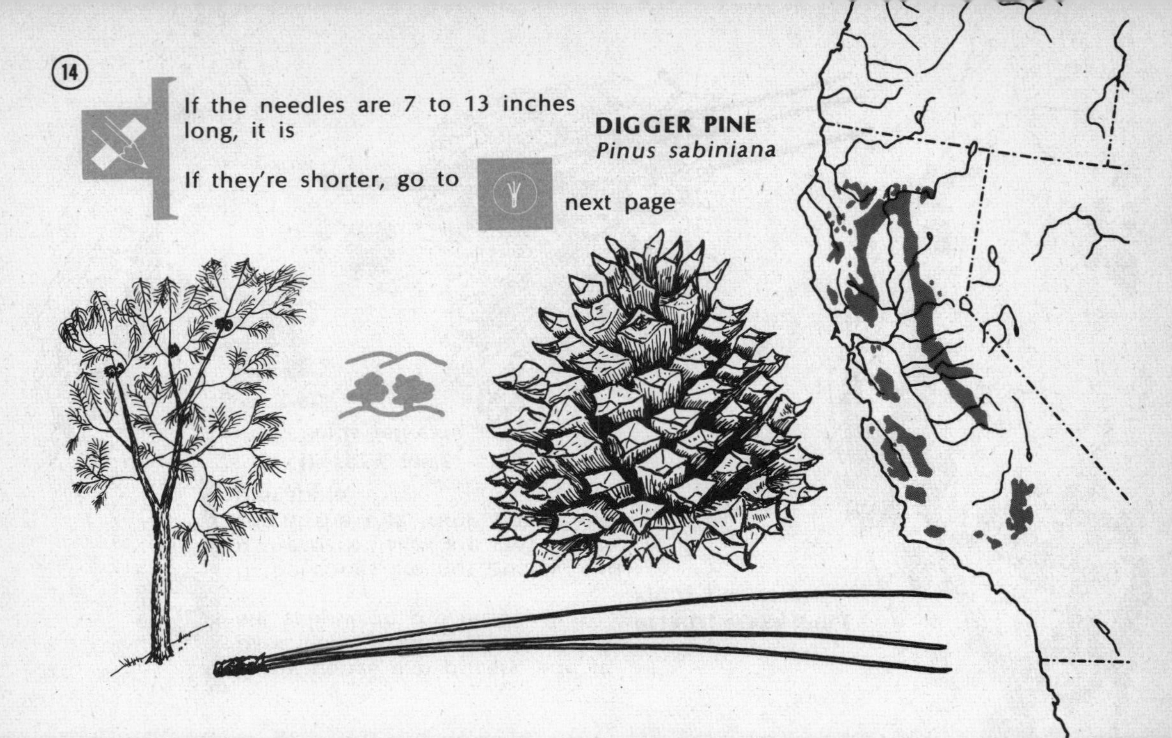

If the foliage is sparse, light green, and the needles are twisted, it is

KNOBCONE PINE
Pinus attenuata

If there is dense, dark green foliage and blackish bark, it is

MONTEREY PINE
Pinus radiata

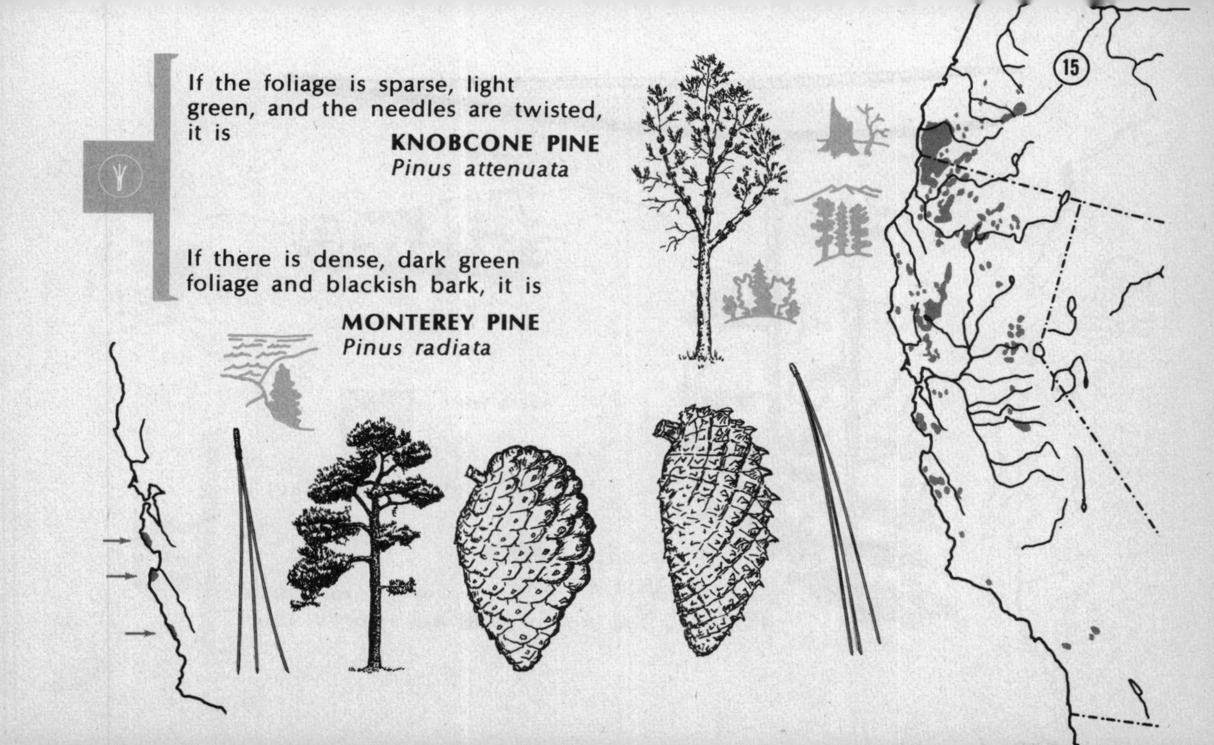

If the needles are three to six inches long, it is

BISHOP PINE
Pinus muricata

If they're shorter, and twisted, go to next page

If the tree is small or shrubby, and it grows near sea level, it is

SHORE PINE
BEACH PINE
Pinus contorta var. *contorta*

If the tree is larger, or if it grows inland above 3,000 ft. elevation, it is **LODGEPOLE PINE**
TAMRAC PINE
Pinus contorta var. *murrayana*

Cones and needles of these two pines look alike.

In the Cascades north of the Columbia River, you'll find Rocky Mountain Lodgepole Pine (*Pinus contorta* var. *latifolia*).

In the acid, hardpan soils near Mendocino, California, you'll find a pygmy variety called Bolander Pine (*Pinus contorta* var. *bolanderi*).

If there are smooth, round scars where old needles have fallen off the twig, it's a **FIR**. Go to [icon] below

Firs also have resin-filled bark blisters and cones that fall apart on the tree instead of dropping to the ground.

If it's not a fir, go to [icon] page 22

If the needles narrow to a stalk where they join the twig, go to [icon] below

If they're wide at the base, go to [icon] page 21

If the needle tips are sharp spines, it is **SANTA LUCIA FIR**
BRISTLECONE FIR
Abies bracteata

If not, go to [icon] next page

If the needles are dark green and shiny on their topsides, go to

next page

If instead of being shiny, there is a whitish band running along the needle top, it is **WHITE FIR**
Abies concolor

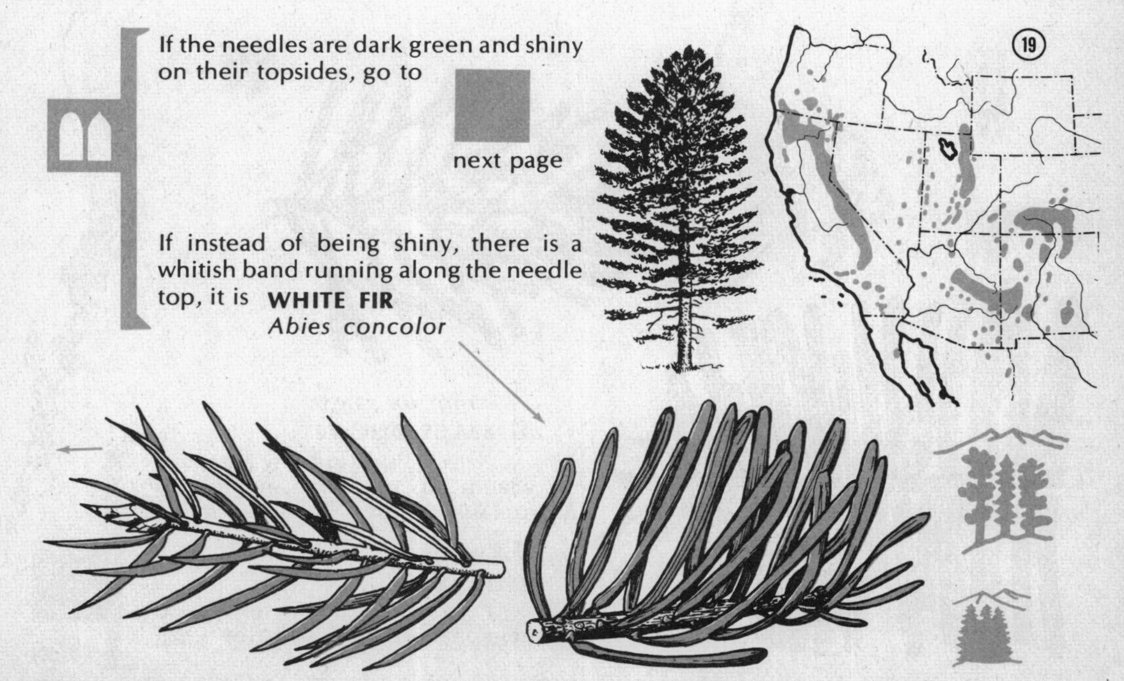

(20)

If the top needles on lower branches point out to the side, it is

GRAND FIR
Abies grandis

If they point upward or toward the end of the twig, and the foliage is silvery underneath, it is

PACIFIC SILVER FIR
Abies amabilis

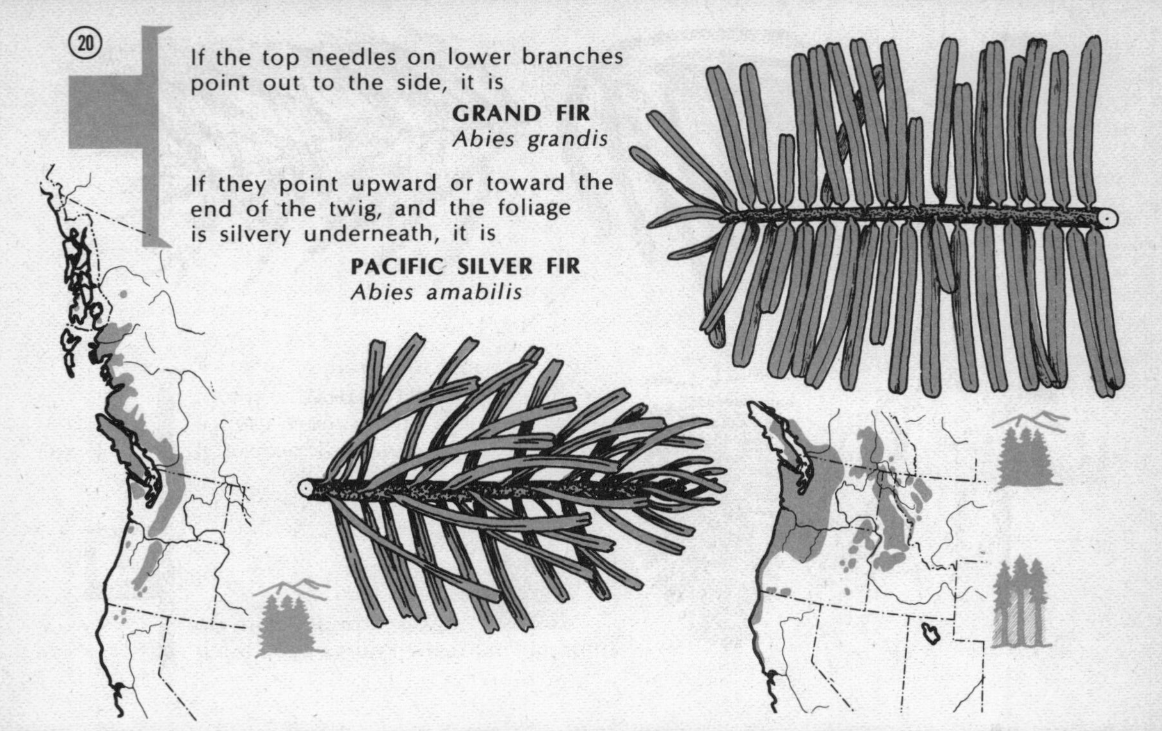

If needles from the lower branches have convex or rounded topsides, and you can twirl them easily between your fingers, it is

CALIFORNIA RED FIR
Abies magnifica

If they're flat and hard to twirl, go to [symbol] below

If the ends of the branchlets have rusty-red bark; or if there are cones over four inches long, it is

NOBLE FIR
Abies procera

If the twig bark is grey, and the cones are shorter, it is

SUBALPINE FIR
Abies lasiocarpa

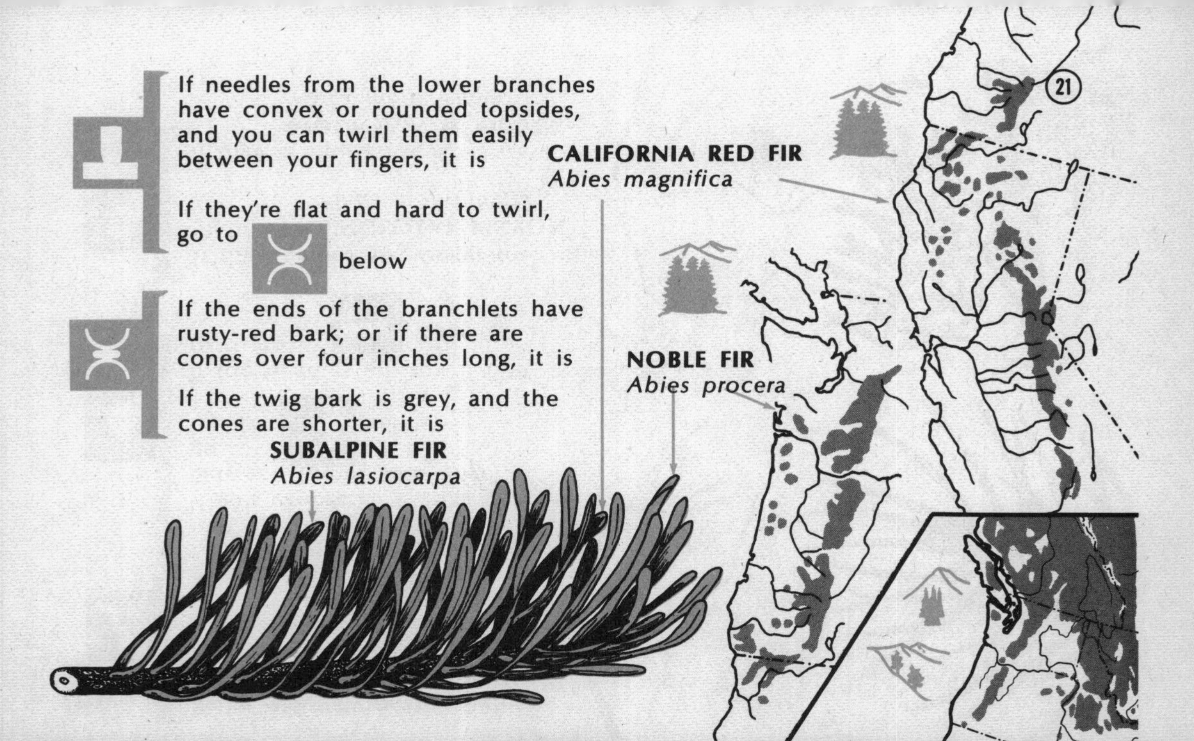

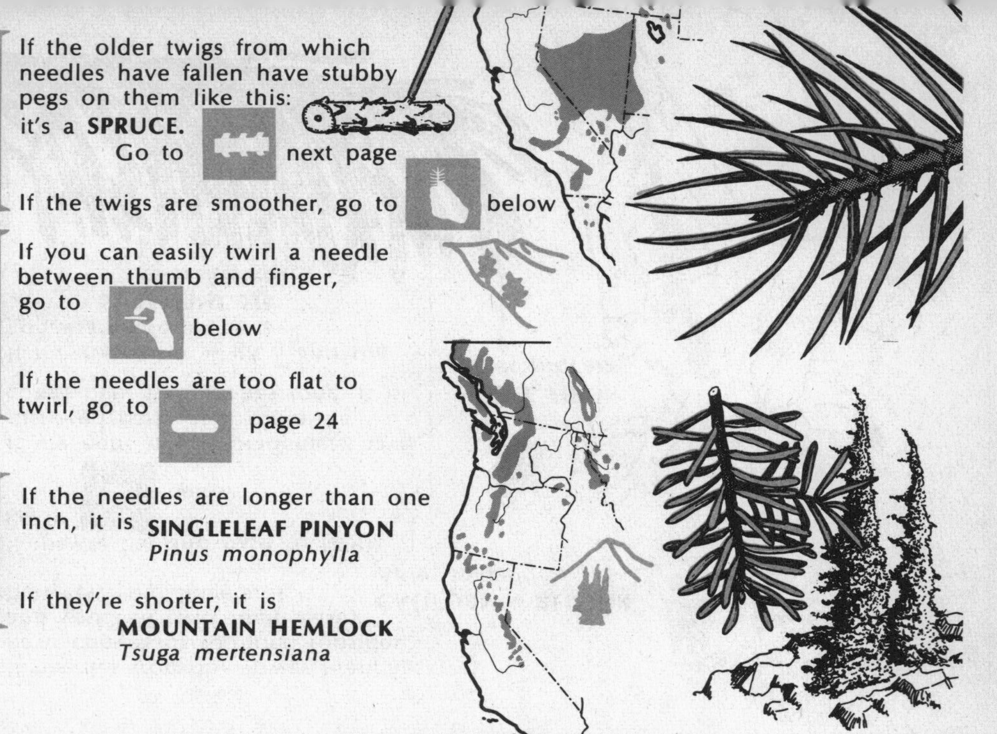

If the older twigs from which needles have fallen have stubby pegs on them like this: it's a **SPRUCE.** Go to next page

If the twigs are smoother, go to below

If you can easily twirl a needle between thumb and finger, go to below

If the needles are too flat to twirl, go to page 24

If the needles are longer than one inch, it is **SINGLELEAF PINYON** *Pinus monophylla*

If they're shorter, it is **MOUNTAIN HEMLOCK** *Tsuga mertensiana*

(23)

If there are many vertically hanging branchlets (up to four feet long) it is **BREWER SPRUCE** **WEEPING SPRUCE** *Picea breweriana*

If the branches don't hang vertically, go to [tree symbol] below

If the needles are four-sided, not flattened, and the same color on all sides, it is **ENGELMANN SPRUCE** *Picea engelmannii*

If the needles are somewhat flattened, and lighter on their topsides, it is **SITKA SPRUCE** *Picea sitchensis*

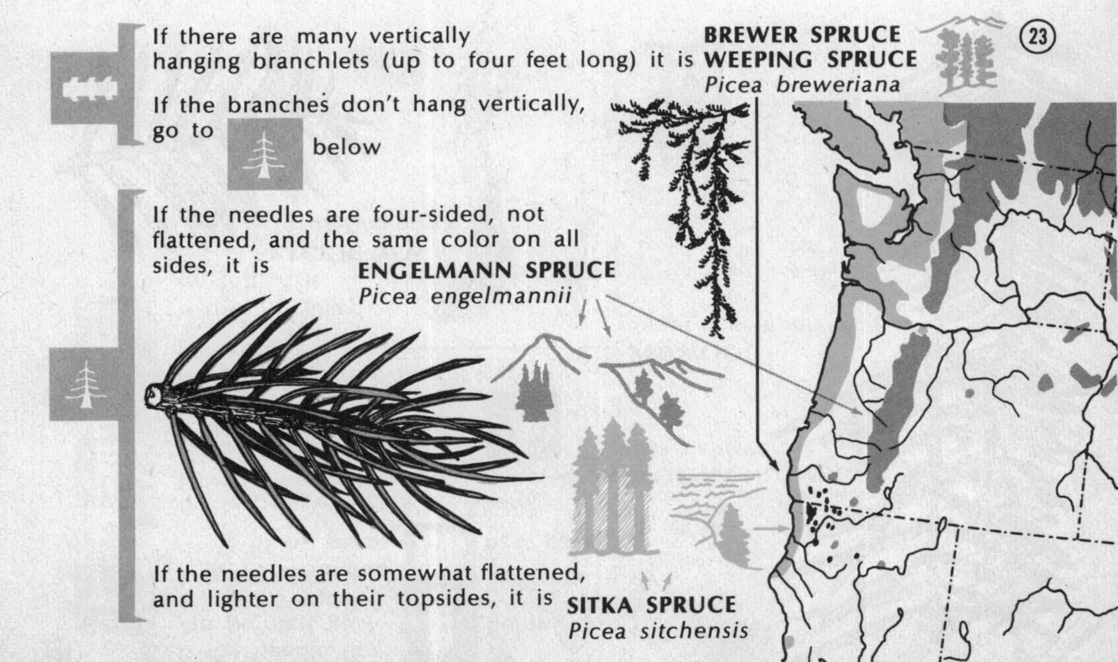

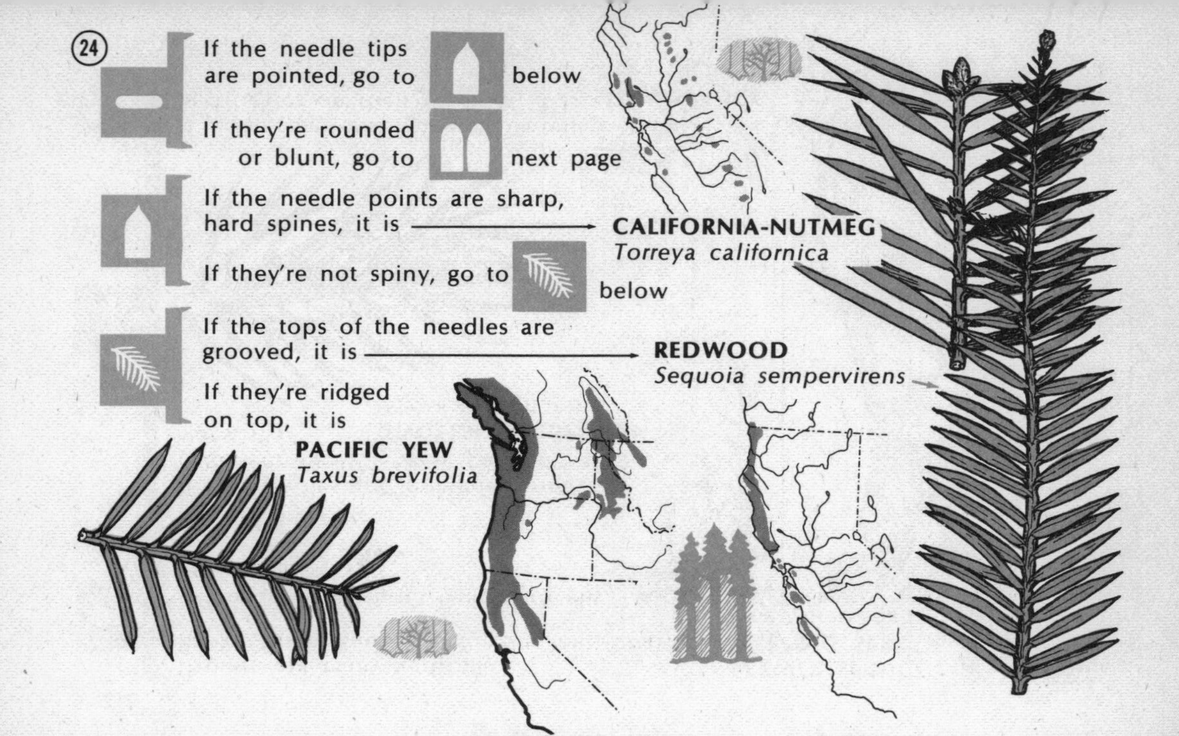

If the needle tips are pointed, go to [pointed-tip symbol] below

If they're rounded or blunt, go to [rounded-tip symbol] next page

If the needle points are sharp, hard spines, it is → **CALIFORNIA-NUTMEG** *Torreya californica*

If they're not spiny, go to [needle-spray symbol] below

If the tops of the needles are grooved, it is → **REDWOOD** *Sequoia sempervirens*

If they're ridged on top, it is **PACIFIC YEW** *Taxus brevifolia*

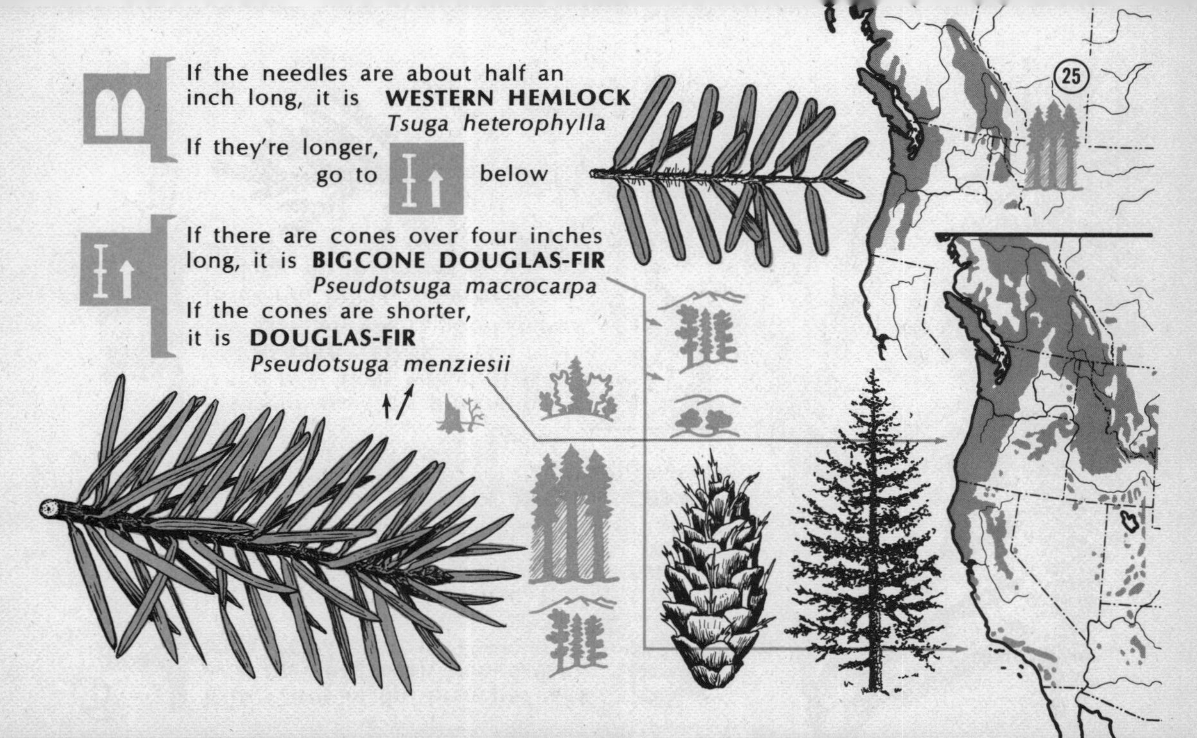

If the needles are about half an inch long, it is **WESTERN HEMLOCK**
Tsuga heterophylla

If they're longer, go to below

If there are cones over four inches long, it is **BIGCONE DOUGLAS-FIR**
Pseudotsuga macrocarpa

If the cones are shorter, it is **DOUGLAS-FIR**
Pseudotsuga menziesii

If the ends of the branches look as if they had been ironed flat, it's a **CEDAR.** Go to → below

If they don't look flattened, go to page 28

If the twig ends look jointed, it is **INCENSE CEDAR** *Calocedrus decurrens*

If they don't look jointed, go to below

If the foliage feels prickly, or if the tree looks wilted, it is **ALASKA-CEDAR** *Chamaecyparis nootkatensis*

If it's not prickly or wilted-looking, go to next page

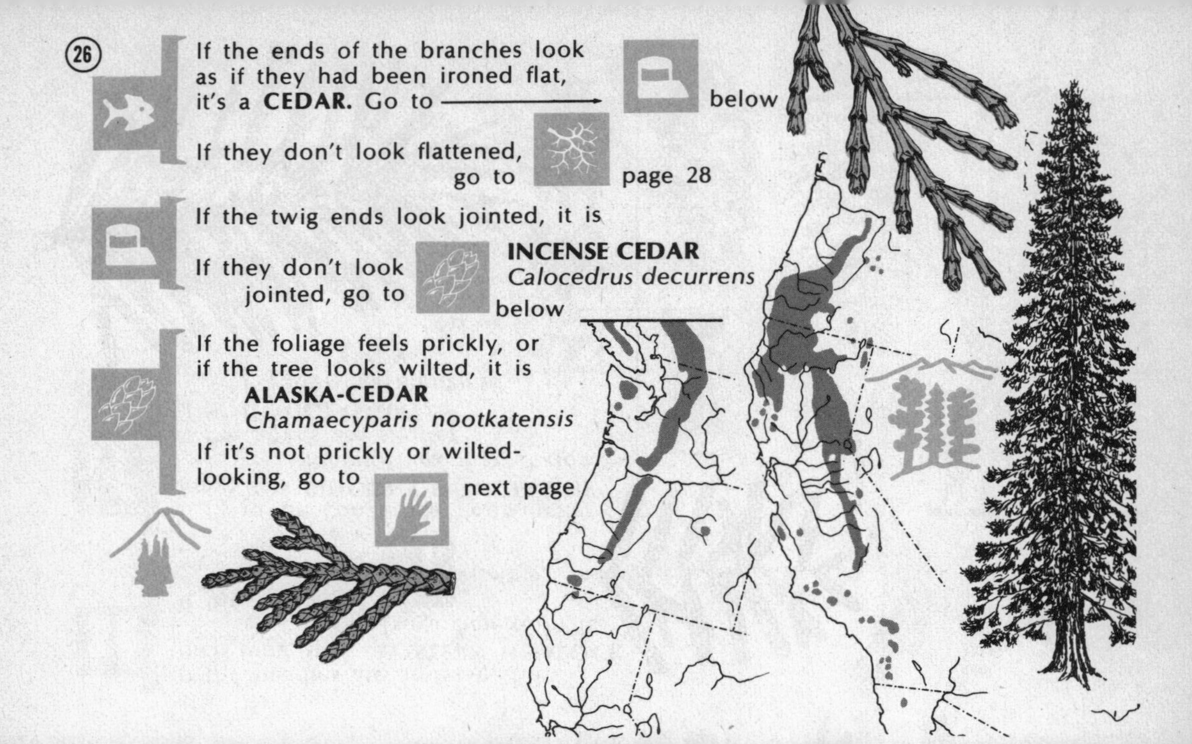

If the foliage is glossy and very fragrant, or if there are leathery, oblong cones, it is

WESTERN RED-CEDAR
Thuja plicata

If you can rub a whitish bloom off the foliage, and there are round cones, it is

PORT-ORFORD-CEDAR
Chamaecyparis lawsoniana

If there are awl-shaped leaves arranged spirally on the twig, it is **GIANT SEQUOIA**
Sequoiadendron giganteum

If the leaves are in opposite pairs instead of a spiral, go to below

If there are roundish, woody, cone-like fruits 1/2 inch or more in diameter, it's a **CYPRESS.** Go to next page

If there are smaller, juicy or pulpy, berry-like fruits, it's a **JUNIPER.** Go to page 30

If you can't find fruit, you may have a male tree. Find a female.

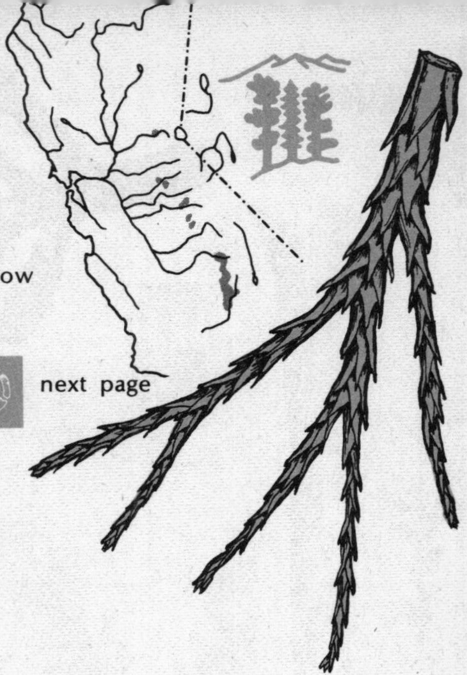

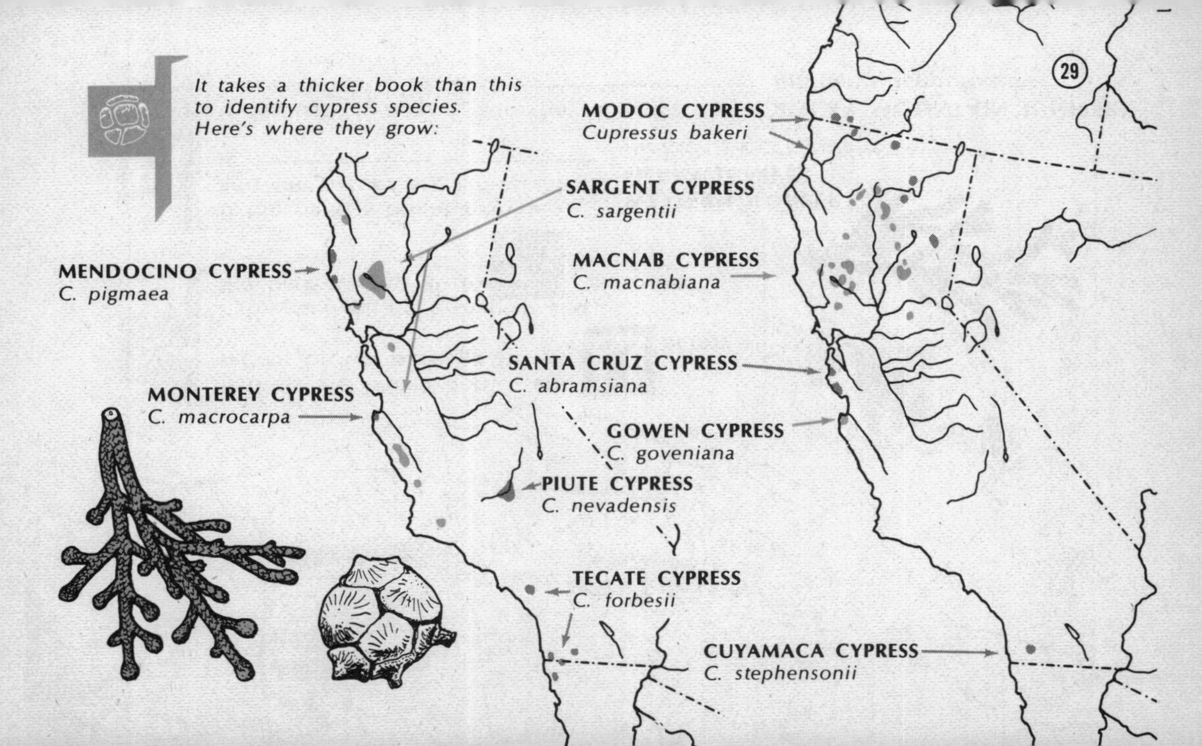
29
It takes a thicker book than this to identify cypress species. Here's where they grow:
MENDOCINO CYPRESS
C. pigmaea
MONTEREY CYPRESS
C. macrocarpa
SARGENT CYPRESS
C. sargentii
MACNAB CYPRESS
C. macnabiana
SANTA CRUZ CYPRESS
C. abramsiana
GOWEN CYPRESS
C. goveniana
PIUTE CYPRESS
C. nevadensis
TECATE CYPRESS
C. forbesii
MODOC CYPRESS
Cupressus bakeri
CUYAMACA CYPRESS
C. stephensonii

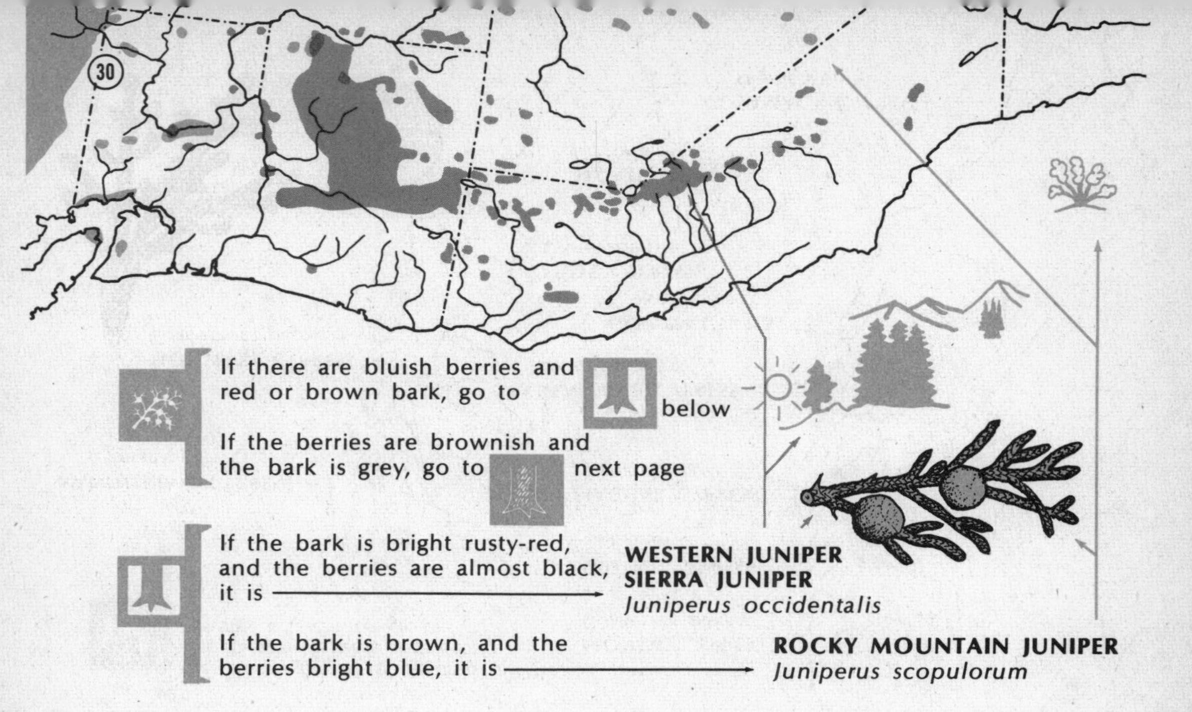

If there are bluish berries and red or brown bark, go to [bark symbol] below

If the berries are brownish and the bark is grey, go to [bark symbol] next page

If the bark is bright rusty-red, and the berries are almost black, it is →
WESTERN JUNIPER
SIERRA JUNIPER
Juniperus occidentalis

If the bark is brown, and the berries bright blue, it is →
ROCKY MOUNTAIN JUNIPER
Juniperus scopulorum

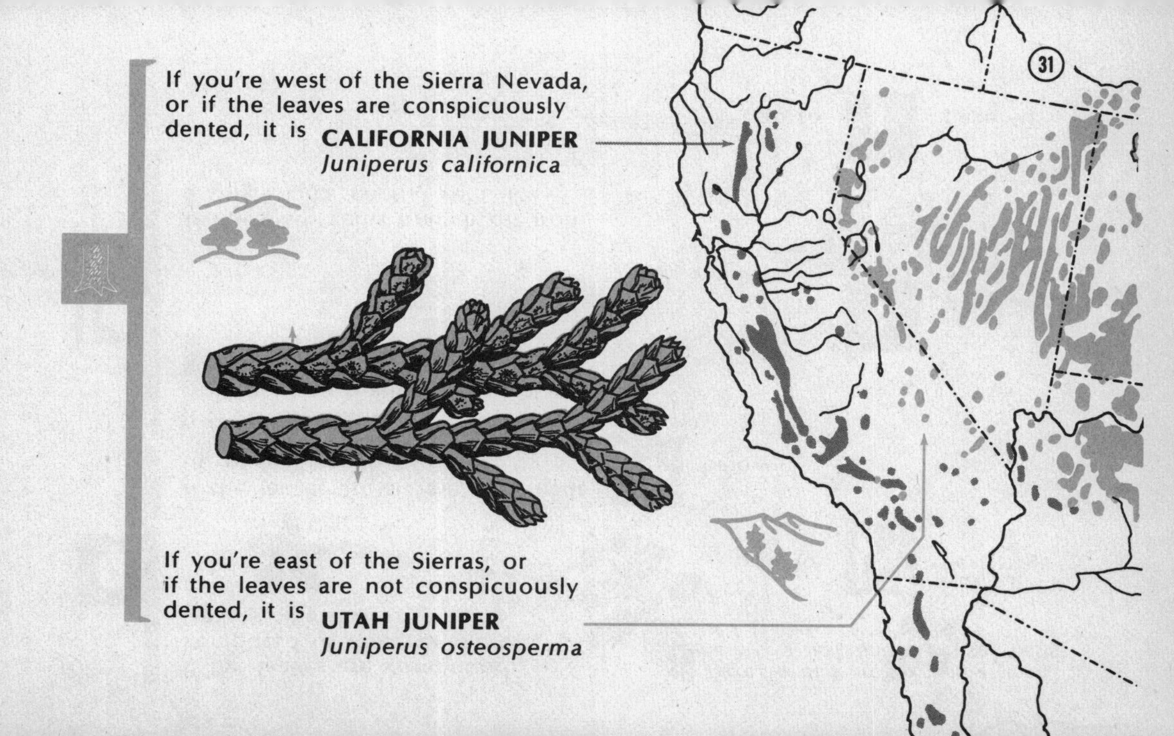

If you're west of the Sierra Nevada, or if the leaves are conspicuously dented, it is **CALIFORNIA JUNIPER** *Juniperus californica*

If you're east of the Sierras, or if the leaves are not conspicuously dented, it is **UTAH JUNIPER** *Juniperus osteosperma*

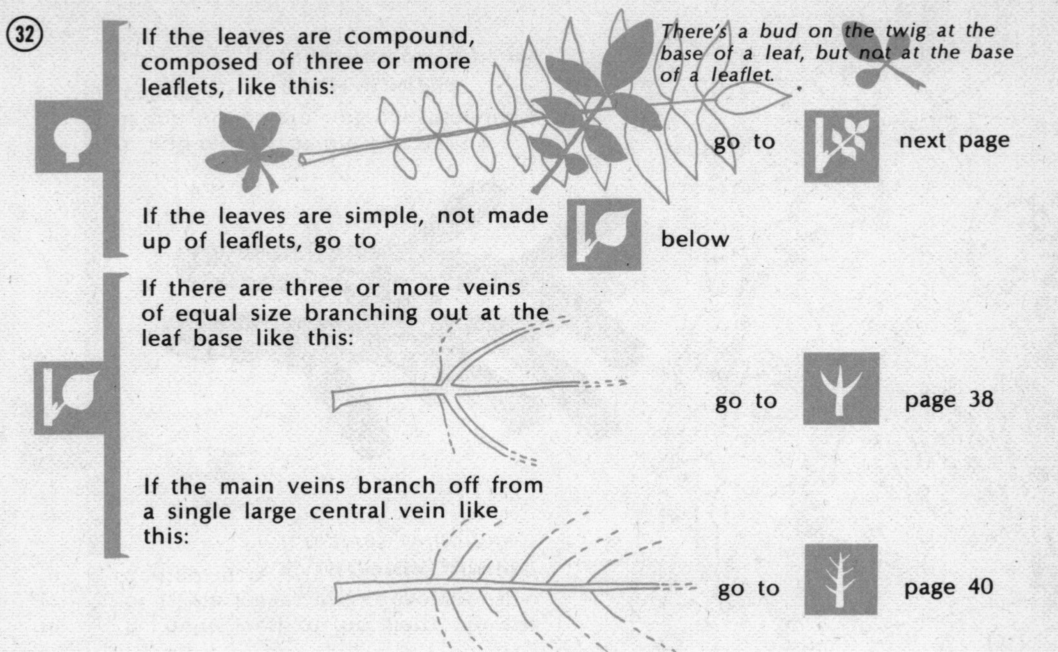

If the leaves are compound, composed of three or more leaflets, like this:

There's a bud on the twig at the base of a leaf, but not at the base of a leaflet.

go to next page

If the leaves are simple, not made up of leaflets, go to below

If there are three or more veins of equal size branching out at the leaf base like this:

go to page 38

If the main veins branch off from a single large central vein like this:

go to page 40

If the leaves have eight of more leaflets, go to [icon] below

If there are fewer leaflets, go to [icon] page 35

If the leaflet margins are saw-toothed, it's a **WALNUT.** Go to [icon] next page

If they're not saw-toothed, go to [icon] below

If there are rounded leaflets and thorns, it is **BLACK LOCUST**
Robinia pseudoacacia

If not, go to [icon] below

If the leaves smell bad, it is **AILANTHUS**
Ailanthus altissima

If they smell spicy, it is **CALIFORNIA PEPPER TREE**
Schinus molle

34

If the leaves are longer than ten inches (or if it's a large tree), it is **HINDS WALNUT** *Juglans hindsii*

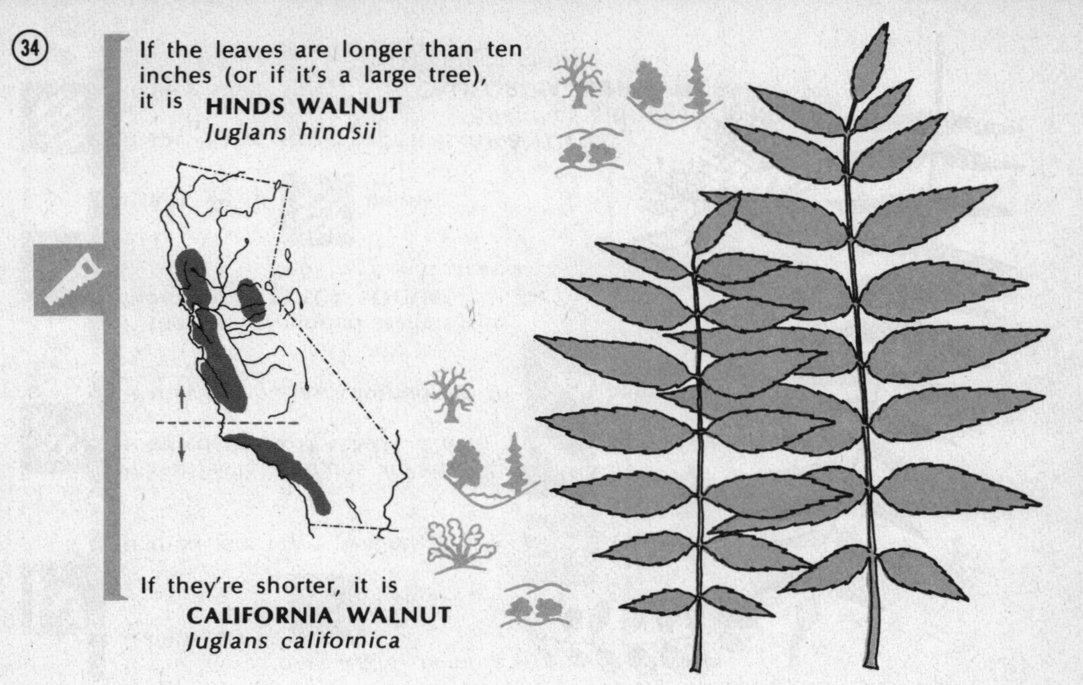

If they're shorter, it is **CALIFORNIA WALNUT** *Juglans californica*

If the leaflets all fan out from the same point, go to [symbol] below

If they don't go to [symbol] next page

If the leaflets are jagged, it is
BOXELDER
Acer negundo

If not, go to [symbol] below

If the leaves have three leaflets, it is **HOP TREE**
Ptelea crenulata

If they have more, it is
CALIFORNIA BUCKEYE
Aesculus californica

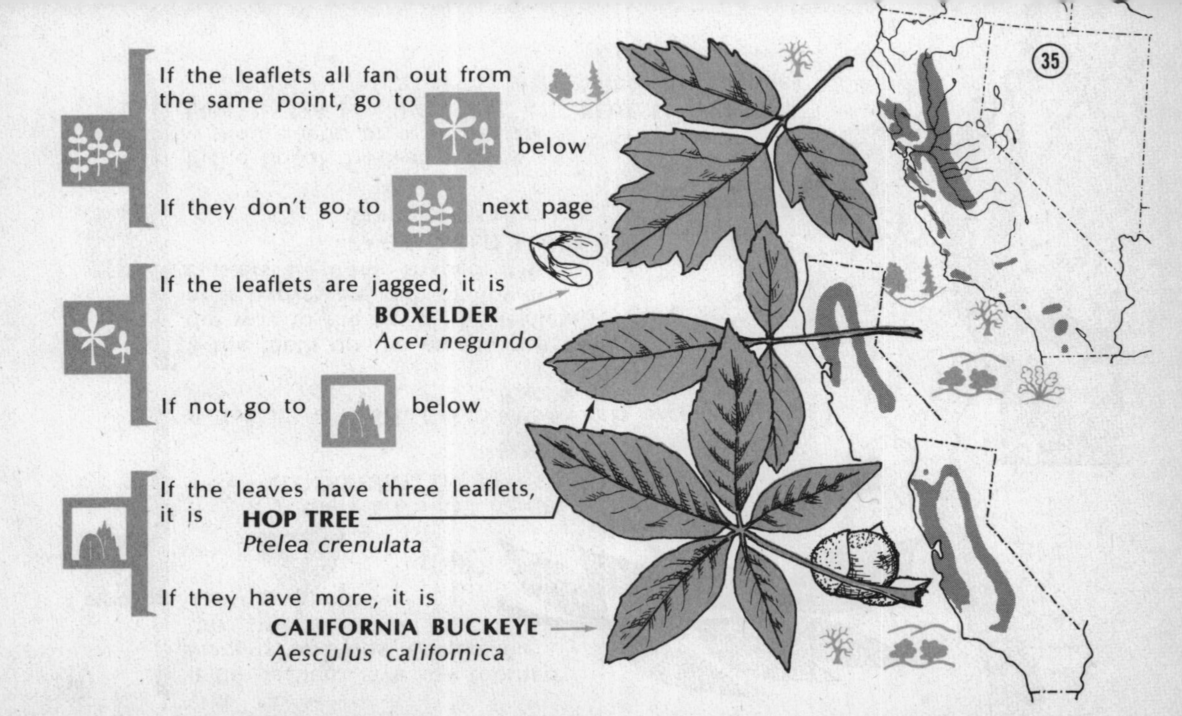

If the leaflets have saw-toothed margins, and tips tapered like this:

. . . or if there are small berries, it's an **ELDERBERRY.** Go to [icon] below

If not, it's an **ASH.** Go to [icon] next page

If the teeth on the margin run all the way to the tip of the leaflet; or if berries are red, or flower clusters are dome-shaped, it is

PACIFIC RED ELDER
Sambucus callicarpa

If the tip of the leaflet is without teeth; or if berries are blue, or flower clusters flat, it is **BLUE ELDERBERRY**
Sambucus caerulea

If the leaflets have rounded tips with saw-toothed margins, it is

TWO-PETAL ASH
FOOTHILL ASH
Fraxinus dipetala

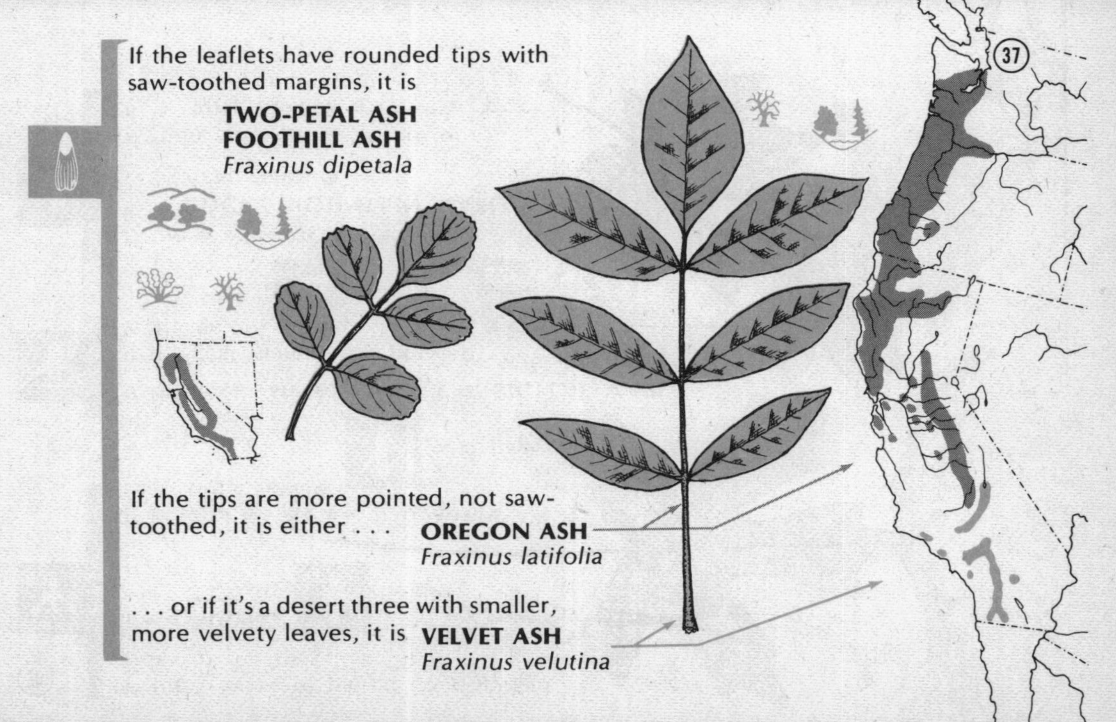

If the tips are more pointed, not saw-toothed, it is either . . . **OREGON ASH** *Fraxinus latifolia*

. . . or if it's a desert three with smaller, more velvety leaves, it is **VELVET ASH** *Fraxinus velutina*

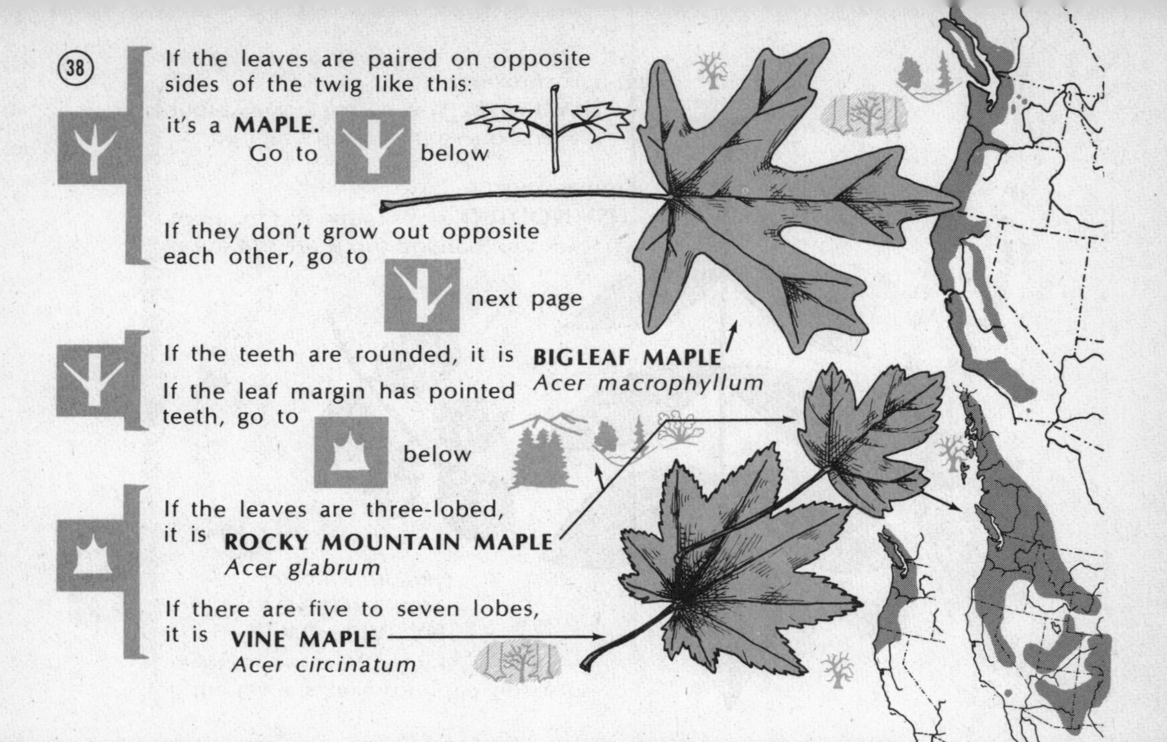

If the leaves are paired on opposite sides of the twig like this:

it's a **MAPLE.** Go to [symbol] below

If they don't grow out opposite each other, go to [symbol] next page

If the teeth are rounded, it is **BIGLEAF MAPLE** *Acer macrophyllum*

If the leaf margin has pointed teeth, go to [symbol] below

If the leaves are three-lobed, it is **ROCKY MOUNTAIN MAPLE** *Acer glabrum*

If there are five to seven lobes, it is **VINE MAPLE** *Acer circinatum*

If the leaves are lobed go to [lobed-leaf symbol] below

If they're not lobed, go to [round-leaf symbol] below

If the leaves are almost round, it is **CALIFORNIA REDBUD**
Cercis occidentalis

If they're narrower (or if you see blue flowers), it is
BLUEBLOSSOM
Ceanothus thyrsiflorus

If the leaves are over four inches wide, it is **CALIFORNIA SYCAMORE ALISO**
Platanus racemosa

If they're smaller, and fuzzy, it is **FLANNELBUSH**
Fremontodendron californicum

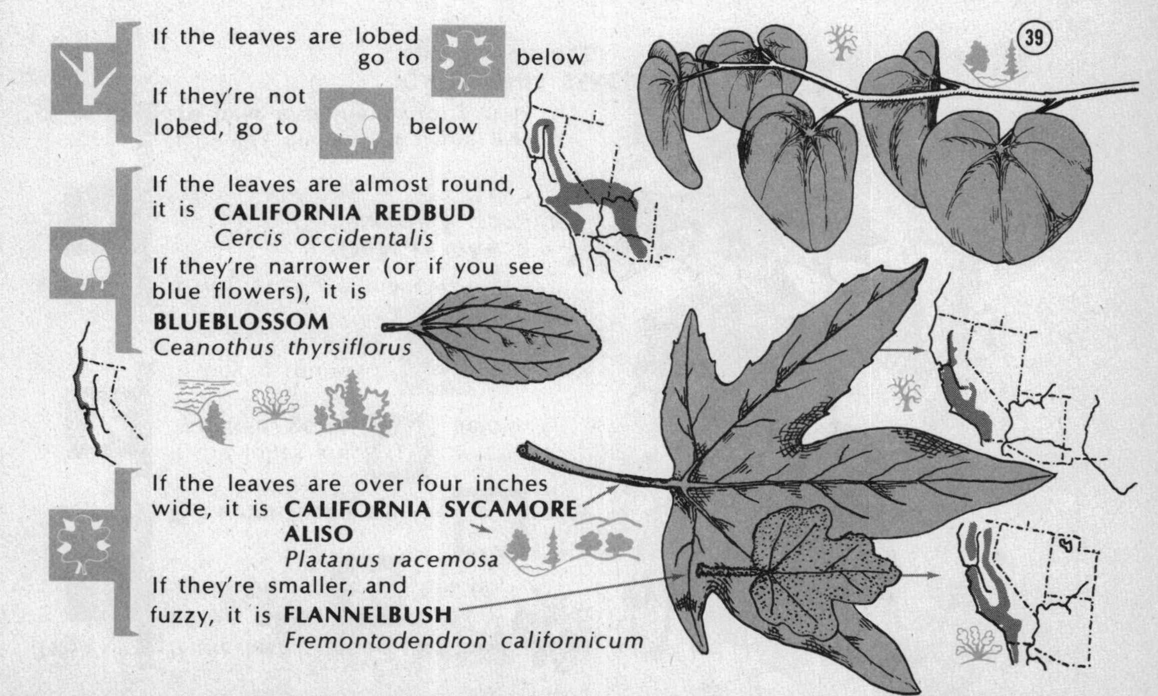

If the leaf is lobed like this: it's an **OAK.** Go to [lobed-leaf symbol] below

If it's not lobed, go to [square symbol] page 42

If the lobes are pointed, go to [Λ symbol] below

If they're rounded, go to [∩ symbol] next page

If the lobes are shallow, it is

ORACLE OAK
Quercus X morehus

If they're deeper; or if the leaves are over four inches long, it is

CALIFORNIA BLACK OAK
Quercus kelloggii

C

If the leaves have soft hairiness on the topsides, and 7 to 11 deeply cut lobes; and if the trunk bark is deeply checkered into squarish plates; or if there are long, hanging branches or long acorns, it is **VALLEY OAK**
Quercus lobata

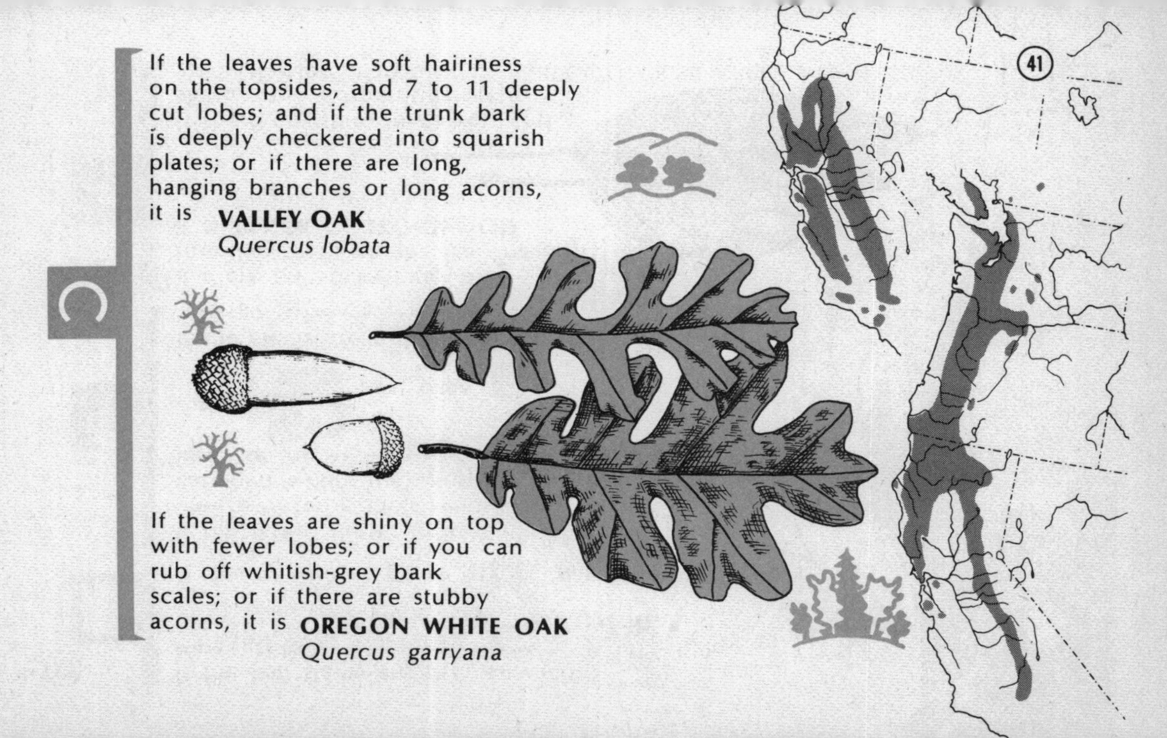

If the leaves are shiny on top with fewer lobes; or if you can rub off whitish-grey bark scales; or if there are stubby acorns, it is **OREGON WHITE OAK**
Quercus garryana

If the leaf stems are over an inch long, go to → below

If they're shorter, go to page 44

If the leaves flutter in a gentle breeze because their stems are flattened where they join the leaf like this →

go to next page

If the stems are not flattened that way, go to → below

If there are sticky twigs and rounded teeth on the leaf margin, it is **BLACK COTTONWOOD**
Populus trichocarpa

If there are shiny red twigs and sharp, outward-pointing teeth along the leaf margin, it is OREGON CRAB APPLE (see p. 56)

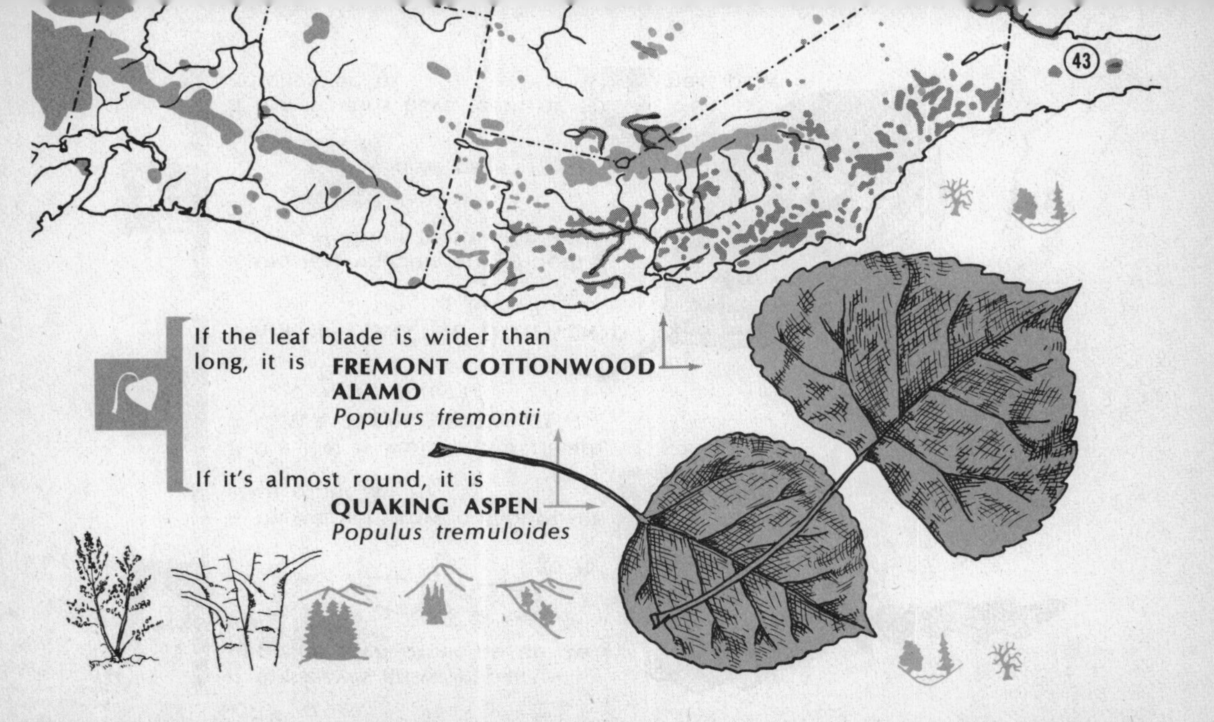

If the leaf blade is wider than long, it is **FREMONT COTTONWOOD ALAMO**
Populus fremontii

If it's almost round, it is **QUAKING ASPEN**
Populus tremuloides

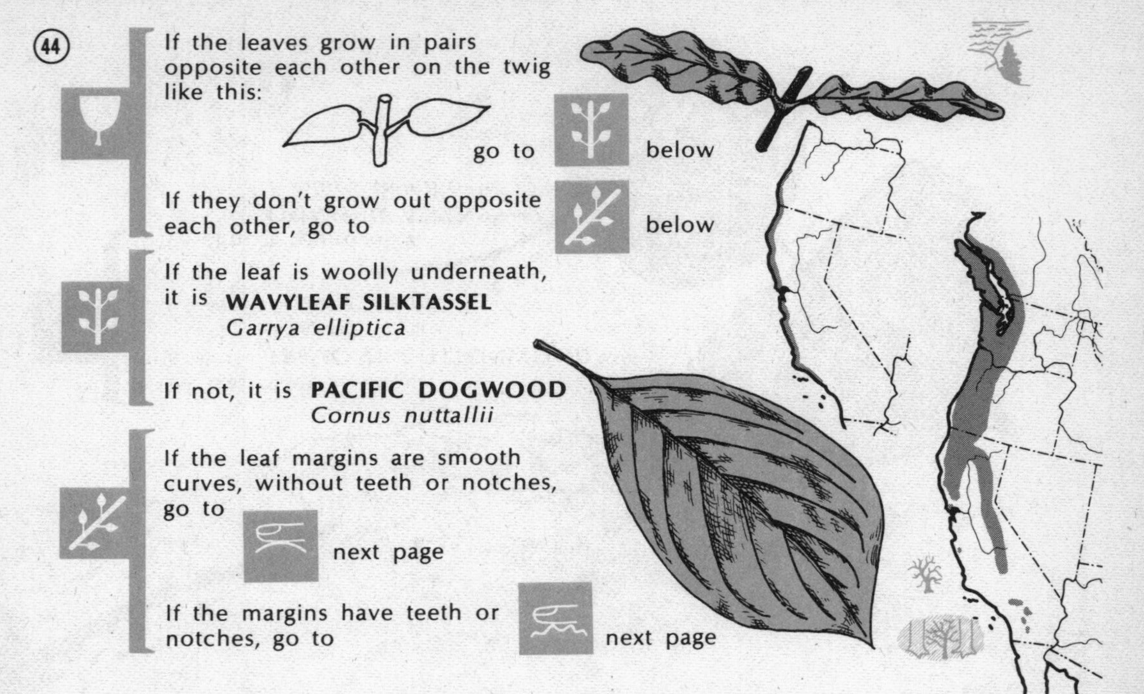

If the leaves grow in pairs opposite each other on the twig like this:

go to [icon] below

If they don't grow out opposite each other, go to [icon] below

If the leaf is woolly underneath, it is **WAVYLEAF SILKTASSEL** *Garrya elliptica*

If not, it is **PACIFIC DOGWOOD** *Cornus nuttallii*

If the leaf margins are smooth curves, without teeth or notches, go to [icon] next page

If the margins have teeth or notches, go to [icon] next page

If the leaf has a strong, penetrating odor when you crush it, go to below

If not, go to next page

If the leaf is dark green with a blunt tip, it is **CALIFORNIA LAUREL**
PEPPERWOOD
BAY TREE
OREGON MYRTLE
Umbellularia californica

If it's pale green with a sharp tip, it is **EUCALYPTUS**
Eucalyptus sp.

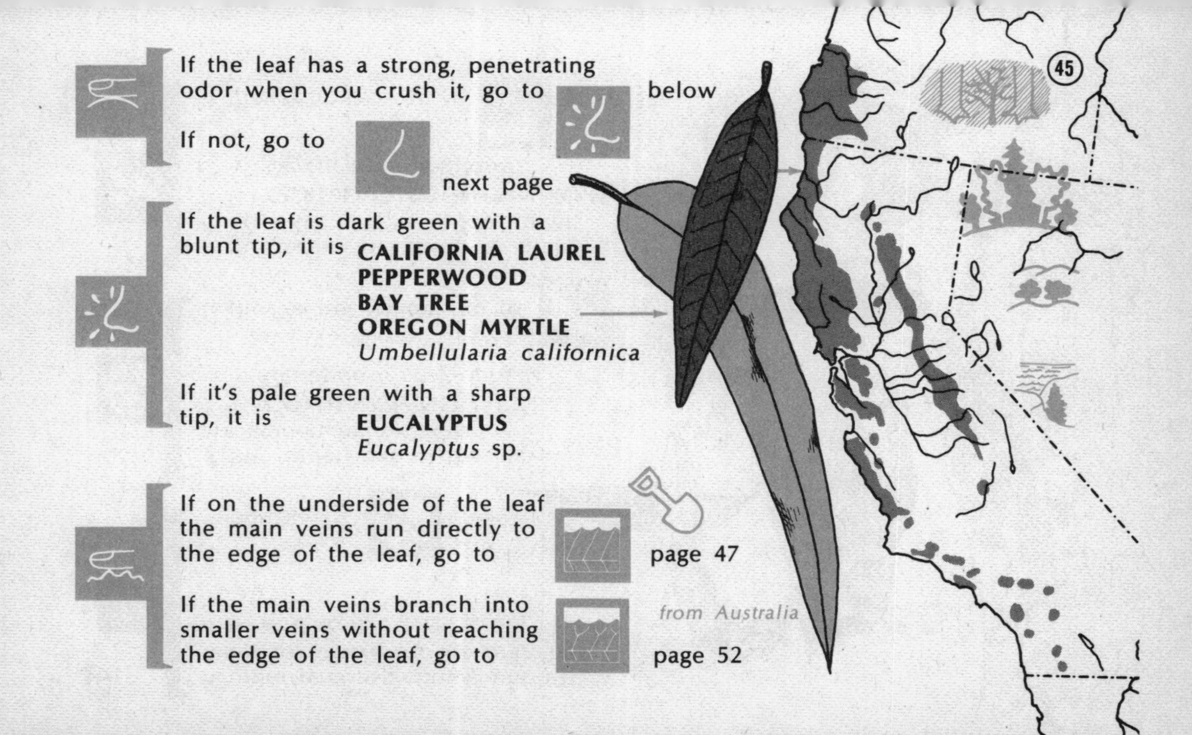

If on the underside of the leaf the main veins run directly to the edge of the leaf, go to page 47

If the main veins branch into smaller veins without reaching the edge of the leaf, go to page 52

If there is conspicuous, smooth, red-brown bark on the branches, it is MADRONE (see p. 57)

If not, go to below

If the undersides of the leaves are golden-yellow, it is
GOLDEN CHINQUAPIN
Castanopsis chrysophylla

If they're not yellow, go to below

If the leaves are about an inch long, with margins rolled under, it is **CURLLEAF MOUNTAIN MAHOGANY**
Cercocarpus ledifolius

If they're longer, go to page 52

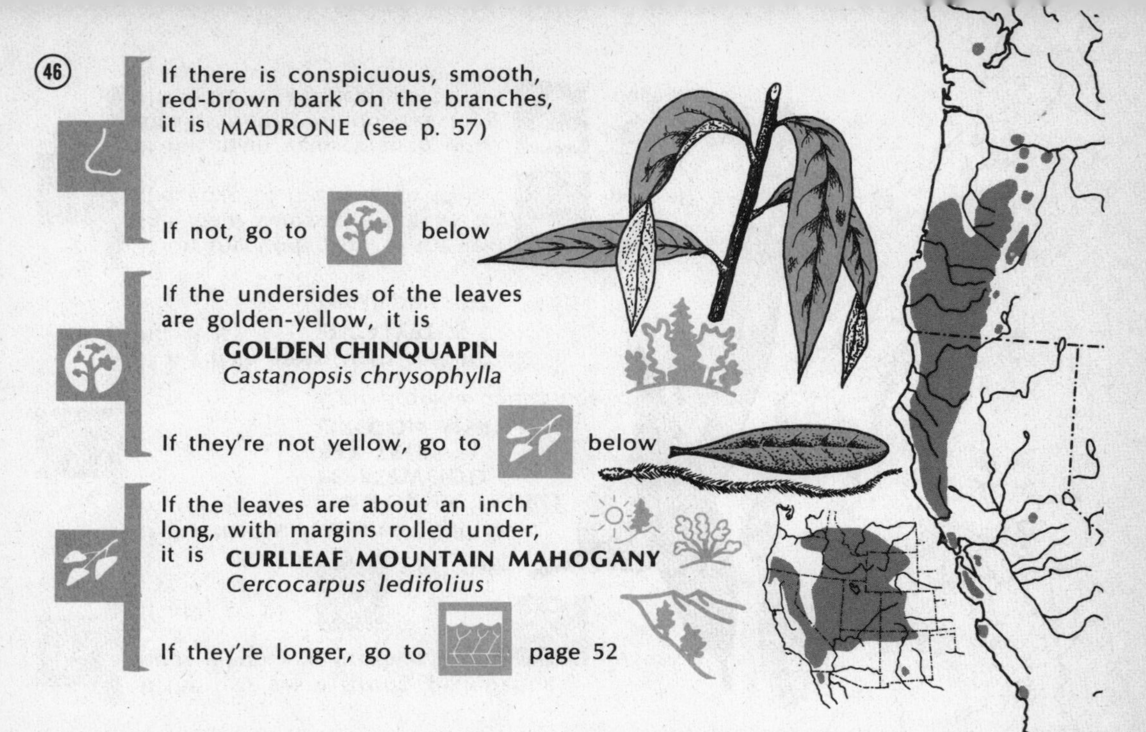

If the leaf blades are shorter than two inches, go to [icon] below

If they're longer, go to [icon] next page

If the leaves are oval with curved veins, it is **PACIFIC SERVICEBERRY**
Amelanchier florida

If they're not oval, and the veins are straighter, go to [icon] below

If the leaf has a wedge-shaped base and a velvety underside, it is
BIRCHLEAF MOUNTAIN MAHOGANY
Cercocarpus betuloides

If the leaf base is rounded, it is
WATER BIRCH
Betula occidentalis

If the leaf stem (or the whole leaf) is woolly or very hairy, go to [sheep symbol] below

If not, go to [scissors symbol] next page

If there's a stubby spine at the end of each main vein, it is

TANOAK
Lithocarpus densiflorus

If there are many small, soft teeth on the margin, it is

CALIFORNIA HAZEL
Corylus cornuta var. *californica*

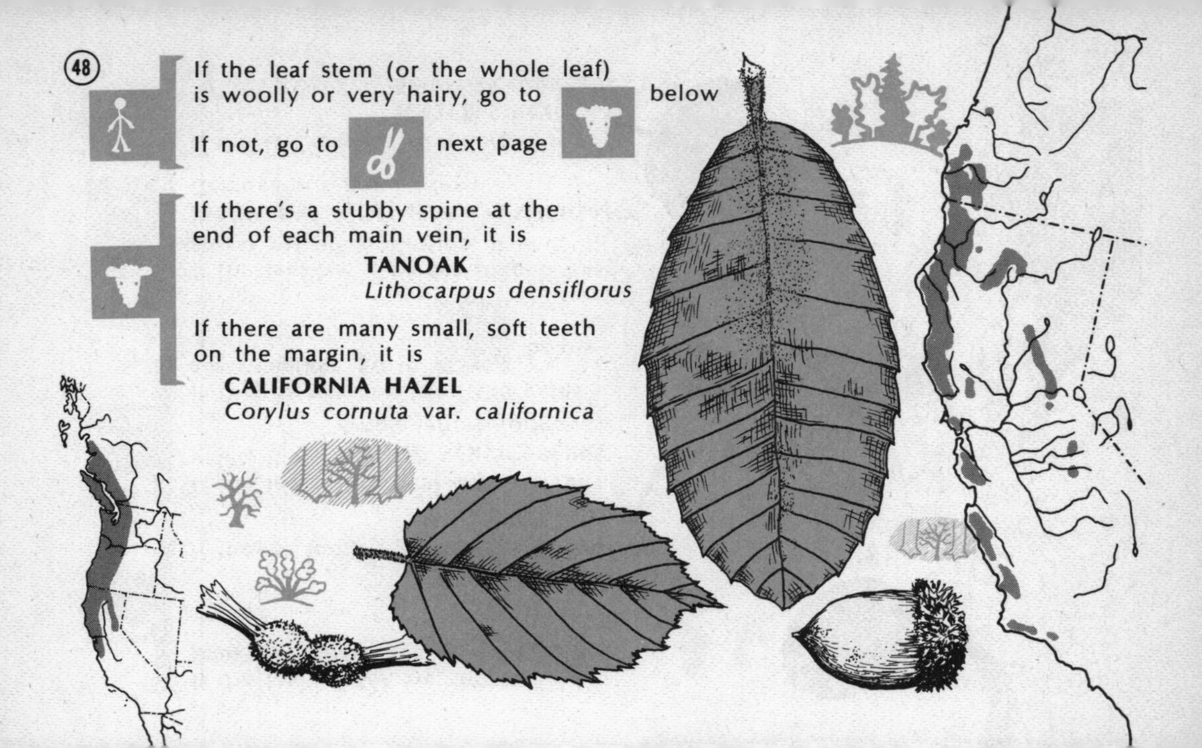

If the trunk has white bark, it is

PAPER BIRCH
Betula papyrifera

If the bark isn't white, go to [icon] below

If the leaf margin has sharply pointed teeth and V-shaped notches, go to [icon] below

If the teeth or notches are rounded, go to [icon] page 51

If the tree has thorns, it is

BLACK HAWTHORN
Crataegus douglasii

If not, go to [icon] next page

If the undersides of the outermost leaves are glossy and sticky, it is

SITKA ALDER
Alnus sinuata

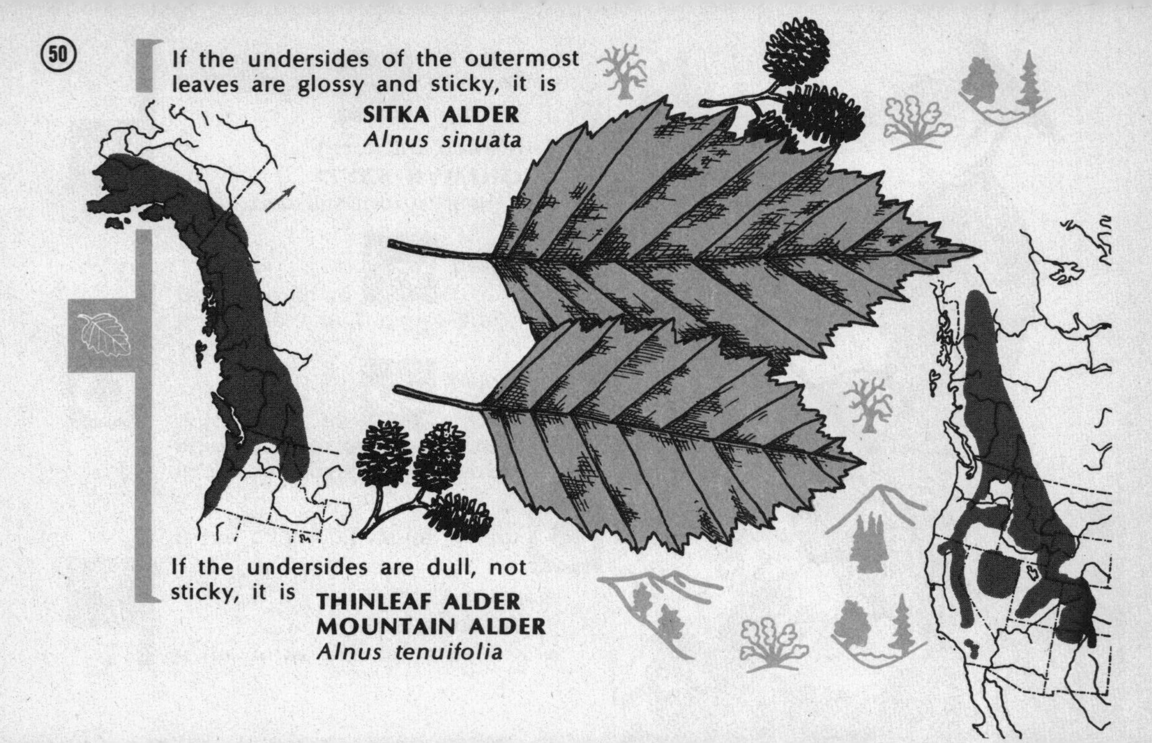

If the undersides are dull, not sticky, it is

THINLEAF ALDER
MOUNTAIN ALDER
Alnus tenuifolia

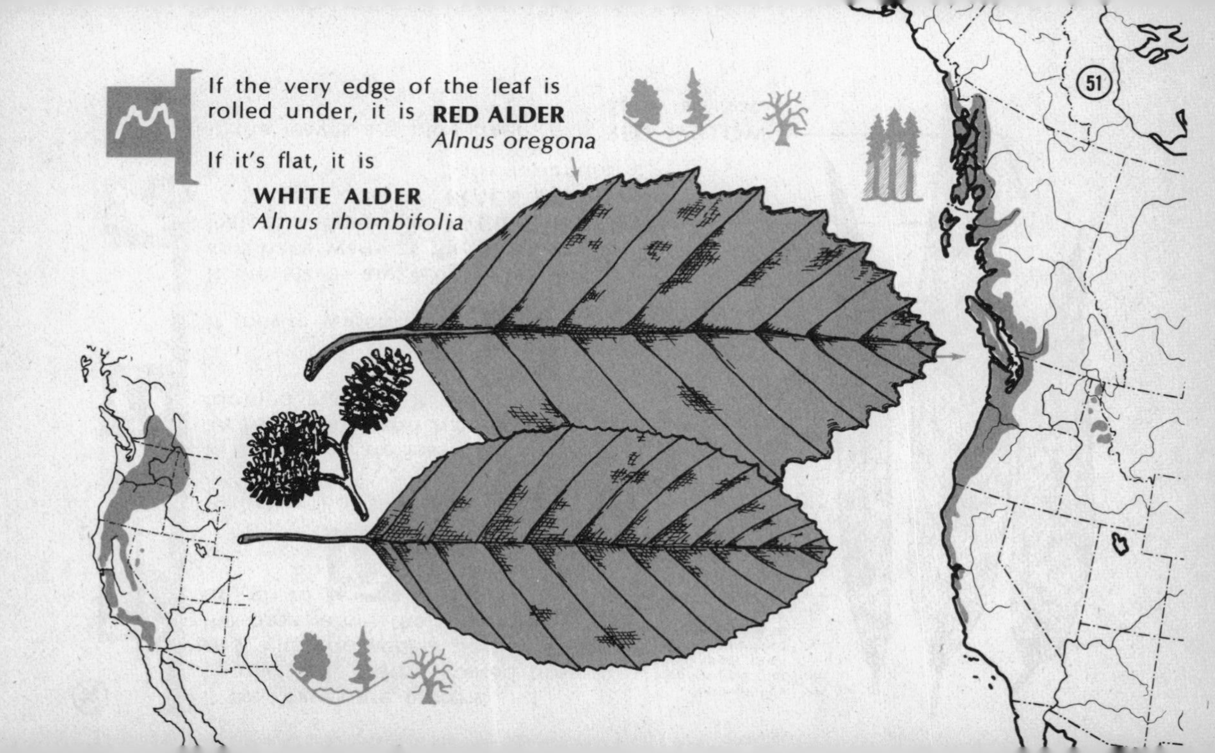
51
If the very edge of the leaf is rolled under, it is RED ALDER
Alnus oregona
If it's flat, it is
WHITE ALDER
Alnus rhombifolia

If the leaves are narrow and bendy, with sharp, tapered tips; and with the widest portion toward the base rather than toward the tip, go to below

If they're not like that, go to next page

If the leaves are less than half an inch wide, and have saw-toothed margins, it is **BLACK WILLOW** *Salix gooddingii*

If they're wider, go to below

If the leaves are yellow-green and have warts at the junction of leaf and stem, it is **PACIFIC WILLOW BLACK WILLOW** *Salix lasiandra*

If the leaves are blue-green, it is **RED WILLOW** *Salix laevigata*

Note: Willows are so variable that even experts can't always identify them by leaves alone.

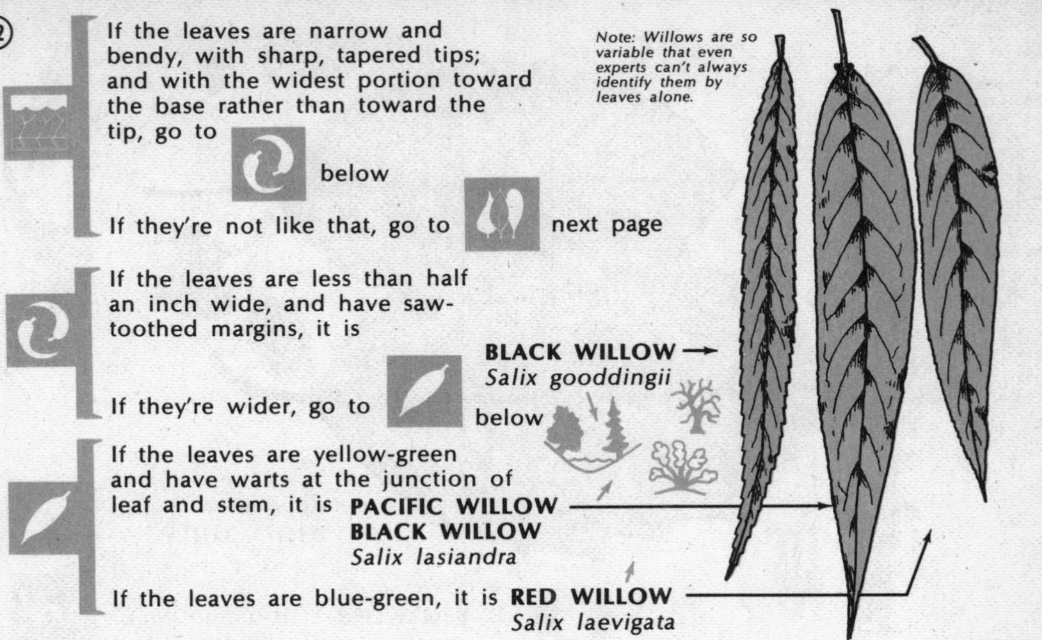

If the leaves are narrow and paddle-shaped—wider toward the tip, and with a wedge-shaped base like this: go to below

If they're some other shape, go to page 55

If all leaves have easy-to-see teeth on their margins, go to below

If the teeth are minute or sometimes absent, go to next page

If the leaves are longer than two inches, it is **PACIFIC BAYBERRY WAX MYRTLE** *Myrica californica*

If they're shorter, it is **BITTER CHERRY** *Prunus emarginata*

If the undersides of the leaves are covered with velvety, white hair, it is **SITKA WILLOW**
SILKY WILLOW
Salix sitchensis

If not, go to     below

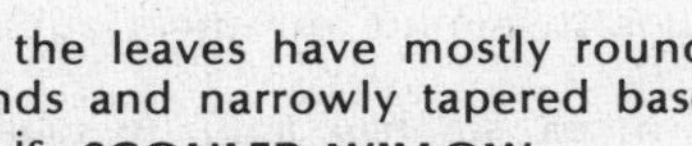

If the leaves have mostly rounded ends and narrowly tapered bases, it is **SCOULER WILLOW**
Salix scouleriana

If they have more pointed ends, wider bases, and rolled-under margins, it is

ARROYO WILLOW
Salix lasiolepis

  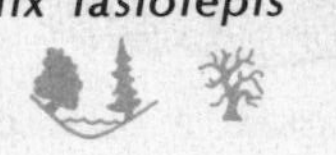

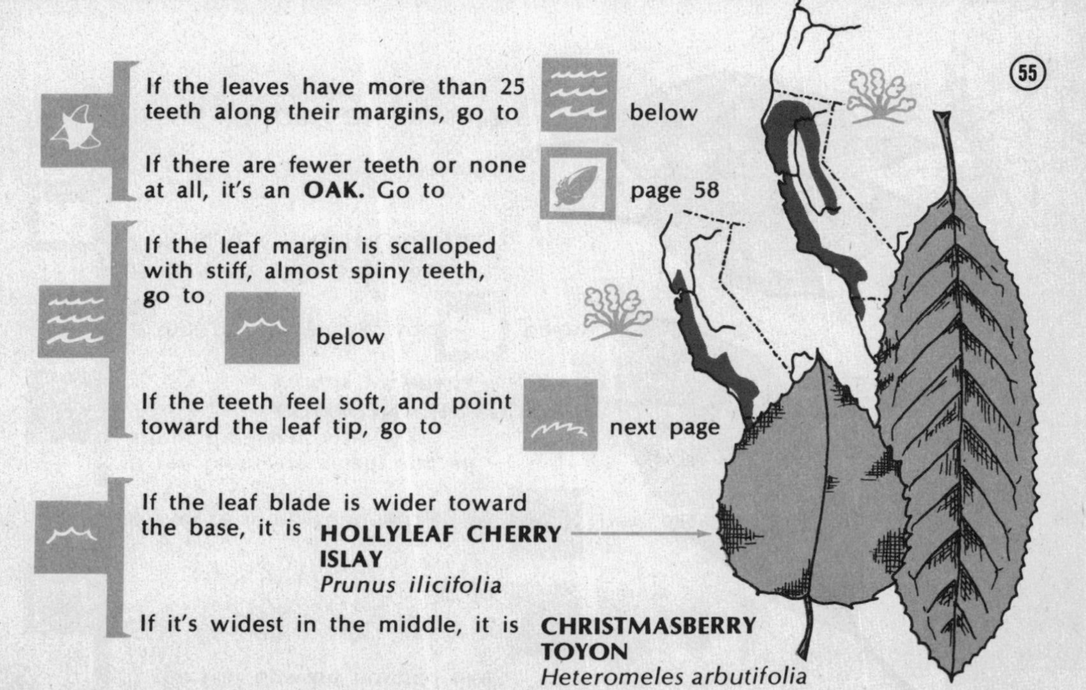

If the leaves have more than 25 teeth along their margins, go to below

If there are fewer teeth or none at all, it's an **OAK.** Go to page 58

If the leaf margin is scalloped with stiff, almost spiny teeth, go to below

If the teeth feel soft, and point toward the leaf tip, go to next page

If the leaf blade is wider toward the base, it is **HOLLYLEAF CHERRY**
ISLAY
Prunus ilicifolia

If it's widest in the middle, it is **CHRISTMASBERRY**
TOYON
Heteromeles arbutifolia

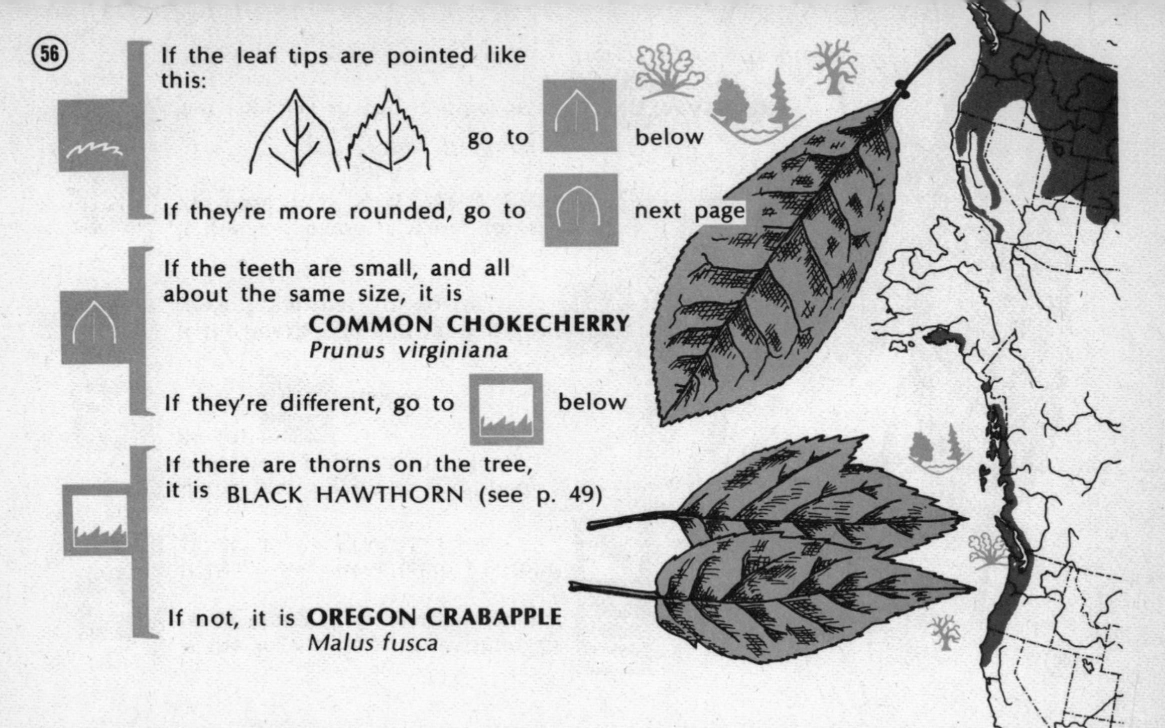

If the leaf tips are pointed like this: go to [pointed-tip symbol] below

If they're more rounded, go to [rounded-tip symbol] next page

If the teeth are small, and all about the same size, it is
COMMON CHOKECHERRY
Prunus virginiana

If they're different, go to [uneven-teeth symbol] below

If there are thorns on the tree, it is BLACK HAWTHORN (see p. 49)

If not, it is **OREGON CRABAPPLE**
Malus fusca

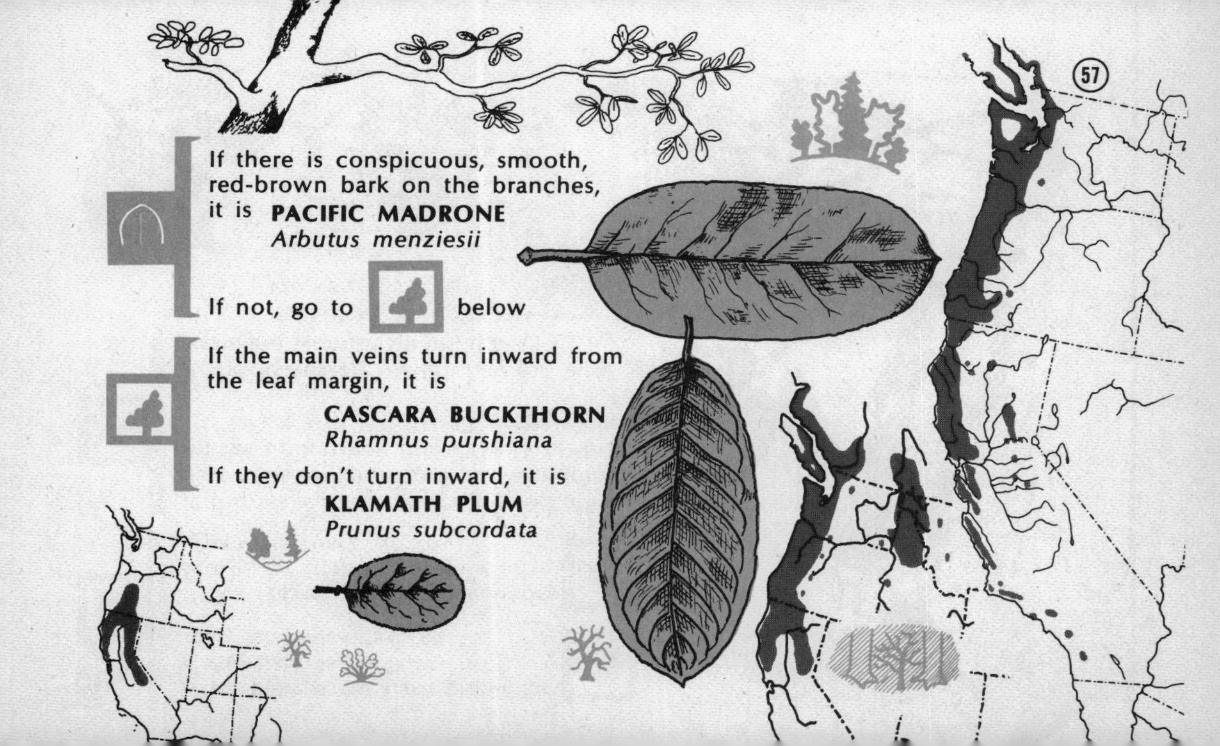

If there is conspicuous, smooth, red-brown bark on the branches, it is **PACIFIC MADRONE**
Arbutus menziesii

If not, go to [symbol] below

If the main veins turn inward from the leaf margin, it is
CASCARA BUCKTHORN
Rhamnus purshiana

If they don't turn inward, it is
KLAMATH PLUM
Prunus subcordata

58

If the leaves are dark green; or if the bark is blackish, not scaly or checkered, go to below

If the leaves are light green or bluish; or if there is scaly or checkered bark, go to next page

If the leaves are convex on top and have tufts of hair where the veins join on the undersides, it is **COAST LIVE OAK**
Quercus agrifolia

If the leaves are flatter, hairless, and some are without spines, it is
INTERIOR LIVE OAK
Quercus wislizenii

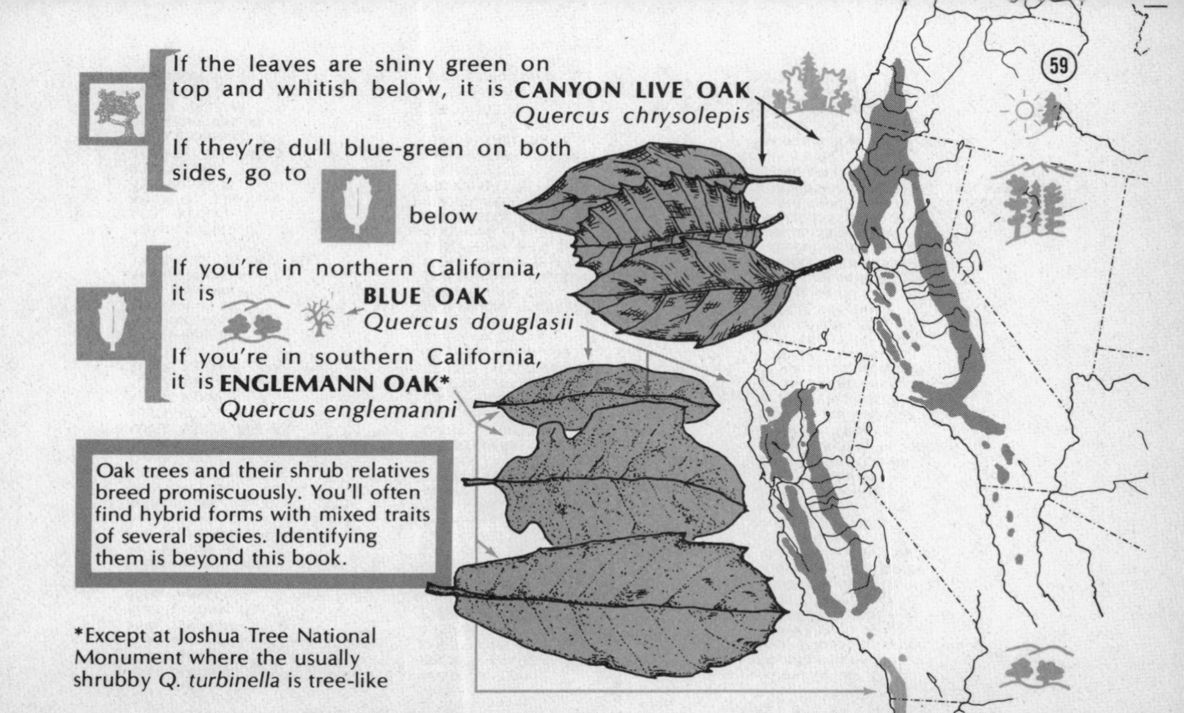

If the leaves are shiny green on top and whitish below, it is **CANYON LIVE OAK**
Quercus chrysolepis

If they're dull blue-green on both sides, go to below

If you're in northern California, it is **BLUE OAK**
Quercus douglasii

If you're in southern California, it is **ENGLEMANN OAK***
Quercus englemanni

Oak trees and their shrub relatives breed promiscuously. You'll often find hybrid forms with mixed traits of several species. Identifying them is beyond this book.

*Except at Joshua Tree National Monument where the usually shrubby *Q. turbinella* is tree-like

INDEX

WINTER TREE FINDER

By May Theilgaard Watts
Tom Watts

A MANUAL FOR IDENTIFYING DECIDUOUS TREES IN WINTER

TO USE THIS BOOK

1. Select a typical twig of the tree you wish to identify. Avoid freaks. (If you cut the twig, do it straight across and sharply to prevent distortion of the pith and damage to the tree.)
2. Begin on page 6 and proceed step by step, considering each choice. (There is a scale for measuring on the cover.)
3. When you have made the final choice, arriving at the name of the tree, compare your twig with the illustration, and check other features shown.

Advice: examine pages 1 to 5 before starting on page 6.

Area covered by this book

This book is for deciduous trees in Winter. For evergreens, or when trees have leaves, use the MASTER TREE FINDER.

THE PARTS OF A TWIG

(Twig illustrations in this book are about 2/3 life-size.)

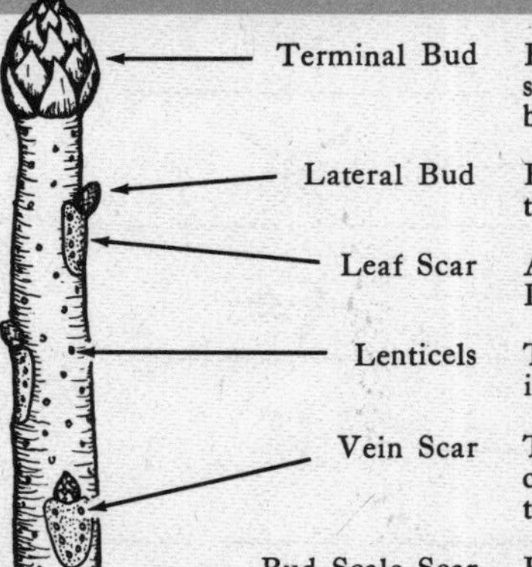

Terminal Bud	From this bud the twig will grow longer in spring. It is often much larger than the lateral buds, but is absent from the twigs of some trees.
Lateral Bud	From this bud a side branch will grow—shorter than the growth from the terminal bud.
Leaf Scar	A leaf was attached here last summer. Leaf scars have many shapes and sizes.
Lenticels	These cork-filled pores permit the green, living inner bark to breathe.
Vein Scar	These dots on the leaf scars are the broken-off, cork-filled ends of the tubes that supplied water to the leaf.
Bud Scale Scar	From this scar the scales of last winter's terminal bud fell last spring. From the tip of the twig to the first bud scale scar is one year's growth. From the tip back to the second scar is two years' growth, and so on. The scale scars encircle the twig.
Pith	This is the soft, inner core of the twig.

2

The map next to each twig illustration shows the area where that tree grows naturally. The kinds of places within that area where the tree is likely to grow — the habitat — is shown by one of the following symbols:

Streambanks, Lakeshores	Trees of these habitats often grow fast and make long twigs.
Lowlands	
Tall Forest Trees	These are often narrow-crowned trees without lower branches.
Under Taller Trees	These trees are often horizontally-branched.
High Altitudes	These trees are also abundant in lowland forests of the far north.
Bogs	
Sand and Gravel Soil	These tend to grow slowly and make short twigs.
Upland	
Edge of the Forest	These are often small and thorny trees.
Pioneer in Disturbed Areas	In time these may hide a parking lot — even a billboard.

The place where some trees grow depends on what people have done, as shown by the following symbols:

3

Trees are planted in parks, yards, and around houses

. . . where winters are cold,

. . . where winters are mild.

Some trees came from across the sea.

Some tolerate the conditions of cities

Pioneer trees begin to grow in a place after

soil has been disturbed,

fire,

cattle have grazed,

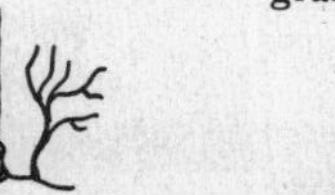

logging.

4 Sometimes a conspicuous feature or the location of a tree makes identification easier.

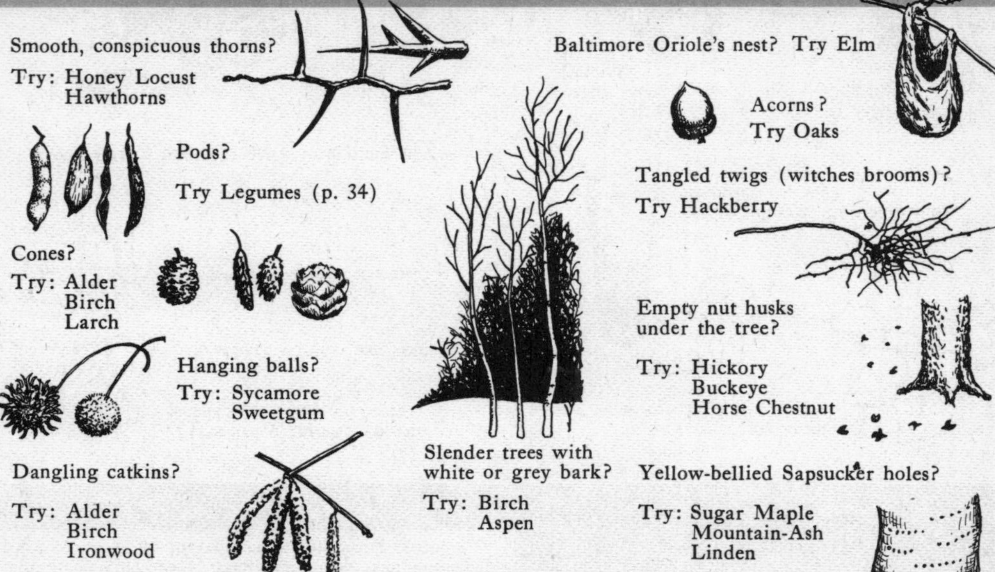

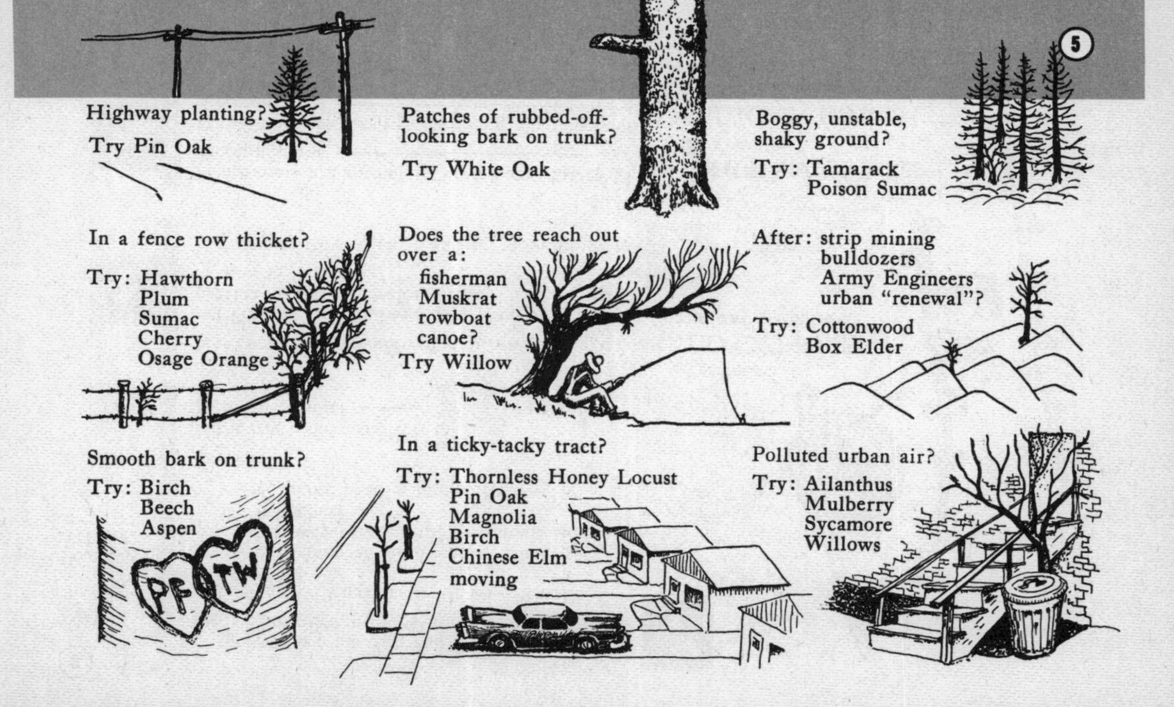
5
Highway planting?
Try Pin Oak
Patches of rubbed-off-
looking bark on trunk?
Try White Oak
Boggy, unstable,
shaky ground?
Try: Tamarack
Poison Sumac
In a fence row thicket?
Try: Hawthorn
Plum
Sumac
Cherry
Osage Orange
Does the tree reach out
over a:
fisherman
Muskrat
rowboat
canoe?
Try Willow
After: strip mining
bulldozers
Army Engineers
urban "renewal"?
Try: Cottonwood
Box Elder
Smooth bark on trunk?
Try: Birch
Beech
Aspen
PF
TW
In a ticky-tacky tract?
Try: Thornless Honey Locust
Pin Oak
Magnolia
Birch
Chinese Elm
moving
Polluted urban air?
Try: Ailanthus
Mulberry
Sycamore
Willows

BEGIN HERE →

If the tree is a conifer, and needle-bearing, but sheds its needles in the winter, go to this symbol below

Conifers will have some or all of these:

—cones
—evergreen shape (central trunk all the way to the top, and small side branches)
—withered needles under the tree

If the tree is not a conifer, go to this symbol → next page

If the cones are globular, soon disintegrating, it is **BALD CYPRESS** ***Taxodium distichum***

(The tree usually has a buttressed base, and often grows in water, where it puts up "knees".)

If the cones are persistent, and not globular, go to 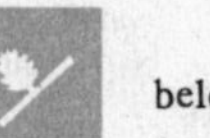 below

If the cones are an inch or more long; the twigs drooping, it is → **EUROPEAN LARCH** ***Larix decidua***

If the cones are about ½ inch long, the twigs not drooping, it is → **AMERICAN LARCH or TAMARACK** ***Larix laricina***

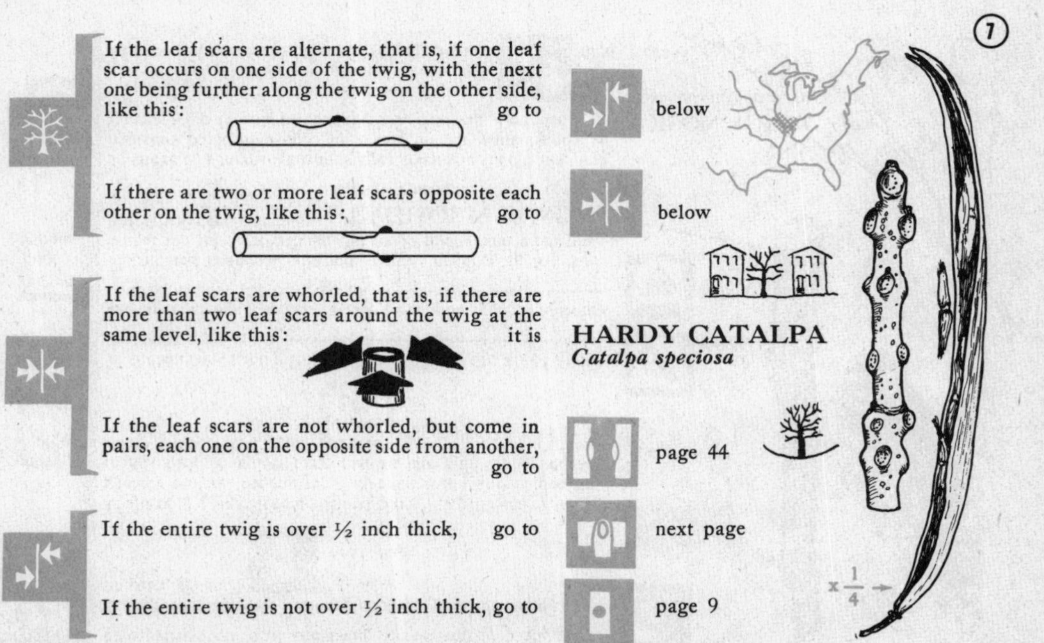

If the leaf scars are alternate, that is, if one leaf scar occurs on one side of the twig, with the next one being further along the twig on the other side, like this: go to below

If there are two or more leaf scars opposite each other on the twig, like this: go to below

If the leaf scars are whorled, that is, if there are more than two leaf scars around the twig at the same level, like this: it is

HARDY CATALPA
Catalpa speciosa

If the leaf scars are not whorled, but come in pairs, each one on the opposite side from another, go to page 44

If the entire twig is over ½ inch thick, go to next page

If the entire twig is not over ½ inch thick, go to page 9

(8)

If a cross-section of the twig shows mostly pith, go to — below

If a cross-section of the twig shows a smaller proportion of pith, go to — next page

If there is a line, like a fold of bark (stipule scar), completely encircling the twig at each bud; and if the terminal bud is much larger than the side buds, it is a MAGNOLIA. Go to — page 42

If there is not such a line, and if the buds are all of about the same size, go to → below

If the leaf scar is somewhat heart-shaped, or shield-shaped, below the bud, go to → below

If the leaf scar is C-shaped, almost encircling the bud, and if the new growth on the twigs is covered with matted, woolly hair, it is

STAGHORN SUMAC
Rhus typhina

If there is a terminal bud larger than the side buds, and mottled bark in a tree in a bog, wash your hands in strong soap if you have handled the twig, because it is

POISON SUMAC
Toxicodendron vernix

If there is no terminal bud, relax, Go to — next page

If the leaf scars are marked with 3 to 5 vein scars; and two buds, depressed, looking like craters on the Moon, push out above the leaf scar; and if the pith is thick and salmon-colored, it is

KENTUCKY COFFEE TREE
Gymnocladus dioicus

(Mature bark has sharp, curved ridges.)

If the leaf scars are marked with many vein scars, like dots, it is

TREE OF HEAVEN
Ailanthus altissima

(In early winter look for the heavy clusters of winged seeds. This tree usually grows in the soot and grime of cities. The bark is smooth, with pale stripes.)

If the twig is stout and tough, difficult to break, with light-colored lenticels and tan or brown pith; and if the leaf scars are large, pale, and somewhat heart-shaped or shield-shaped; and the end bud is larger than the side buds, go to page 36

If the twig does not have this combination of characteristics, go to next page

(10)

If several buds of different sizes are clustered irregularly at the tip of the twig, like this go to below

If the buds are not clustered, go to below

If there are many light-colored, raised lenticels that become horizontal on the older parts of the tree, and if there are three vein scars on the leaf scar, it is → **PIN CHERRY** *Prunus pensylvanica*

(Pin-like flowering spurs appear in second year. Inner bark is bright green, with bitter taste.)

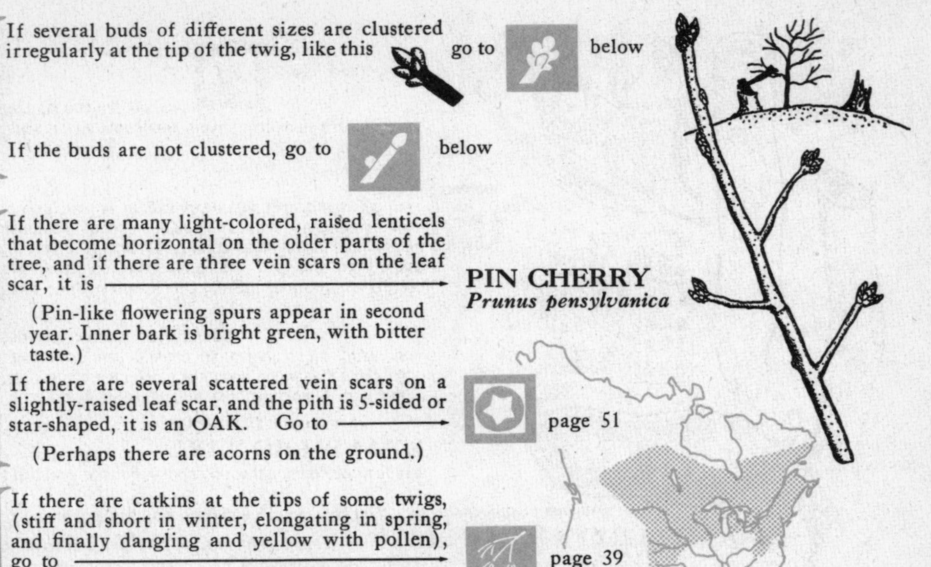

If there are several scattered vein scars on a slightly-raised leaf scar, and the pith is 5-sided or star-shaped, it is an OAK. Go to → page 51

(Perhaps there are acorns on the ground.)

If there are catkins at the tips of some twigs, (stiff and short in winter, elongating in spring, and finally dangling and yellow with pollen), go to → page 39

If there are no catkins, go to next page

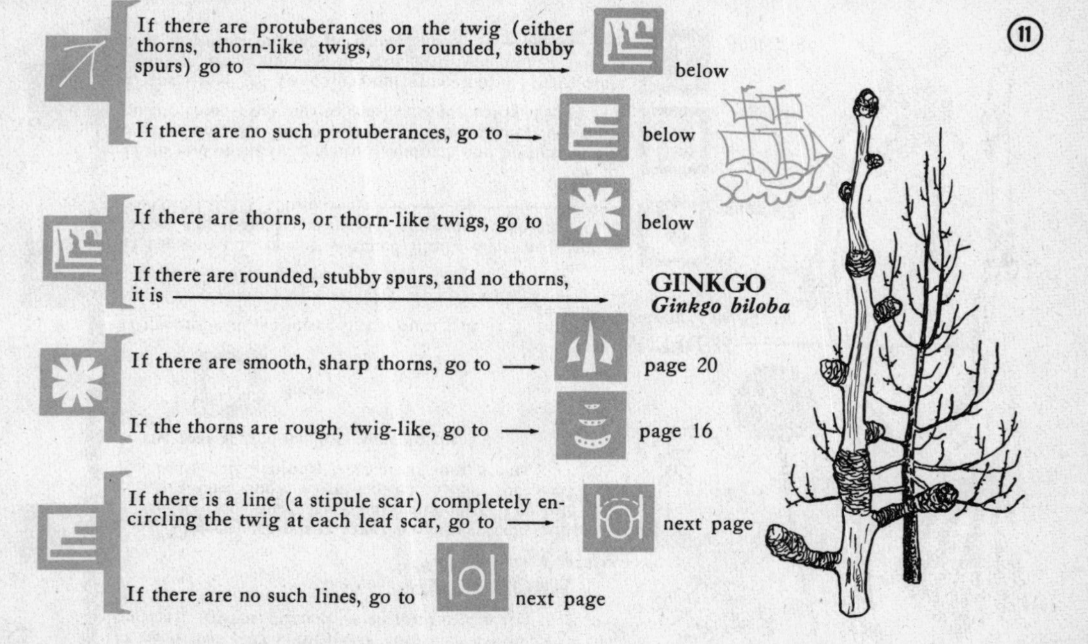

If there are protuberances on the twig (either thorns, thorn-like twigs, or rounded, stubby spurs) go to → below

If there are no such protuberances, go to → below

If there are thorns, or thorn-like twigs, go to → below

If there are rounded, stubby spurs, and no thorns, it is → **GINKGO** ***Ginkgo biloba***

If there are smooth, sharp thorns, go to → page 20

If the thorns are rough, twig-like, go to → page 16

If there is a line (a stipule scar) completely encircling the twig at each leaf scar, go to → next page

If there are no such lines, go to next page

⑫

If each leaf scar completely encircles a bud; and the buds are brown, conical, with only one scale, it is

SYCAMORE
Platanus occidentalis

(The smooth white inner bark has flecks and patches of older bark adhering to it. The big branches look whitewashed. Look for seed balls still hanging from their long stems.)

If the leaf scar does not encircle the bud, go to

below

If the end bud is shaped like a duck bill, it is

TULIP TREE
Liriodendron Tulipifera

(The main trunk usually rises straight from base to tree-top.)

If the end bud is not flattened like a duck bill, but is large, egg-shaped, arrowhead-shaped, or oblong, it is MAGNOLIA. Go to ⟶  page 42

If the end of the twig is blunt, slanted, and budless (with neither terminal bud nor lateral bud; or if there are pods on the tree, it belongs to the Legume family. Go to page 34

If the tip of the twig does not appear blunt or budless (though there may be no true terminal bud, a lateral bud is almost in that position), go to ⟶  next page

If each bud is enclosed in a single cap-like scale, it is a willow. Go to ⟶ page 32

(Usually a tree of bottomlands, with slender twigs.)

If the bud is not enclosed in a single cap-like scale, go to ⟶ below

If the bud has no scales at all, but is covered with dense, dark hairs, it is ⟶ **PAWPAW** *Asimina triloba*

If the bud has scales, go to ⟶ below

If the bud is enclosed in 2 scales (hairy inner scales sometimes show at the tip), go to ⟶ page 28

If the bud is enclosed in more than 2 scales, go to below

If the buds are at least 4 times as long as thick, go to ⟶ next page

If buds are not so proportioned, go to ⟶ next page

If the end bud is larger than the side buds, go to ⟶ below

If the end buds are not noticeably larger than the side buds, go to ⟶ next page

If the end buds are long, ½ inch to ¾ inch, tapering very gradually, on a stout twig, go to ⟶ page 30

If the buds are less than ½ inch long, go to ⟶ page 16

If the buds are almost an inch long, grow at a wide angle from the twig, and show 8 or more scales, it is a BEECH. Go to ⟶ below

If the buds lie close against the twig, and are about ½ inch long, showing 5 to 6 scales, it is

(Usually a small tree, often shrub-like, with bark gray with darker long streaks.)

SERVICEBERRY
JUNEBERRY
Amelanchier arborea

If the bark is a light satiny gray, and it is a native tree of rich forests, it is ⟶ **AMERICAN BEECH** ***Fagus grandifolia***

If the bark is a darker, pewter-gray, and it is a planted tree, on a lawn, it is ⟶ **EUROPEAN BEECH** ***Fagus sylvatica***

illustration on next page

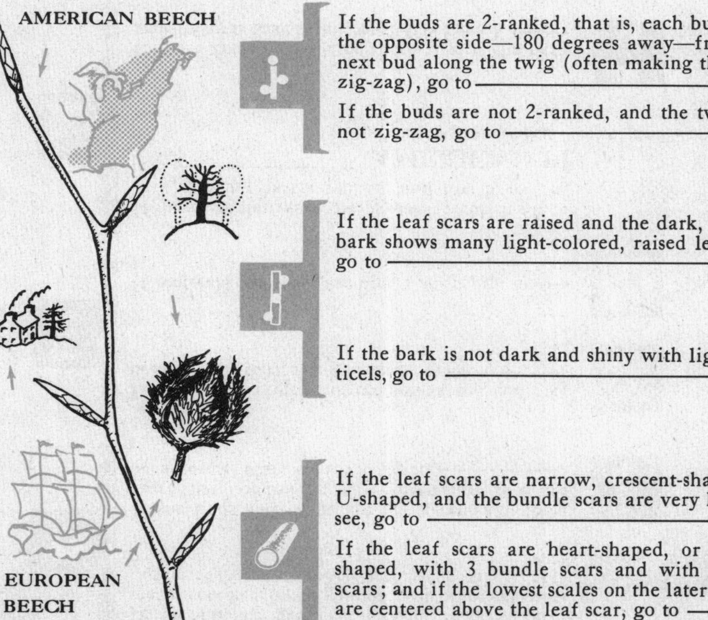

15

If the buds are 2-ranked, that is, each bud is on the opposite side—180 degrees away—from the next bud along the twig (often making the twig zig-zag), go to ⟶ page 24

If the buds are not 2-ranked, and the twigs do not zig-zag, go to ⟶ below

If the leaf scars are raised and the dark, smooth bark shows many light-colored, raised lenticels, go to ⟶ next page

If the bark is not dark and shiny with light lenticels, go to ⟶ below

If the leaf scars are narrow, crescent-shaped or U-shaped, and the bundle scars are very hard to see, go to ⟶ page 19

If the leaf scars are heart-shaped, or shield-shaped, with 3 bundle scars and with stipule scars; and if the lowest scales on the lateral buds are centered above the leaf scar, go to ⟶ page 22

If the buds are green or reddish, on green, aromatic, root beer-tasting twigs; side branches turning up at their tips; one bundle scar only, it is **SASSAFRAS** *Sassafras albidum*

If the buds and twigs are not green, and have more than one bundle scar—often hard to count because leaf scars are small, go to → below

If lenticels are light-colored and raised, conspicuous against dark shiny bark, go to → below

If lenticels and bark are not as above, go to → page 18

If there are thorn-like twigs, dark, reddish-black bark, peeling on the trunks; and low branches, it is → **AMERICAN PLUM** *Prunus americana*

If there are no thorn-like twigs, and if the bark and the buds taste bitter, go to CHERRY → next page

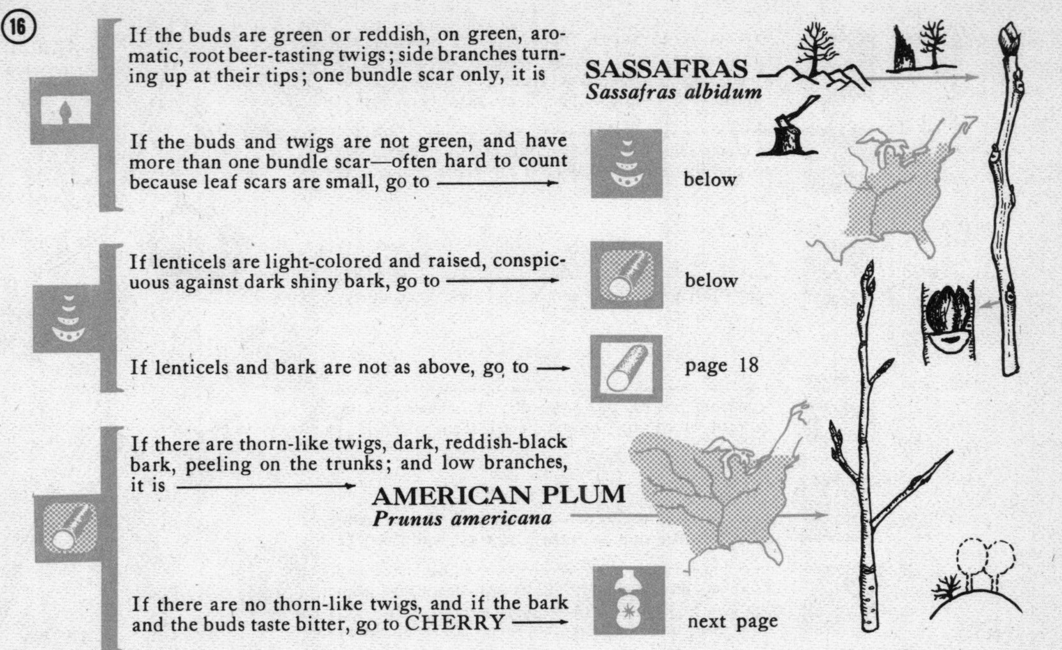

If the buds have gray-margined scales, and the lenticels do not elongate horizontally, a small tree, it is

CHOKE CHERRY
Prunus virginiana

If the bud scales are not gray-margined, and the lenticels *do* elongate horizontally, go to  below

If the bark is dark, peeling in roundish flakes on older trunks, a big tree, it is

BLACK CHERRY
Prunus serotina

If the bark is lustrous orange-red, with the lenticels orange and conspicuous and powdery on the surface, and if a few buds are clustered at the tip of the twig, it is

PIN CHERRY
Prunus pensylvanica

(illustration on p. 10)

If the leaf scar is broadly crescent-shaped or triangular, showing 3 bundle scars, or 3 groups of bundle scars, go to → below

If the leaf scar is very narrow, and bundle scars are very hard to see; many-scarred fruiting spurs, or thorn-like twigs often present, go to → next page

If the leaf scar is brown with lighter bundle scars; and buds are dark with downy tips; end bud only slightly larger than side buds, it is

SOUR GUM or TUPELO
Nyssa sylvatica

(Lower branches are usually declined. Mature trunks have "alligator bark.")

If the leaf scars are not as above; and the pith is 5-sided, go to → below

If bundle scars are white rings with dark center; twigs shiny, aromatic; branchlets developing corky ridges; trunk sometimes exuding an aromatic gum; woody, ball-like fruits hanging on through the winter, it is

SWEET GUM
Liquidambar Styraciflua

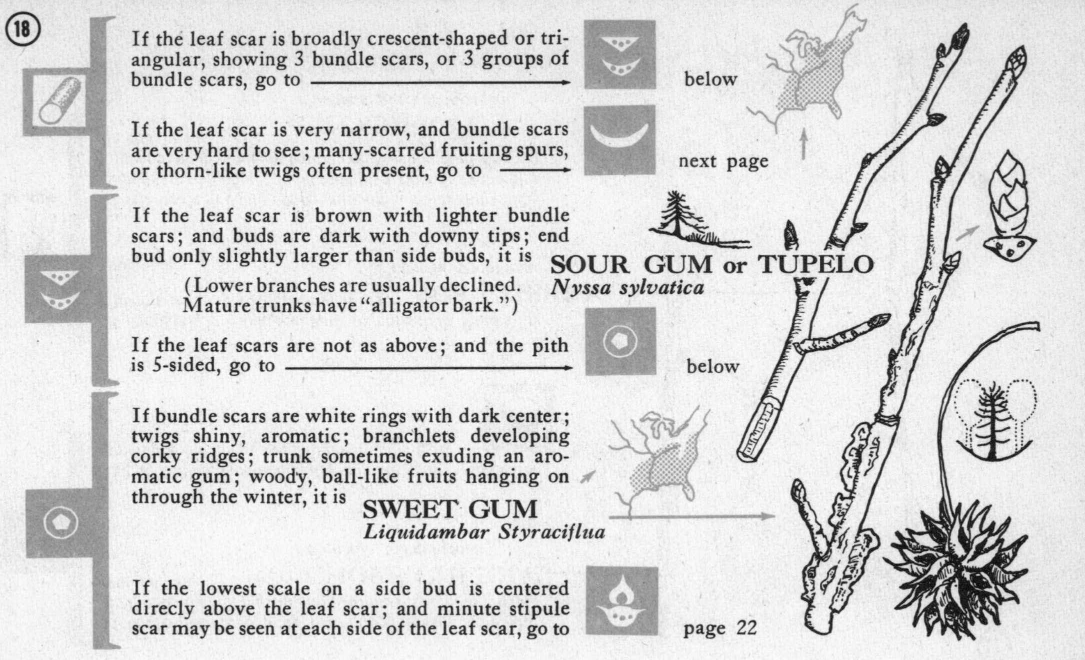

If the lowest scale on a side bud is centered direcly above the leaf scar; and minute stipule scar may be seen at each side of the leaf scar, go to page 22

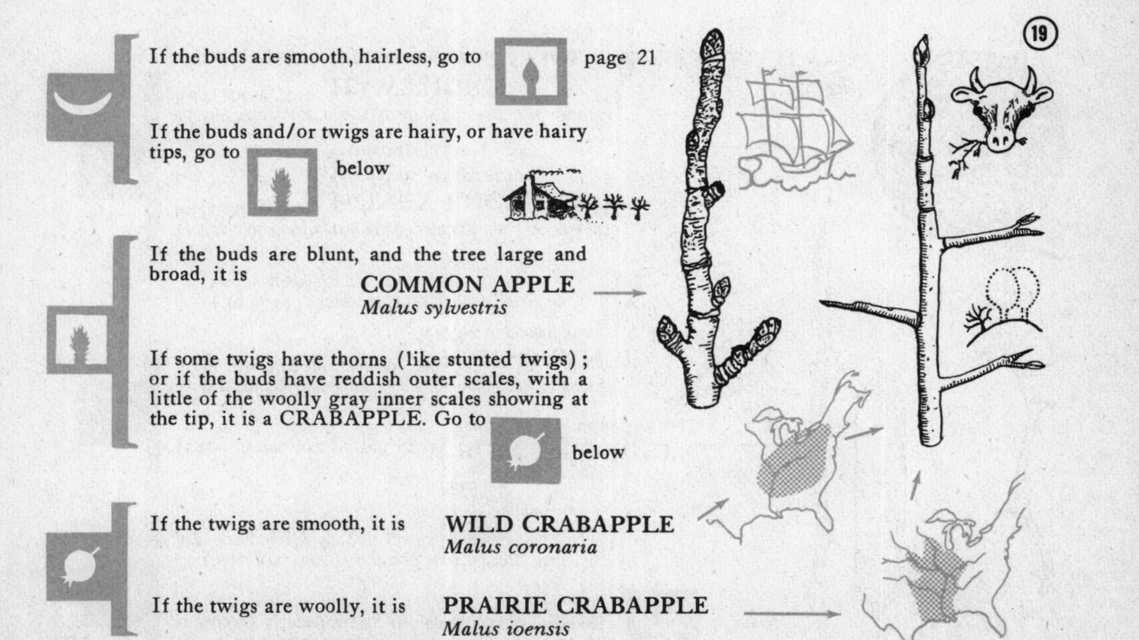

If the buds are smooth, hairless, go to page 21

If the buds and/or twigs are hairy, or have hairy tips, go to below

If the buds are blunt, and the tree large and broad, it is **COMMON APPLE** *Malus sylvestris*

If some twigs have thorns (like stunted twigs); or if the buds have reddish outer scales, with a little of the woolly gray inner scales showing at the tip, it is a CRABAPPLE. Go to below

If the twigs are smooth, it is **WILD CRABAPPLE** *Malus coronaria*

If the twigs are woolly, it is **PRAIRIE CRABAPPLE** *Malus ioensis*

20

If the thorns are short (less than ¾ inch), and regularly spaced along the twig, go to ⟶ below

If there are thorns over ¾ inch long, and they are irregularly spaced go to below

If the thorns are paired, it is **BLACK LOCUST** *Robinia Pseudo-Acacia*

If the thorns are single, on a twig that zig-zags from thorn to thorn, it is **OSAGE ORANGE** *Maclura pomifera*

(Some old Osage Orange trees also have warty growths on the twigs.)

If some of the thorns are branched, and no winter buds show, it is **HONEY LOCUST** *Gleditsia triacanthos*
(illustration on p. 34)

If the thorns are not branched, and the winter buds show, it is **HAWTHORN**
(illustration on next page)

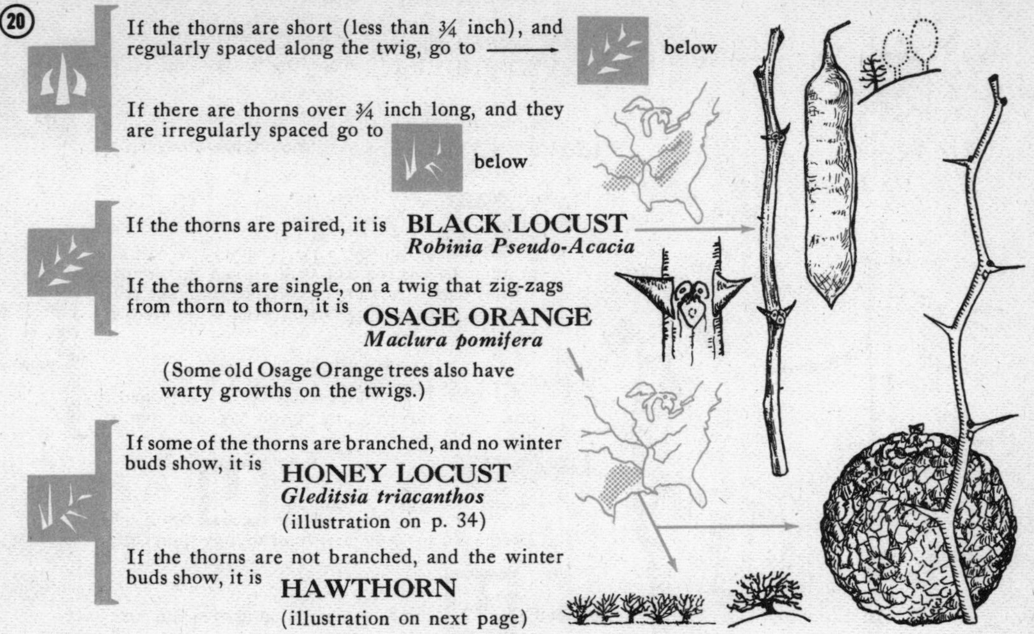

21

If the buds are smooth, pointed; and side buds are pointed away from the twig, it is **COMMON PEAR**
Pyrus communis

If the buds are globular, and red, it is **HAWTHORN**

Usually this tree bears sharp smooth thorns.

Hawthorns are far too numerous to cover here. You will probably be seeing one of these more common forms:

DOWNY HAWTHORN
Crataegus mollis

THICKET HAWTHORN
Crataegus pruinosa

COCKSPUR HAWTHORN
Crataegus crus-galli

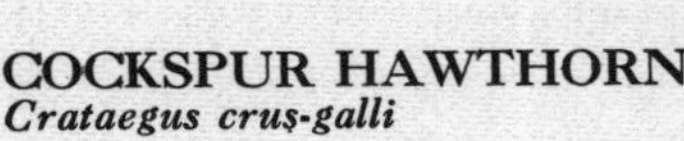

WASHINGTON HAWTHORN
Crataegus Phaenopyrum

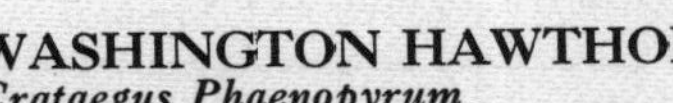

DOTTED HAWTHORN
Crataegus punctata

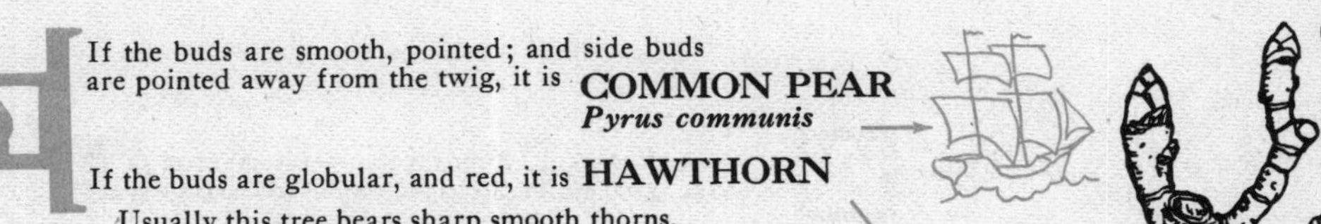

If the buds and twigs have a dense, white, cottony covering, easily rubbed off; and the tree has smooth, whitish bark with black markings, it is ⟶

WHITE POPLAR
Populus alba

(There is a narrow form with ascending branches called Bolleana Poplar.)

If the tree has no such dense white covering, and it is either spire-shaped or small, go to ⟶  below

If the tree is spire-shaped, with many ascending small branches, it is

LOMBARDY POPLAR
Populus nigra **variety *italica***

If the trees are small (with light gray bark, darker at the base), often forming colonies, go to ⟶ next page

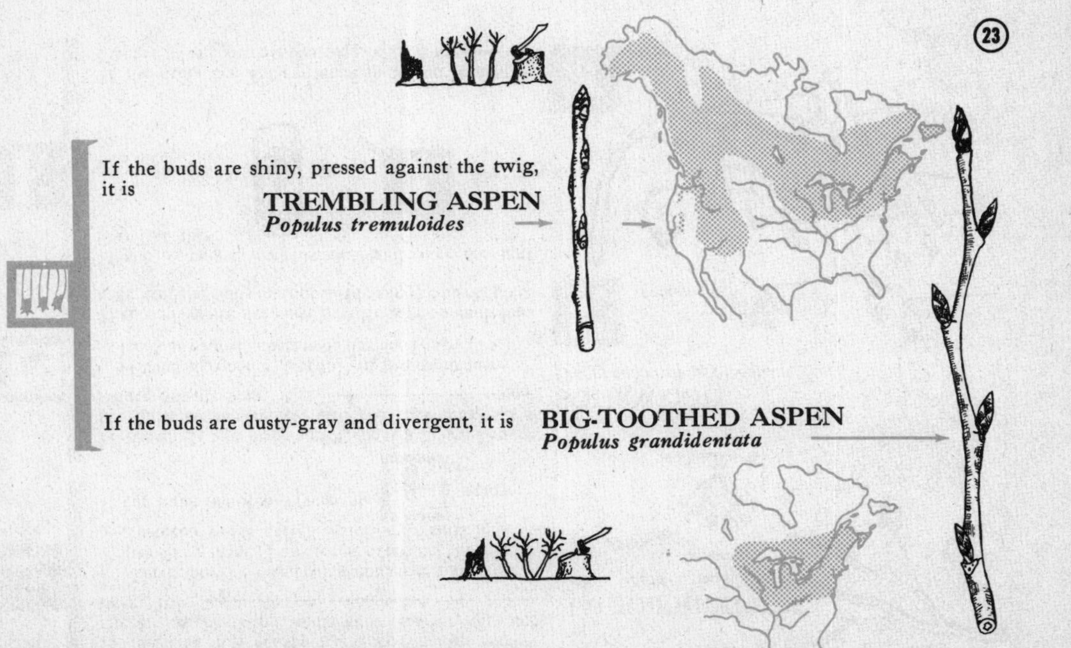

If the buds are shiny, pressed against the twig, it is

TREMBLING ASPEN
Populus tremuloides

If the buds are dusty-gray and divergent, it is

BIG-TOOTHED ASPEN
Populus grandidentata

If the tree has warty bark, becoming warty-ridged on the trunk, with very slender, zig-zag twigs, it is ——→

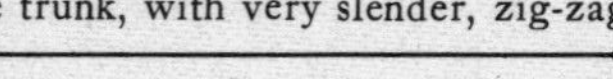

HACKBERRY
Celtis occidentalis

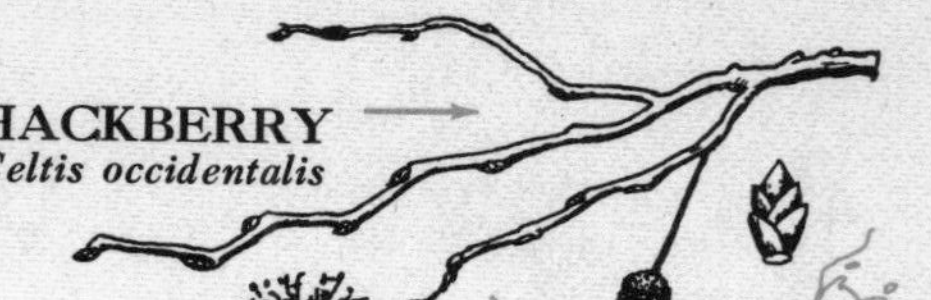

(Dark, cherry-like fruit sometimes hangs on into the winter. The tree is often marked by clustered twigs called witches brooms.)

If the bark is not warty, go to  below

If the buds are very small, partially sunken in the bark of the twigs; and the leaf scar has a single bundle scar, it is ——→

SOURWOOD
Oxydendrum arboreum

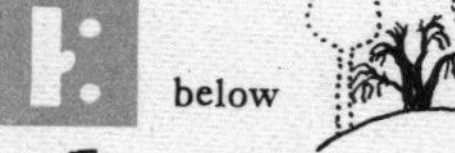

(Often shrublike, but tall in the mountains. Look for loose clusters of dry seed capsules.)

If there is more than one bundle scar on each leaf scar, and the buds are not hidden in the bark, go to below

If the buds are roughly centered over the leaf scar like this:

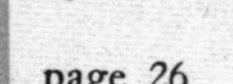

go to next page

If the buds are *not* centered over the leaf scar, but are to one side, it is an ELM. Go to ——→ page 26

If the side buds are about the same width as the twig, the twigs light brown, go to → below

(A full-sized tree with milky juice in spring.)

If the side buds are wider than the twig; the leaf scars small, narrow, with unequal stipule scars, go to → below

(A small tree without milky juice in spring.)

If the twigs are downy, and if the buds are longer than wide with with brown-margined bud scales, and spread away from the twig, it is **RED MULBERRY** *Morus rubra*

If the twigs are not downy; and if the buds are pressed against the twig, almost as wide as long, often with additional small buds on either side, it is **WHITE MULBERRY** *Morus alba*

If there are about 6 scales on each bud; and if the bark peels vertically in ½ inch strips, it is **IRONWOOD**
(illustration on p. 39)

If the trunk is like grey stone sculptured into muscles and sinews, with about 12 scales on each bud, it is **BLUE BEECH**
AMERICAN HORNBEAM *Carpinus caroliniana*

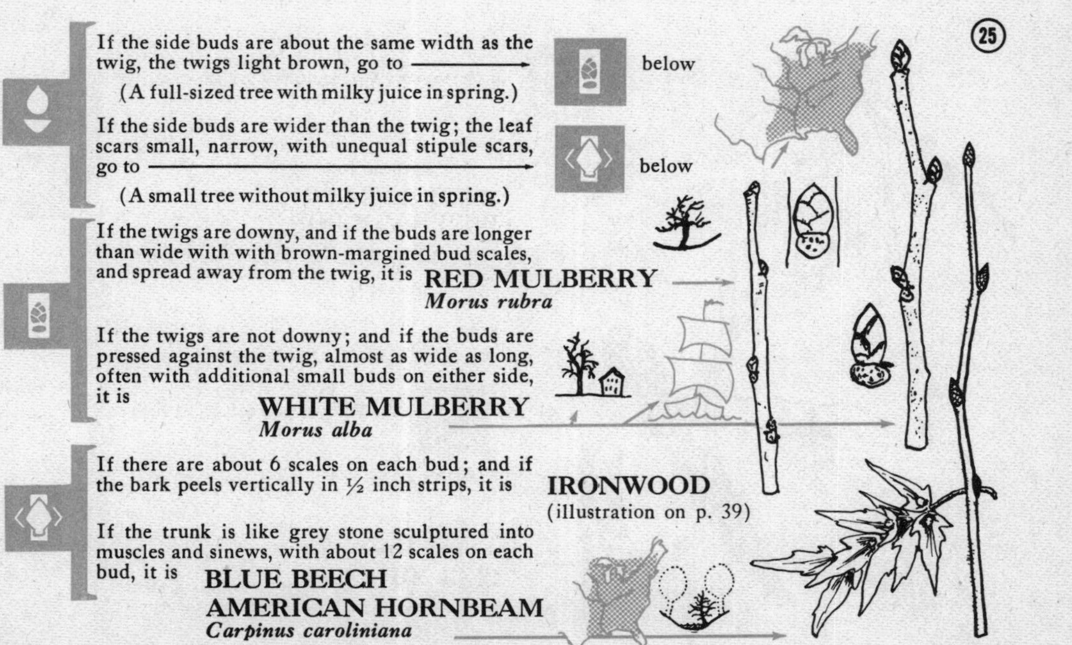

If the older twigs are corky-winged, or have corky growths, it is

CORK ELM
Ulmus Thomasi

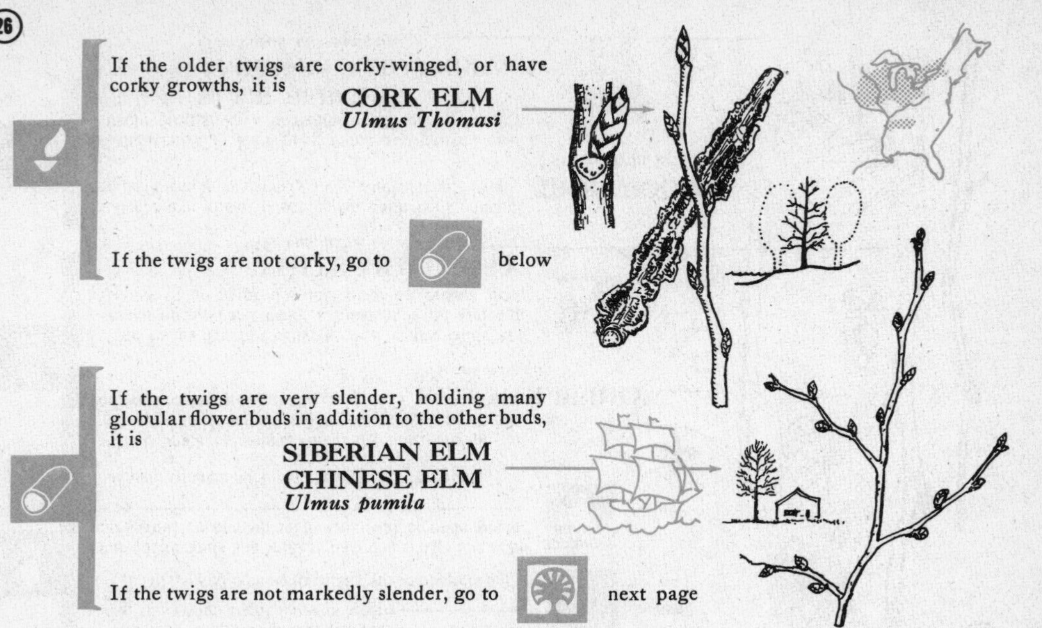

If the twigs are not corky, go to [symbol] below

If the twigs are very slender, holding many globular flower buds in addition to the other buds, it is

SIBERIAN ELM
CHINESE ELM
Ulmus pumila

If the twigs are not markedly slender, go to [symbol] next page

27

If the buds are downy and dark, and the inner bark slimy, it is

SLIPPERY ELM
Ulmus rubra

If the buds are brown, not downy, it is

AMERICAN ELM
Ulmus americana

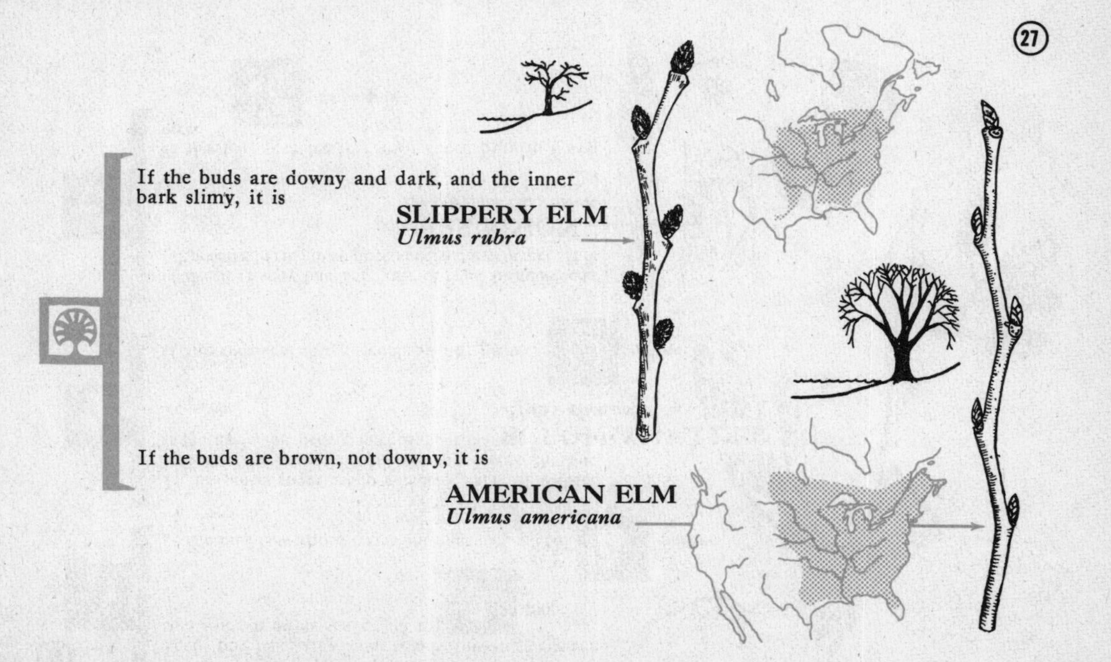

If the bud has hairy inner scales showing between two smooth outer scales, go to page 30

If the bud is without hairy inner scales, go to below

If the scales meet as do the two parts of a duck bill, and are smooth reddish-brown; and the bud is stalked; the pith triangular, it is **EUROPEAN ALDER** *Alnus glutinosa*

If the two scales are overlapping, go to below

If the leaf scar has only one curved bundle scar (shrivelled fruit may persist into the winter), it is **PERSIMMON** *Diospyros virginiana*

If the leaf scar has three or more bundle scars, go to next page

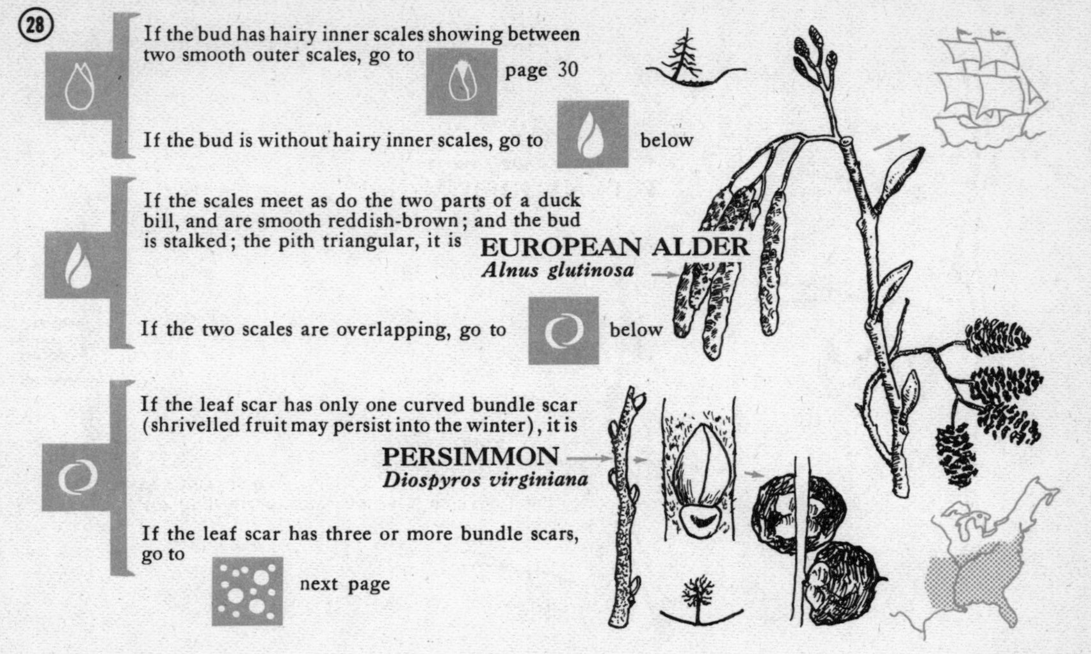

If the buds are chestnut-brown on a chestnut-brown twig; pith five-sided; lenticels numerous, raised, white, it is **CHESTNUT** *Castanea dentata* *

If the buds are red, or red and green; twig zig-zag, it is a BASSWOOD. Go to [symbol] below

(There may be round, tan fruits suspended from a leaf-like wing.)

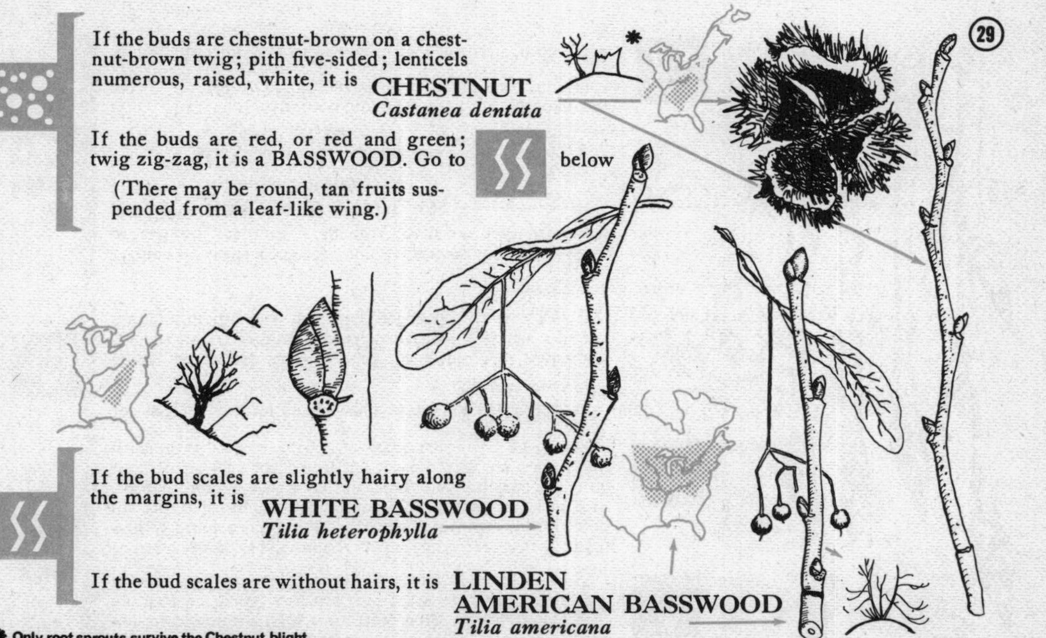

If the bud scales are slightly hairy along the margins, it is **WHITE BASSWOOD** *Tilia heterophylla*

If the bud scales are without hairs, it is **LINDEN AMERICAN BASSWOOD** *Tilia americana*

* Only root sprouts survive the Chestnut blight.

If the end bud is hairy and has its tip turned slightly to one side; and the bark is marked with conspicuous light-colored lenticels; and the leaf scars are narrow, raised, it is a MOUNTAIN ASH. Go to  below

If the end bud is symmetrical; leaf scar crescent-shaped, with 3 bundle scars (or 3 groups of bundle scars); and the small branches are light-colored, smooth; the pith 5-sided; and a small stipule scar may be seen on each side of the leaf scar; and the lowest scale on a side bud is centered and directly above the leaf scar, go to ⟶  below

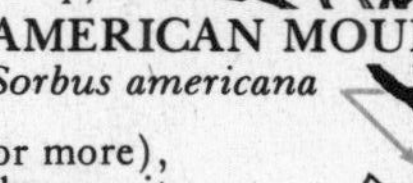

If the buds and twigs are woolly, it is **EUROPEAN MOUNTAIN-ASH** *Sorbus aucuparia*

If the twigs are smooth, and the outer bud scales are sticky; but the inner scales, protruding at the tip, are hairy, and the tree is rather shrublike, it is **AMERICAN MOUNTAIN-ASH** *Sorbus americana*

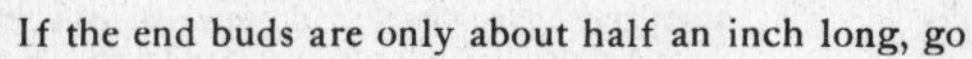

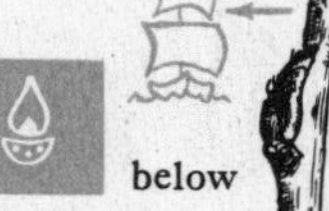

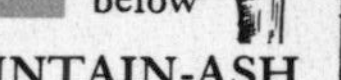

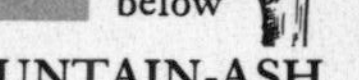

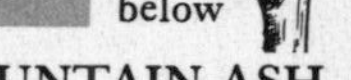

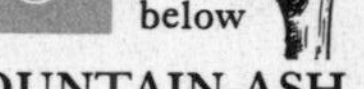

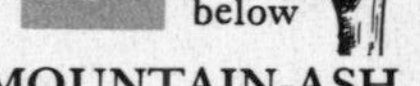

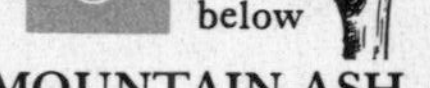

If the end buds are very long (often an inch or more), excessively resinous, fragrant; twigs reddish brown, it is either: **BALSAM POPLAR** ***Populus balsamifera***

or: **BALM OF GILEAD** ***Populus gileadensis***

(the cultivated horticultural tree grown only from cuttings or sprouts—maturing no seeds)

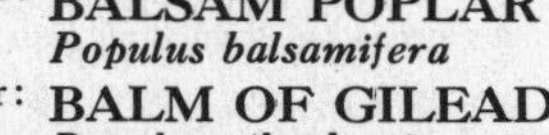

If the end buds are only about half an inch long, go to  next page

If the buds taper to both ends; twigs yellow to yellow-brown, go to ⟨◊⟩ below

If the buds are broadly egg-shaped; twigs brownish-gray, it is

SWAMP COTTONWOOD
Populus heterophylla

If the buds are sticky, it is

EASTERN COTTONWOOD
Populus deltoides

If the buds are slightly hairy, it is

PLAINS COTTONWOOD
Populus deltoides occidentalis

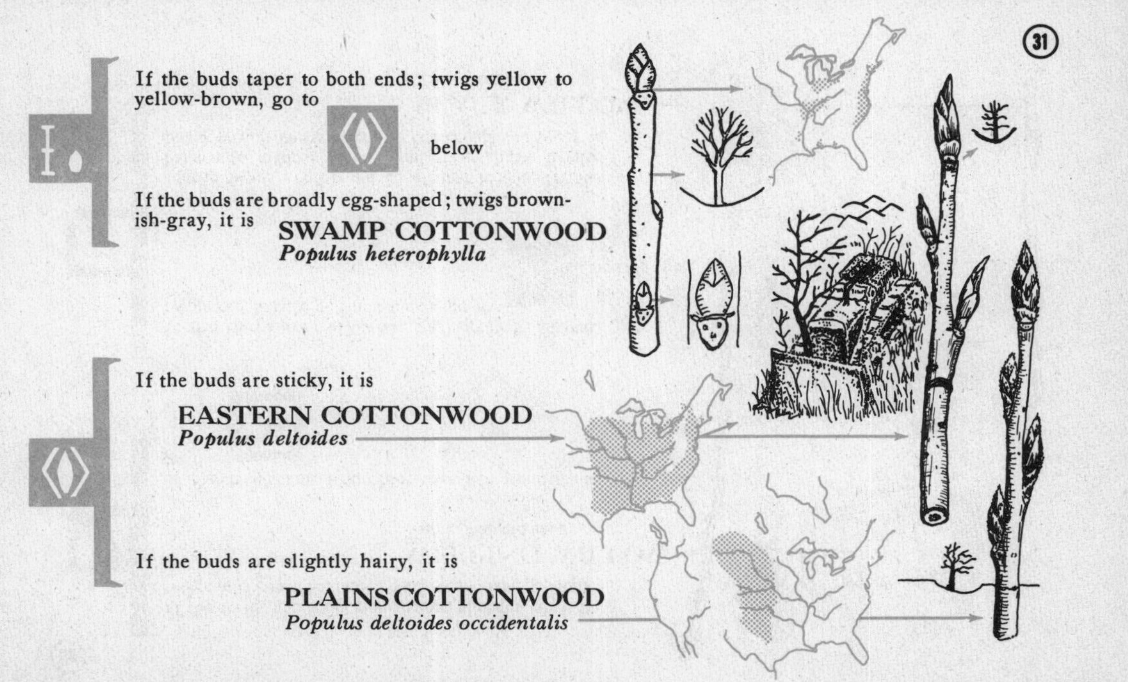

If the twigs are long, pendulous, slender, and the twigs and branchlets are yellow to orange, it is

WEEPING WILLOW
Salix babylonica

If the twigs and branchlets are not pendulous, go to below

If the twigs are yellowish, bark gray to brown, twigs not brittle at their bases, go to next page

If the twigs are brown to almost black; trunks brown to almost black; and twigs have brittle bases which cause them to break off easily, it is

BLACK WILLOW
Salix nigra

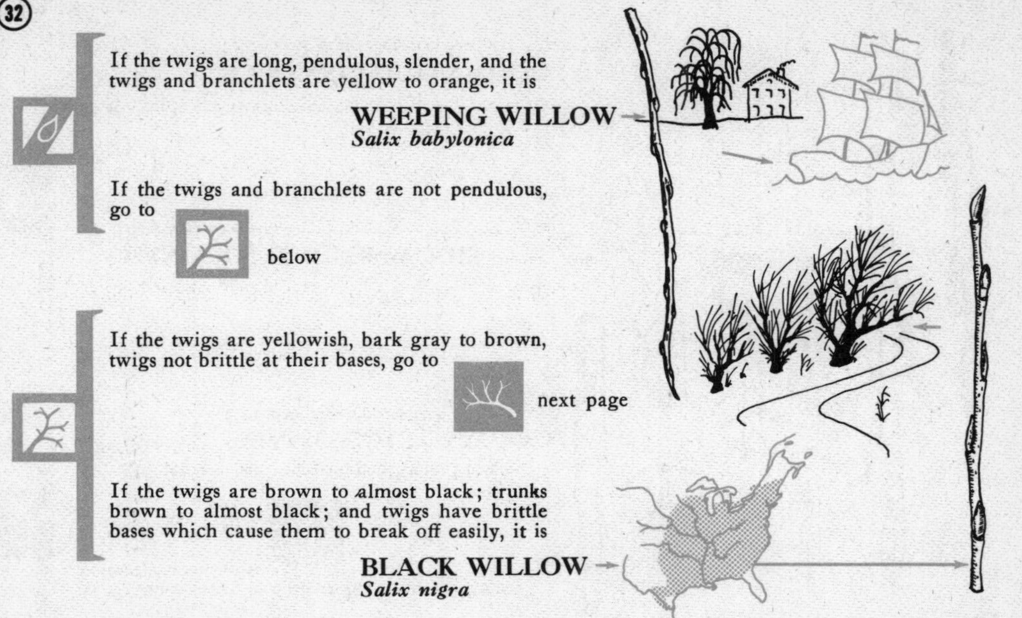

If the twigs are greenish to yellow, with fine silky hairs, it is

WHITE WILLOW
Salix alba

(One of the varieties of White Willow, selected for especially golden color, is known as Golden Willow.)

If twigs are yellow to yellow-brown, with large buds; leaf-scars U-shaped, it is

PEACH-LEAVED WILLOW
Salix amygdaloides

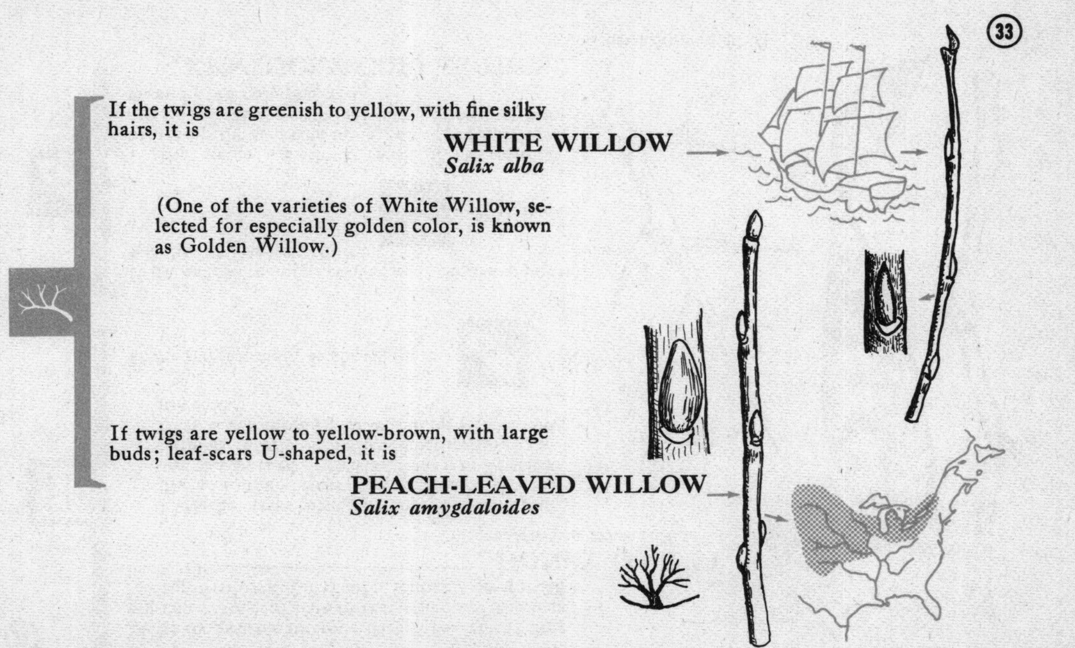

If the twigs are a lustrous red-brown, and if they zig-zag from leaf scar to leaf scar; and the tree has light-colored, horizontal lenticels on smooth bark, it is ——→

HONEY LOCUST
Gleditsia triacanthos

(Mature trees usually have a spreading, dished top, and bear long, branched thorns, and flat, curved or twisted pods 6 to 8 inches long. A thornless, podless horticultural variety is commonly planted along streets and in parks.)

If the twigs are not as above, go to below

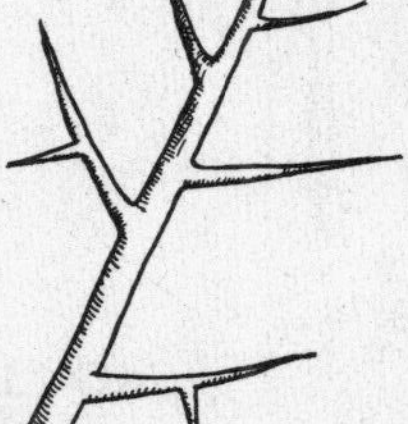

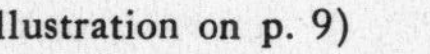

If the twigs are not as above; or if there are pods 4 inches or less long, go to next page

If the twigs are thick, with thick, salmon-colored pith; two side buds, one above the other, can be seen above each leaf scar, appearing sunken and crater-shaped, it is

KENTUCKY COFFEE-TREE

(illustration on p. 9)

If the tree has an extremely broad and flat top; or if there are pods with the lower tip extremely long-tapered, it is **MIMOSA SILK TREE** *Albizia julibrissin*

If the top is not extremely broad and flat, go to [key symbol] below

If each winter bud is almost completely encircled by a leaf scar, it is **YELLOWWOOD** *Cladrastis kentukea*

If the winter bud is not encircled; and if there are globular flower buds appearing in many places along the bark — even sometimes on the trunk — it is **REDBUD** *Cercis canadensis*

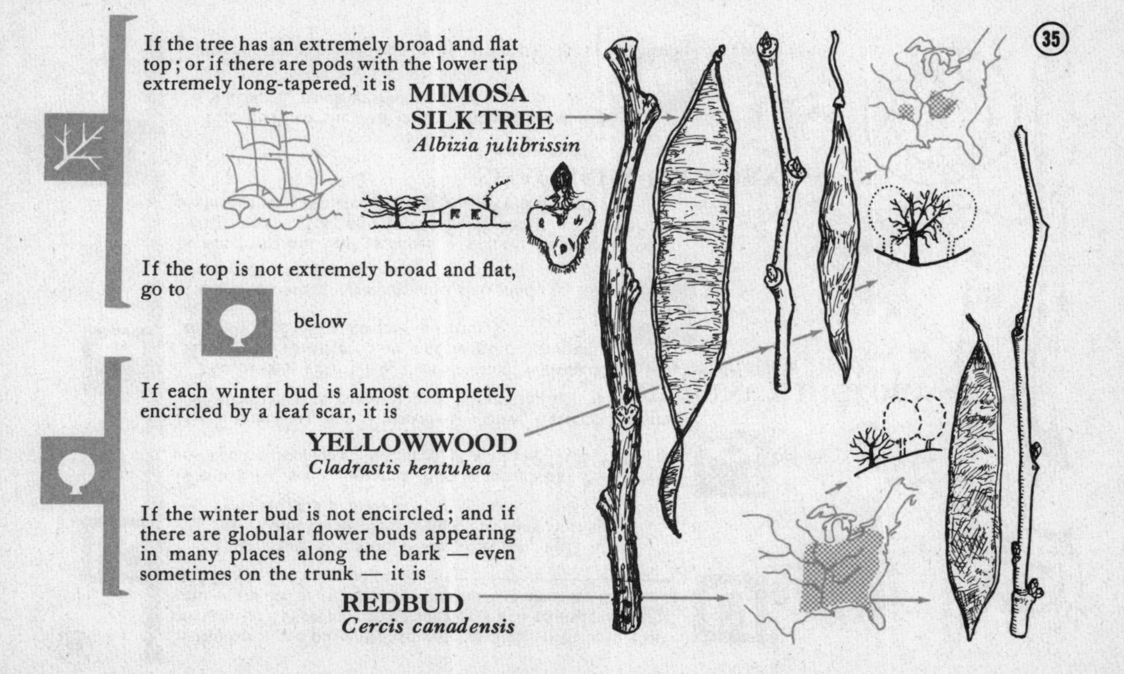

If the buds are pale and downy; and the pith is in thin, horizontal layers; and the lenticels are round; and the vein scars form three crescents on the leaf scar, it is a WALNUT. Go to page 38

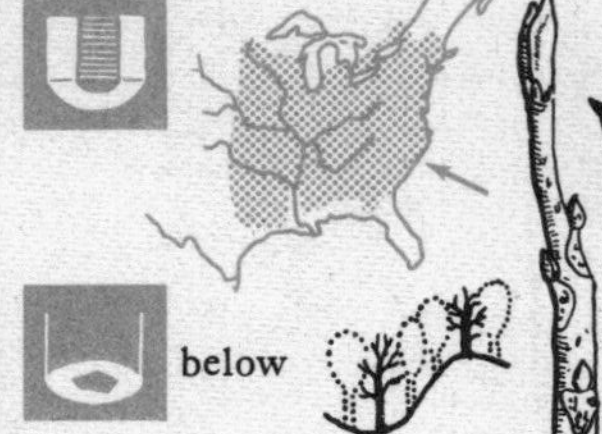

(Any nuts you find under the tree will have husks that do not split open, but they will stain your fingers brown.)

If the pith is not layered, but is somewhat five-sided, and the lenticels are elongated, it is a HICKORY. Go to below

If the terminal bud is mustard-yellow, flattened, granular, and the tree is usually on bottomland, it is

BITTERNUT HICKORY
Carya cordiformis

(The husk is yellowish, thin-skinned, 4-ribbed above the middle. The nut is globe-shaped, thin-shelled. The kernel is bitter.)

If the buds are not yellow and flattened, go to below

If the terminal bud is large ($\frac{1}{2}$ inch or more), with dark outer scales; and if the bark peels in great thick plates, giving the tree a shaggy appearance, it is

SHAGBARK HICKORY
Carya ovata

(The husk of the nut is dark brown; the nut is 4-ribbed, thickwalled.)

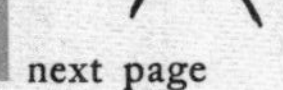

If the terminal bud is not large and dark, go to next page

If the twigs and buds are somewhat hairy, go to below

If the twigs and buds are smooth; side buds almost at right angles to the twig, it is

PIGNUT HICKORY
Carya glabra

(The end bud has loose, brown, outer scales. The fruit is pear-shaped.)

If the terminal bud has scales that meet without overlapping; the twig is reddish-brown; the bark has flattened, interlacing ridges; a bottomland tree, it is

PECAN
Carya illinoensis

(Husk is thin-skinned, 4-winged, often remains on the tree through winter; nut is thin-shelled, kernel sweet.)

If the terminal bud is almost globular, an upland tree, it is

MOCKERNUT HICKORY
Carya tomentosa

(Husk reddish-brown, thick; nut long, thick-walled.)

If the end bud is cream-colored and 1 to 2 times as long as it is wide; and the leaf scars have a velvety strip across the top; and the pith is dark brown, with layers as thick as the spaces between the layers; and if the bark has light-colored, flattened ridges making a network against the darker brown, it is

BUTTERNUT
WHITE WALNUT
Juglans cinerea

(The fruit is oblong.)

If the end bud is gray, short; and the side buds are set in a notch in the upper edge of the leaf scar; and if the pith is light brown, with layers much smaller than the spaces between the layers; and if the bark is dark and furrowed, it is

BLACK WALNUT
Juglans nigra

(The fruit is globular.)

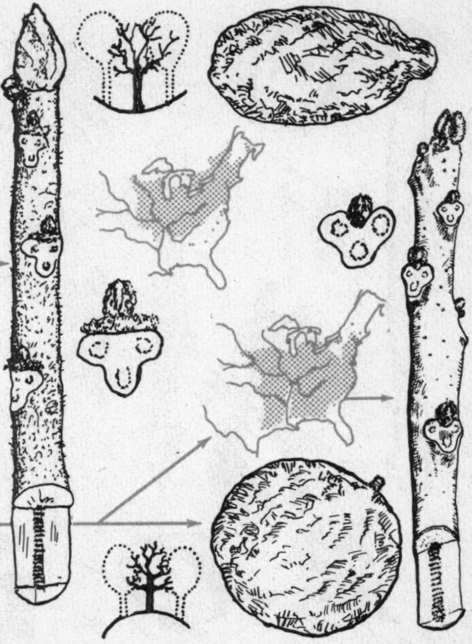

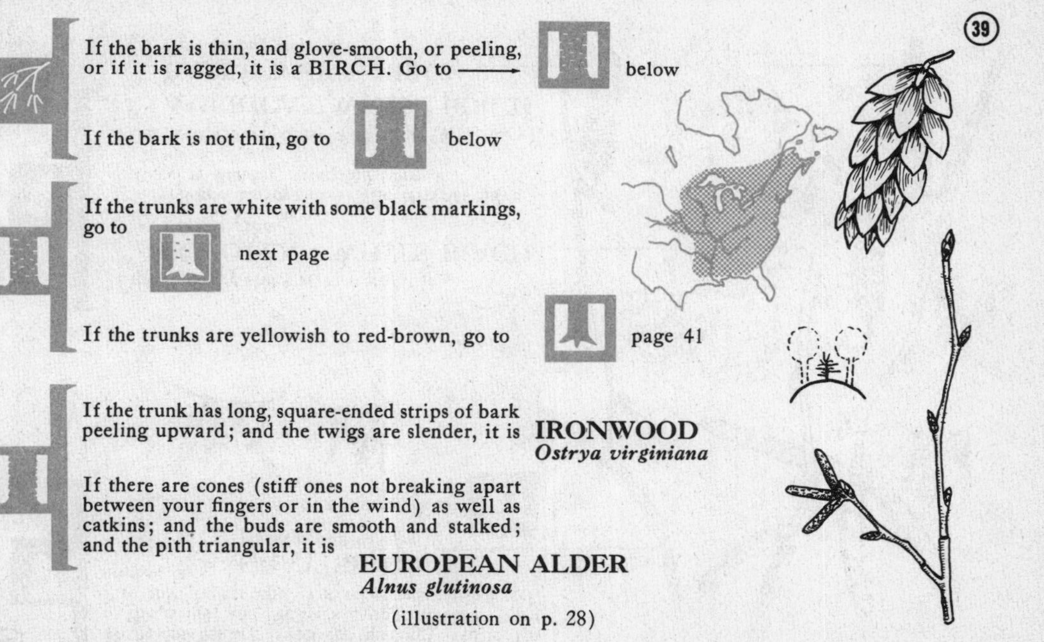

If the bark is thin, and glove-smooth, or peeling, or if it is ragged, it is a BIRCH. Go to ——→ below

If the bark is not thin, go to below

If the trunks are white with some black markings, go to next page

If the trunks are yellowish to red-brown, go to page 41

If the trunk has long, square-ended strips of bark peeling upward; and the twigs are slender, it is **IRONWOOD**
Ostrya virginiana

If there are cones (stiff ones not breaking apart between your fingers or in the wind) as well as catkins; and the buds are smooth and stalked; and the pith triangular, it is

EUROPEAN ALDER
Alnus glutinosa

(illustration on p. 28)

If the catkins are usually borne singly at the tips of the twigs; and the bark cannot be easily split into thin layers and is marked with black triangles, it is

GRAY BIRCH
Betula populifolia

If the bark peels into thin layers, go to [icon] below

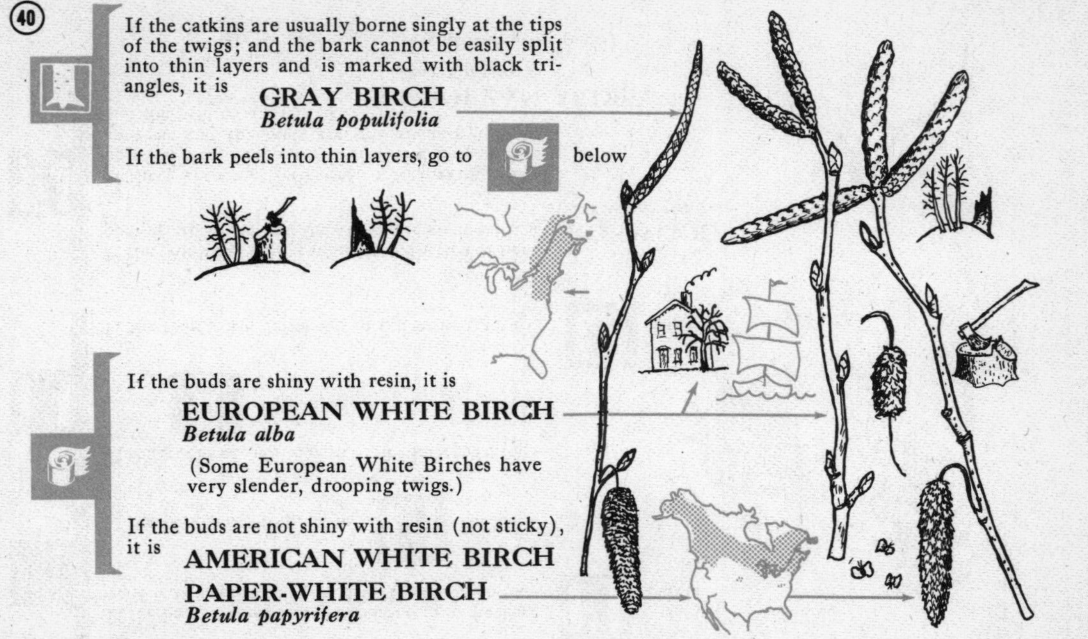

If the buds are shiny with resin, it is

EUROPEAN WHITE BIRCH
Betula alba

(Some European White Birches have very slender, drooping twigs.)

If the buds are not shiny with resin (not sticky), it is

AMERICAN WHITE BIRCH

PAPER-WHITE BIRCH
Betula papyrifera

If the bark is peeling, and silvery-yellow to copper-red, go to [symbol] below

If the bark is dark brown, not peeling, and the tree resembles a cherry tree (the twigs and buds are good to chew for a strong wintergreen taste; the cones are upright and thick and persist into the winter) it is

CHERRY BIRCH
Betula lenta

If the tree trunk is excessively ragged; and the twigs are hairy, it is

RED BIRCH
RIVER BIRCH
Betula nigra

(The cones have matured and fallen apart during the summer.)

If the bark is silvery to pale yellow, somewhat ragged, and the twigs have a slight wintergreen flavor, it is

YELLOW BIRCH
Betula alleghaniensis

If the end bud is hairy or woolly, go to — next page

If the end bud is smooth, go to — below

If the end bud is 1½ to 2 inches long; the bark thin, dark brown, it is **MOUNTAIN MAGNOLIA** *Magnolia Fraseri*

If the end bud is 1 inch long, with its tip pointed and curved; the bark thick, gray; the tree often branching at base, it is **UMBRELLA MAGNOLIA** *Magnolia tripetala*

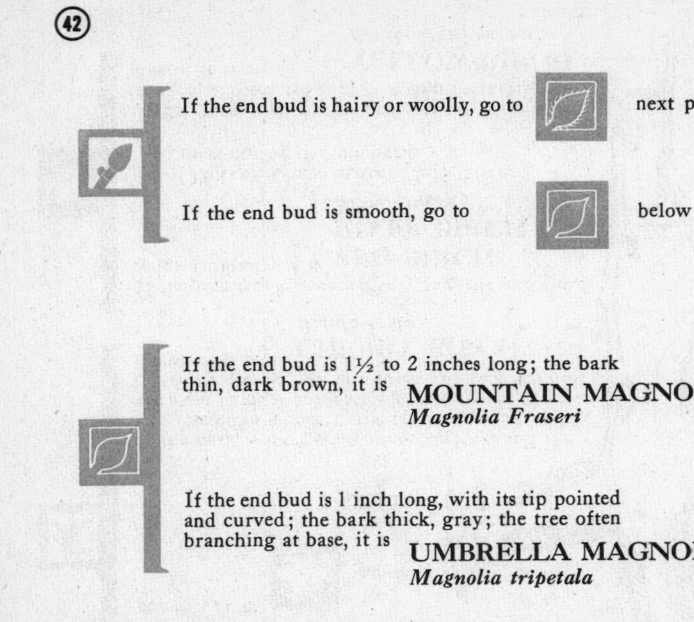

If the hairy covering is silky, go to [leaf symbol] below

If the hairy covering is woolly, matted; the buds are 1¾ to 2 inches long; the new growth light yellow-green, it is

LARGE-LEAVED MAGNOLIA
Magnolia macrophylla

If the end bud is oblong, ½ to ¾ inch long; densely covered with olive-gray hairs; the new growth a shining reddish-brown; the bark dark gray-brown, furrowed; the tree pyramidal, it is

CUCUMBER MAGNOLIA
Magnolia acuminata

If the end bud is egg-shaped, silky, gray; the new growth reddish-brown, the bark gray, smooth, it is

SAUCER MAGNOLIA
Magnolia soulangeana

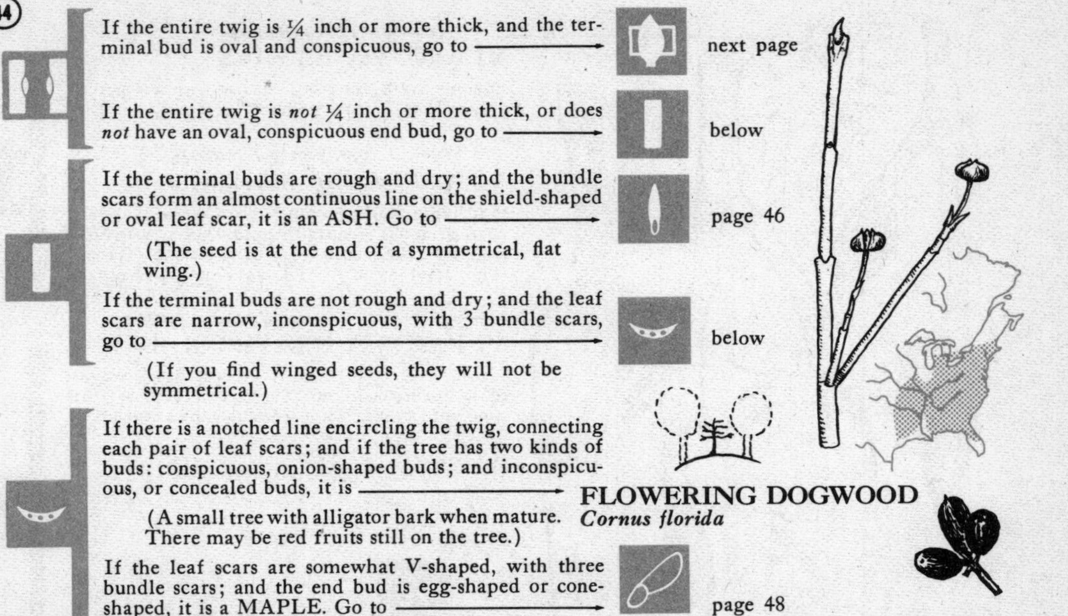

If the entire twig is ¼ inch or more thick, and the terminal bud is oval and conspicuous, go to → next page

If the entire twig is *not* ¼ inch or more thick, or does *not* have an oval, conspicuous end bud, go to → below

If the terminal buds are rough and dry; and the bundle scars form an almost continuous line on the shield-shaped or oval leaf scar, it is an ASH. Go to → page 46

(The seed is at the end of a symmetrical, flat wing.)

If the terminal buds are not rough and dry; and the leaf scars are narrow, inconspicuous, with 3 bundle scars, go to → below

(If you find winged seeds, they will not be symmetrical.)

If there is a notched line encircling the twig, connecting each pair of leaf scars; and if the tree has two kinds of buds: conspicuous, onion-shaped buds; and inconspicuous, or concealed buds, it is → **FLOWERING DOGWOOD** *Cornus florida*

(A small tree with alligator bark when mature. There may be red fruits still on the tree.)

If the leaf scars are somewhat V-shaped, with three bundle scars; and the end bud is egg-shaped or cone-shaped, it is a MAPLE. Go to → page 48

If the terminal bud is sticky, dark, smooth, and ¾ inch or more long, it is

HORSE CHESTNUT
Aesculus Hippocastanum

If the terminal bud is not as above, go to [symbol] below

If the bud scales are keeled, like a boat bottom, and have fine-hairy edges; and if the twigs, when bruised, have a fetid odor, it is

OHIO BUCKEYE
Aesculus glabra

(In fall look on the ground for the spiny husks holding single seeds with large, pale scars.)

If the bud scales are not keeled, it is

SWEET BUCKEYE
YELLOW BUCKEYE
Aesculus octandra

(In fall look on the ground for leathery husks which usually hold 2 smooth seeds.)

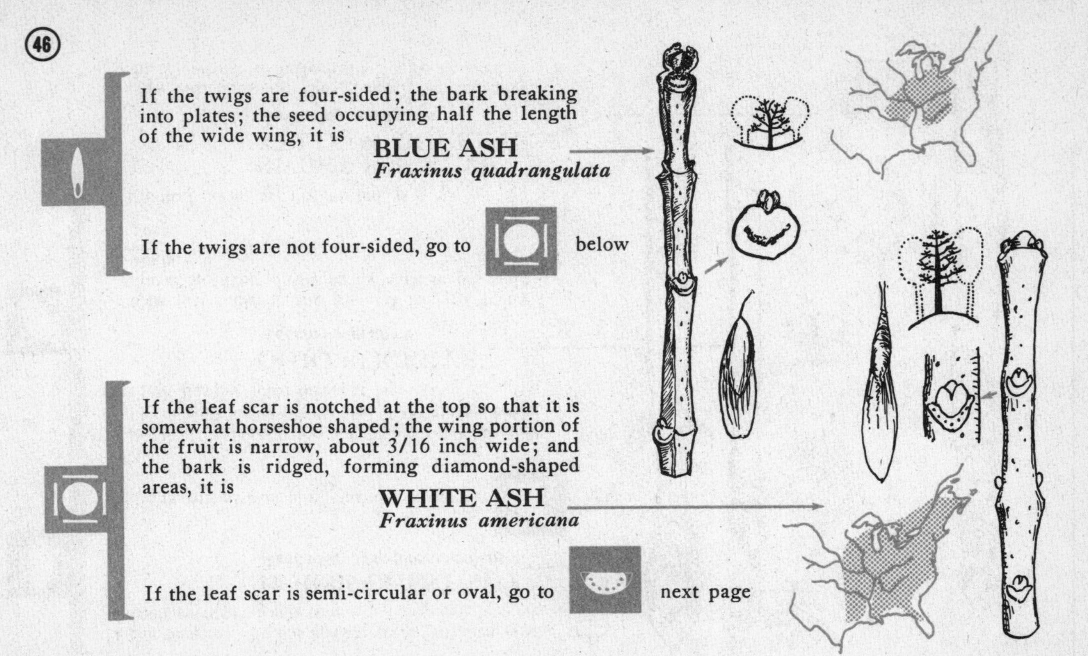

If the twigs are four-sided; the bark breaking into plates; the seed occupying half the length of the wide wing, it is

BLUE ASH
Fraxinus quadrangulata

If the twigs are not four-sided, go to below

If the leaf scar is notched at the top so that it is somewhat horseshoe shaped; the wing portion of the fruit is narrow, about 3/16 inch wide; and the bark is ridged, forming diamond-shaped areas, it is

WHITE ASH
Fraxinus americana

If the leaf scar is semi-circular or oval, go to next page

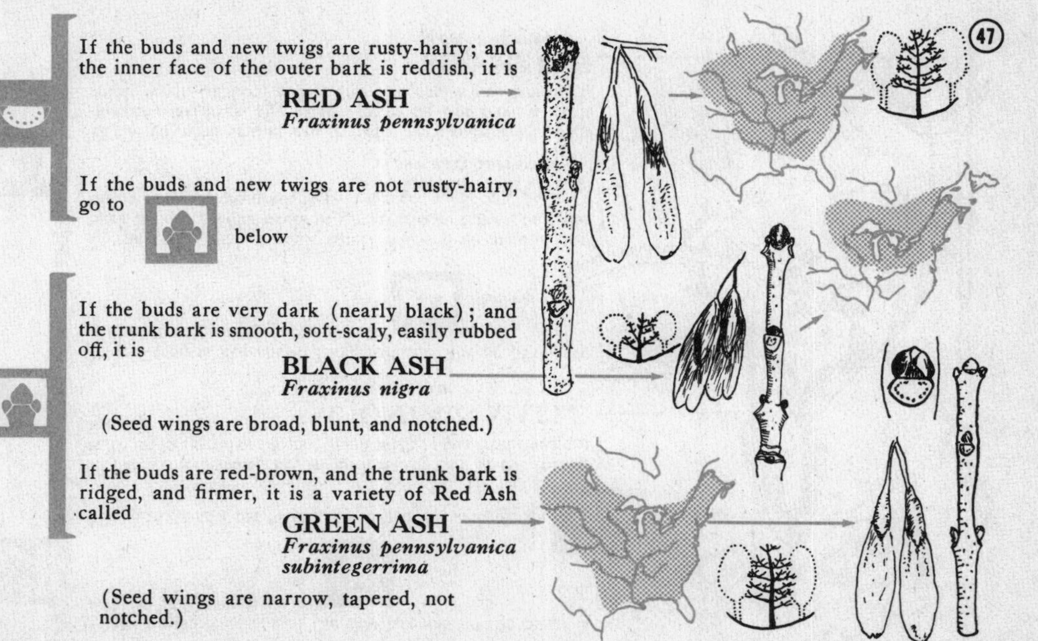

If the buds and new twigs are rusty-hairy; and the inner face of the outer bark is reddish, it is

RED ASH
Fraxinus pennsylvanica

If the buds and new twigs are not rusty-hairy, go to [symbol] below

If the buds are very dark (nearly black); and the trunk bark is smooth, soft-scaly, easily rubbed off, it is

BLACK ASH
Fraxinus nigra

(Seed wings are broad, blunt, and notched.)

If the buds are red-brown, and the trunk bark is ridged, and firmer, it is a variety of Red Ash called

GREEN ASH
Fraxinus pennsylvanica subintegerrima

(Seed wings are narrow, tapered, not notched.)

If the buds are red; and the new growth on the twigs is red, or red-brown, go to below

If the buds and the new growth are not red, go to  next page

If the tree is shrub-like, an understory tree of the forest, with densely-hairy twigs (often with fruits that hang on into the winter), it is

MOUNTAIN MAPLE
Acer spicatum

If the tree is not shrub-like, and the flower buds are globular and conspicuous, go to below

If the twigs give a rank smell when broken, and the bark on old trunks peels in great shaggy flakes, and the bud scales are pointed, it is

SILVER MAPLE
Acer saccharinum

If the younger trunks are smooth, very pale gray, with darker markings, and if the twigs do not have a rank smell when broken, and if the bud scales are rounded, it is

RED MAPLE
Acer rubrum

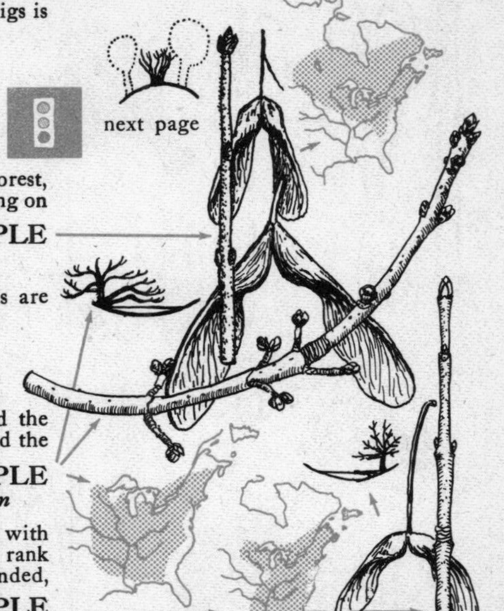

If the buds are whitish and woolly; and the twigs are purplish or greenish; and the leaf scars from opposite sides of the twig meet at their tips, forming a tooth-like point, it is **BOX ELDER** *Acer Negundo*

If the buds are not whitish and woolly, go below to

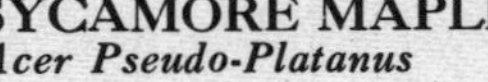

If the twigs are stout, with end buds making a broad, low triangle, smooth, green or partly green, go to below

If the buds are longer-pointed, and brown to reddish-brown, go to next page

If the buds are marked with green and some red-brown; and the fruits which may still be clinging to the tree are joined in pairs at a wide angle so that they resemble a miniature coat hanger, it is **NORWAY MAPLE** *Acer platanoides*

(In early spring the tree is conspicuous with clusters of yellow-green flowers. At that time one can easily identify this tree by its milky juice.)

If the end buds are big and green, it is **SYCAMORE MAPLE** *Acer Pseudo-Platanus*

(No milky juice.)

If the tree is small, shrublike (usually on sandy soil); and the bark is striped with light lines; and the buds have short stalks; and the end bud has two scales that meet at their edges but do not overlap; and the bud scales are keeled, it is

STRIPED MAPLE
Acer pensylvanicum

If the tree is not shrublike; and if the buds are brown to grayish-brown; the twigs slender; the bark stone-gray with large scales peeling off sideways on the old trunks (usually marked by horizontal rows of yellow-bellied-sapsucker holes), it is

SUGAR MAPLE
Acer saccharum

(If the twigs are rough-hairy; and the buds are dark gray to black; and the bark is very dark, almost black, it may be a tree similar to Sugar Maple called

BLACK MAPLE
Acer nigrum

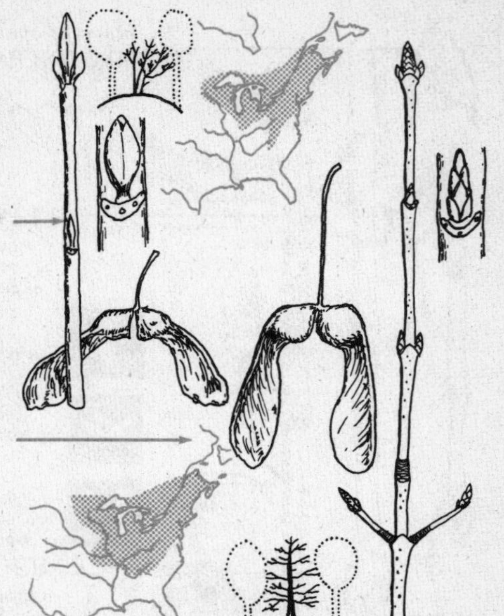

If the bark is light gray on younger parts, flaky or ridged and darker gray on older parts; and if the buds are only about 1/8 to 1/4 inch long, go to below

(Leaves you may find will *not* be bristle-tipped. The acorn ripens in one year. The inside of the acorn cup is smooth.)

If the bark is dark, smooth and shiny on the younger parts, becoming ridged on the older parts; and if the buds are conical or ovate, 1/8 to 1/2 inch long, go to page 54

(The leaves will usually be bristle-tipped. The acorns, which are bitter, take two years to ripen. So you may find both young ones on the branches, and ripe ones on the ground. The acorn cup is silky or woolly inside, and has thin scales.)

If the buds are rounded, go to next page

If the buds are pointed, go to below

If the buds are chestnut-brown with hairless scales, and the bark flaky; the crown narrow, and dense; and the tree has a buttressed base (often grows on limestone ridges), it is

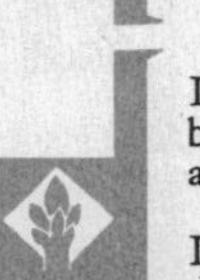

CHINQUAPIN OAK
Quercus Muehlenbergii

If the buds are dark red with hairy scales; and the bark is deeply fissured, not flaky; and the inner bark is red; and the tree has an open, spreading crown, it is

CHESTNUT OAK
Quercus Prinus

If you can easily rub off a handful of bark scales from the trunk, go below →

If the trunk bark is furrowed, but has few scales to rub off, go to next page →

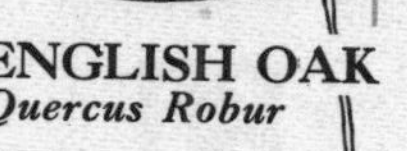

If the twigs are smooth, and the tree has a broad, rugged crown, go below →

If the young twigs are covered with a coarse, orange-brown down; and the tree is often scrubby, irregular, and usually on dry, sandy or rocky upland, it is →

POST OAK
Quercus stellata

(Look for durable, leathery leaves, lobed to form a sort of cross-shape. Acorn cup is bowl-shaped, and half encloses the nut.)

If the acorns are long, and paired on long stalks; and the tree is planted in a park or parkway, it is

ENGLISH OAK
Quercus Robur

If the acorns are not stalked, and the tree is a native, it is →

WHITE OAK
Quercus alba

(Look for right-angled branching. The pale tan leaves cling far into winter. The acorns will be hard to find, because they are sweet squirrel food. White Oaks are often unmistakably marked by a belt of worn-looking bark on the trunk [caused by fungus].)

If the twigs are thick and somewhat hairy, developing corky ridges with age; and the buds are hairy, it is

BUR OAK
Quercus macrocarpa

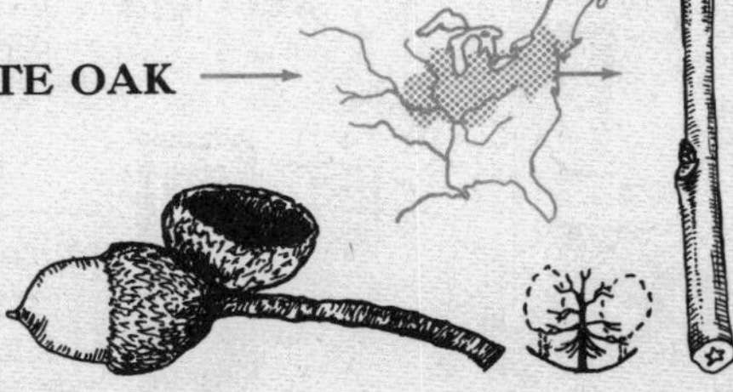

(The end buds often show thread-like stipules longer than the scales. Look for acorns almost covered by the fringed acorn cups. This is the most gnarled and rugged-looking of the oaks.)

If the twigs are smooth, and the lower branches hang down, and the tree grows in rather moist soil, and there are often curling scales of bark on the branches, it is

SWAMP-WHITE OAK
Quercus bicolor

(Look for acorns with stems 1 to 4 inches long.)

If the tree is small (never over 30 feet), with a crooked trunk and contorted branches; or if it is shrubby, go to → next page

(These trees usually grow on barren, dry ridges.)

If the tree is of normal shape and size, and not contorted or shrubby, go below →

(These trees usually grow in a forest or in open groves on good upland or bottomland soil.)

If the tree is branched like a pine tree, with a straight central trunk going almost to the very top, and with drooping lower branches, it is → **PIN OAK** ***Quercus palustris***

(Straight-up-growth habit makes this a common tree for planting along roads near power lines.)

If the tree is not branched like a pine tree, go to → below

If the bud scales are covered with a grayish wool; the buds decidedly angular, up to ½ inch long; and the inner bark is yellow, it is → **BLACK OAK** ***Quercus velutina***

(The most reliable way to identify Black Oak is by a fringe, around the edge of the acorn cup, formed by the loose tips of the scales.)

If the bud scales are not covered with a grayish wool (though there may be some hairiness); and if the buds are not noticeably angular; and the inner bark is not yellow, go to → next page

(Acorn cup scales are not loose and form no fringe.)

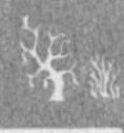

If the buds are all less than ⅛ inch long, it is

SCRUB OAK
BEAR OAK
Quercus ilicifolia

(This tree is shrubby, with abundant small acorns less than ½ inch long.)

If the buds are more than ⅛ inch long, it is **BLACKJACK OAK** ***Quercus marilandica***

(The acorns are about ¾ inch long, light brown, and striated.)

If the lower part of the tree is conspicuously cluttered with dead branches and twigs, it is

HILL'S OAK
JACK OAK
Quercus ellipsoidalis

(The acorn cup is top-shaped.)

If the tree is not conspicuously cluttered, the tree is either Scarlet Oak, Shingle Oak, Water Oak, Red Oak, Spanish Oak, or Willow Oak. To find out which, it is necessary to look at an acorn (or a dry leaf). Go to ⟶

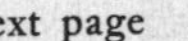

next page

If the acorn cup is top-shaped, like this: go to below

If the acorn cup is more saucer-shaped, like this: go to next page

If the acorns are on short stalk; and the tree has gray-brown, shallowly furrowed bark, and green-brown twigs, brown leaves persisting until spring, it is

SHINGLE OAK
Quercus imbricaria

If there are concentric rings around the tip of the acorn; and if the tree has blackish, deeply furrowed bark and red-brown twigs, it is

(Look for red inner bark.) **SCARLET OAK**
Quercus coccinea

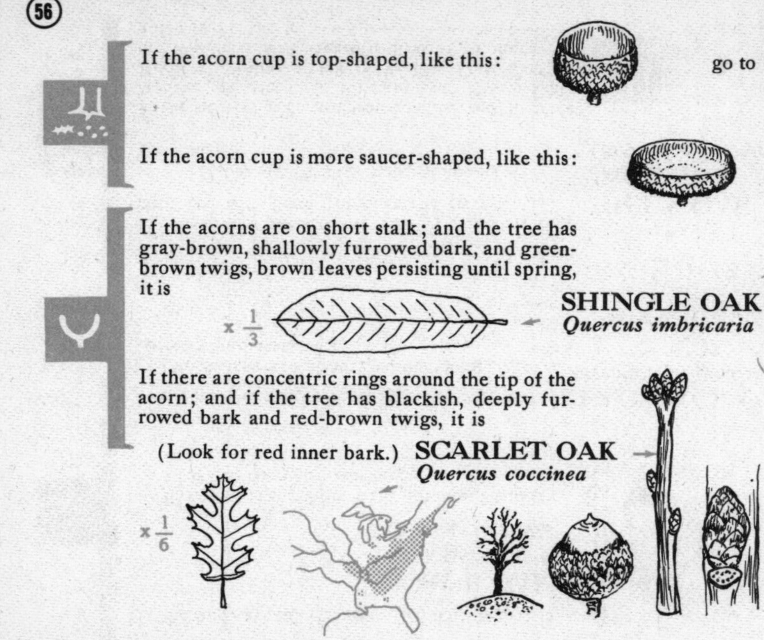

If the acorns are nearly black, with a bright orange kernel, it is

WATER OAK
Quercus nigra

(Leathery leaves of several forms cling on this tree far into the winter.)

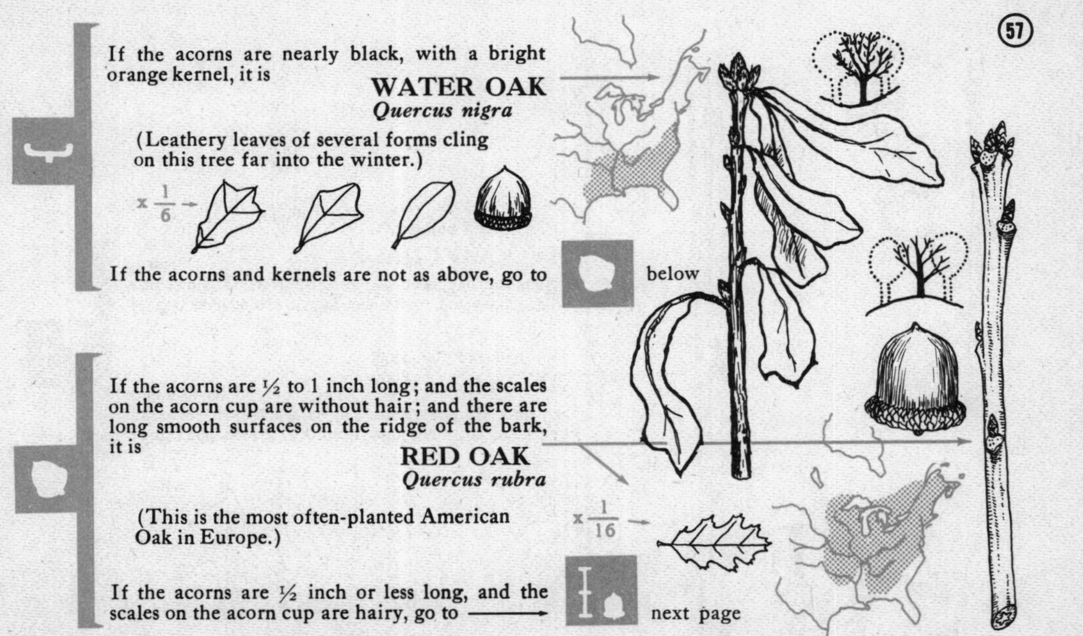

If the acorns and kernels are not as above, go to below

If the acorns are ½ to 1 inch long; and the scales on the acorn cup are without hair; and there are long smooth surfaces on the ridge of the bark, it is

RED OAK
Quercus rubra

(This is the most often-planted American Oak in Europe.)

If the acorns are ½ inch or less long, and the scales on the acorn cup are hairy, go to ⟶ next page

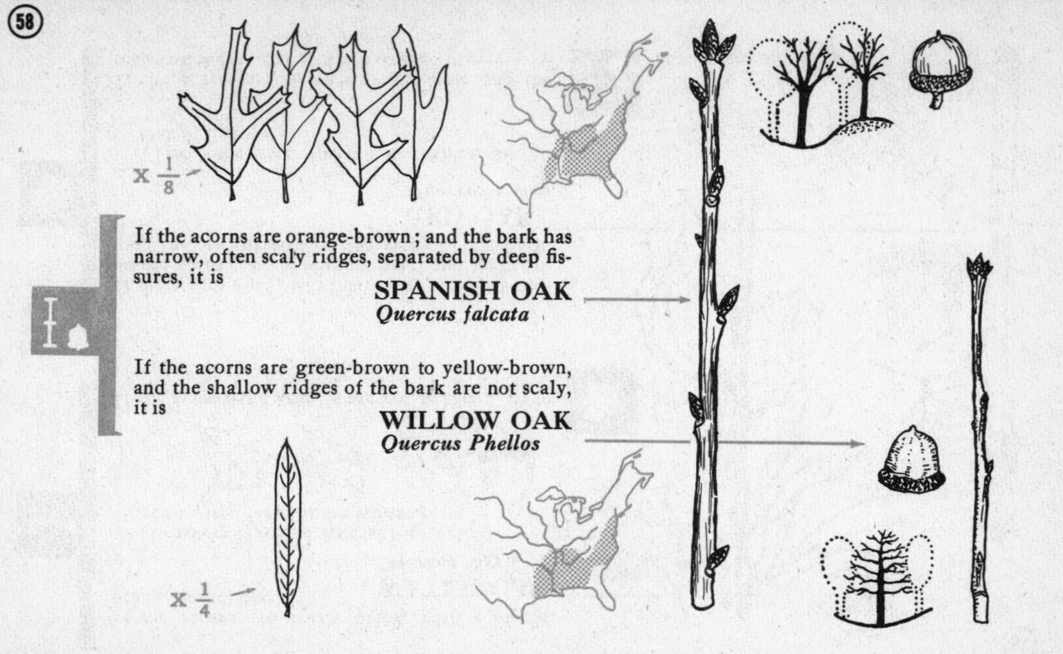

If the acorns are orange-brown; and the bark has narrow, often scaly ridges, separated by deep fissures, it is

SPANISH OAK
Quercus falcata

If the acorns are green-brown to yellow-brown, and the shallow ridges of the bark are not scaly, it is

WILLOW OAK
Quercus Phellos

INDEX